Teacher Growth Trajectory (TGT)

PEDAGOGICAL ENHANCEMENT FOR IMPROVED STUDENT OUTCOMES THROUGH *FEEDING-BACK, FEEDING-FORWARD,* AND *FEEDING-UP*

Purposeful observation practices utilizing collaborative communication toward facilitating sustained teacher growth

A guide for administrators

DR. DON STERNBERG

Sternberg, Don. Teacher Growth Trajectory (TGT). Pedagogical Enhancement for Improved Student Outcomes through Feeding-Back, Feeding-Forward, and Feeding-Up. Purposeful observation practices utilizing collaborative communication toward facilitating teacher growth. A guide for administrators.

ISBN print book: 13: 978-1722654559
ISBN 10: 1722654554

Editing by Demon for Details
Cover design and interior formatting by Woven Red Author Services, www.WovenRed.ca

Published and printed in the United States of America

With sincere dedication to Kathy and Elyssa for
keeping me grounded, focused and giving me purpose.

To Dan Ingram, George Carlin, Gary Larson and Soupy Sales
for putting life in the proper perspective
and to
the Eagles for providing the background music.

About the Author

Recognized as New York State's 2009 Principal of the Year by the National Association of Elementary Principals and by Redbook magazine for leading one of the 72 best elementary schools in the United States, Don Sternberg knows what it takes to walk the high-wire that a school principal faces every day. His 42-plus year career in the public education, as a teacher, assistant principal, principal, college instructor, as well as recognition by peers for his outstanding performance gives Don expertise and credibility that few can match. In *Teacher Growth Trajectory (TGT). Pedagogical Enhancement for Improved Student Outcomes through Feeding-Back, Feeding-Forward and Feeding-Up*, he shares his insights about how to successfully lead within the public education arena keeping the most important constituency, the students, front and center in all he does.

Don is adjunct lecturer in educational administration at the State University of New York at Stony Brook. His writing has appeared in Principal magazine as well as the School Administrators Association of New York State Journal. He is the author of *The Principal: Traversing the High-Wire with No Net Below, 79 Places Where the High-Wire Can Be Greasy.*

Foundational Question

One could ask naively, why should an administrator apply an intense and laborious amount of time and energy to the task of sustaining and monitoring a teacher's pedagogical growth?

It is certainly a fair question, and, setting aside for a moment the inherent, strong commitment a teacher would hopefully feel toward his or her own professional growth, I believe this aspect - - teacher growth - - cannot be left to the caprice of each individual.

If left on their own, teachers would naturally default to old habits and assumptions, and devote varying degrees of intensity and effort toward their pedagogical growth. This inconsistency of application would result in erratic growth, resulting in inconsistent degrees of success - - which would inevitably translate to varying degrees of success for our children.

Nothing jolts me harder, and subsequently drives me toward building Teacher Growth Trajectories, than this palpably true passage written by Haim Ginnott:

I've come to the frightening conclusion that I am the decisive element in the classroom. It's my daily mood that makes the weather. As a teacher, I possess a tremendous power to make a child's life miserable or joyous. I can be a tool of torture or an instrument of inspiration. I can humiliate or humor, hurt or heal. In all situations, it is my response that decides whether a crisis will be escalated or de-escalated and a child humanized or de-humanized.

If you find this as truthful and chilling as I do, then turn the page and let's get started...

Table of Contents

Chapter 2 Taking a Leadership Role in Developing a Teacher Growth Trajectory (TGT) 29

Chapter 5 Teacher Attitudes Toward the Observation Process and How to Ameliorate Them..**103**

Preface

Quality is never an accident; it is always the result of high
intention, sincere effort, intelligent direction and skillful
execution.

~ William Foster

I thought a great preamble for this tome about facilitating teacher growth
by capitalizing on the observation process would be to include how many
observations I conducted during my thirty-five years as a principal. By the
time I factored in full-time staff members, part-timers, and the teachers
shared among different schools within the district, the project became
overwhelming and subsequently unnecessary.

I came to realize that the potentially captivating number of observations paled in comparison to *what I learned* from each experience, and
what I walked away with in terms of learning how *great* pedagogy, when
skillfully applied, propels student learning. What I learned from one experience added to the next observation, and the subsequent dialogue with
each teacher added to my own skill sets.

These observational Lego blocks accumulated, and powered my development into a seasoned and highly effective supporter of quality pedagogical practices. These individual blocks created an assemblage of best
practices, quality pedagogical concepts, and basic understandings of *how
students learn best*. The experience itself shaped my ability to apply those
practices, understandings, and concepts to help sustain teacher pedagogical growth.

Smart Gerbils

During the countless hours spent sitting in those small plastic chairs in the
rear of the classroom - - chairs that were easier to get into than out of as
the years progressed - - I always grew a little as an educator from every

single observation I performed, and from every conversation I had with a teacher.

I had the opportunity to observe some *great* master teachers, who created environments so conducive to learning that even the class pet gerbil stood a better-than-average chance of acing the state assessments. Because, truth be told, not every teacher is a *great* teacher, and not every child (or gerbil, for that matter) will have the benefit of spending 183 days - - give or take a few days - - in a highly effective educational environment.

However, donning the mantle of principal places you squarely in a leadership position, where you are responsible for applying a concerted and continual effort toward making every teacher in the school a *great* teacher.

The Feeding Challenge

Teaching is a challenging and an ever-evolving job. It is not just about standing in front of the room presenting information by writing on the SMART Board, providing an example or two, and then giving students an assessment to see if they learned anything.

A *great* teacher plans thoroughly and with enthusiasm. He or she knows the ability level of each student, challenging each one academically, and then offers meaningful assessments to determine if they understood the concepts and can functionally apply them in a relevant situation.

Astute school leaders know that teachers are the *only significant factor* driving student achievement! And, in order to grow pedagogically, teachers need the right kind of support from their principal, supported by information relevant to their current skill sets, as well as suggestions and recommendations that are actionable, useful, applicable and *directly connected* to student learning.

1) You are feeding-back!
   Providing each teacher with concrete information based upon evidence you collected during your observations.

2) You are feeding-forward!
   You are conferencing, supporting and providing resources to place teachers on a specific professional growth trajectory toward greatness.

3) You are feeding-up!
   You are propelling teachers by providing them with valuable and useable information to increase their pedagogical skill sets, as well

as assisting them in developing an understanding that why, how, and what they are doing has significant influence on every student in the class.

Teacher Observations: The Conduit Toward Success

John Hoyle, Fenwick English, & Betty Steffy (2005) contend that in order for teacher observations to work, teachers have to view them as a positive process that supports the inherent rewards of professional growth. They argue, "True professionals need open, threat-free workplaces that nurture self-expression and respect..." (p. 106).

This is where you, as principal, enter the picture. What can you do to create a highly effective classroom environment (translation: *a classroom with a great teacher, where both kids and gerbils benefit)*?

That is your goal!

What can you do to support your most *outstanding* educators, as well as the ones who should be standing out in the parking lot and not in the classroom? Then factor in all the teachers who occupy the classrooms between the *great* and the not so *great!*

Where do you start? My suggestion is threefold:

1) Start at the beginning by calculating each teacher's most basic pedagogical need. Please be careful to make sure this is done for every teacher in the school.
2) Have a plan and apply due diligence to bringing the plan to positive fruition.
3) Work purposefully and prudently - - and be patient.

This tome is your plan outline and justification. Once you have a plan, the other two will fall into place logically.

If you want people to grow professionally, you have to give them feedback. Giving feedback can be difficult, because you might think, "I might hurt someone's feelings..." or "This might require an uncomfortable conversation..." or "I'm telling someone I really like and respect that they're falling short in some regard..." So you could avoid giving feedback, but it would be a huge mistake, because you would not be fulfilling your commitment to your students.

There will be some teachers who you see soaring to *greatness*, others who are on the threshold of *greatness*, and still others who are mired in the mud of ineptitude and stagnation. In all cases, you are their support system while they self-select to achieve *greatness*, or seek an alternate career, or, at the very least, transfer into another building!

The bottom line is that *you* will be teaching teachers by *engaging and purposefully feeding-back, feeding-forward and feeding-up!* You will be leading today to build a more solid tomorrow for your students. The kids (and the gerbils) are counting on *you!*

Introduction

Greater than the threat of mighty armies is an idea whose time has come.

~ Victor Hugo

DDS

Over a dozen years ago, Kenneth Leithwood and Gene Riehl wrote, "In these times of heightened concern for student learning, school leaders are being held accountable for how well teachers teach and how much students learn" (Leithwood & Riehl, 2003, p. 1).

What has changed since 2003? Nothing! Their statement is as applicable today as it was over fifteen years ago, and I postulate that a dozen years from now the statement will still ring true and be accurate for the era.

Why? I don't know! If I could predict that effectively, I would pick Mega-Power Ball numbers, win, and be writing this book on the beach in Hawaii while lounging in front of my multimillion-dollar condo!

What can you do about it? Nothing, you are too small and insignificant to make such a global change. So, should you quit the field of educational and become a dentist? No, because do you really want to spend a career sticking your hands into the mouth of a stranger?

"Throughout history, most schools have operated within a conventional paradigm that attempts to control teachers' instructional behaviors" (Glickman, Gordon, & Ross-Gordon, 2014, p. 7). However, in recent years, we can see a shift to a more collegial model that focuses more on growth rather than compliance. "When researchers ran the numbers in dozens of different studies, every factor under a school's control produced just a tiny impact, except for one: *which teacher the student had been assigned to...*" (Green, 2010 p. 2).

And herein is the control factor of your professional destiny - - your hill that needs to be climbed, the cross you lug, and the challenge of the productive use of your time, energy and expertise.

In your little corner of the education world, you will seek to create, as principal, an academic environment that is highly responsive to *all* students. You must hire well - - or what I call *hire hard* - - and provide each teacher with a *growth trajectory* toward *greatness*. You will inherit from your predecessor (who is currently sitting at the pool in Boca, no longer worried about those poor-quality teachers he or she hired and has now left behind for you) a cadre of teachers of varying degrees of effectiveness.

How you utilize your time and expertise and the time and expertise of the teachers around you will make all the difference in your success as a principal. <u>The bottom line is, your students can only achieve limited success unless *you achieve full success*</u>. No pressure!

There will be *instructional resources* to maximize, as well as *human resources* in the form of human capital. *The maximization of human capital only comes from a process that is viewed by teachers as collaborative.* They will consider how your feedback is delivered and aligned with your actions - - as *they* perceive them. Both of these are of equal value, and if either one is not performed properly, it will result in a less-than-positive outcome.

Misconception

Being a leader of people means taking the initiative and responsibility for the direction and performance of others. Who will willingly join you on this journey, and who might require being pushed, cajoled, or dragged along?

One of the challenges you will encounter is how to get the person you are pushing, cajoling, or dragging to stand on their own two feet, observe what is happening around them from a pedagogical standpoint, and participate as a collaborative partner in the journey toward pedagogical *greatness*.

Will they walk side-by-side with you? That initial or entrance level of understanding on the part of the teacher is the beginning of mapping their *Teacher Growth Trajectory* (TGT) journey. The map is not developed based upon whim, but rather based upon **evidence** of degrees of performance that you observe and *simply* bring to the teacher's attention in a non-judgmental fashion. Please be aware that the word *simply*, as utilized here, is the largest understatement you will find in this book!

Ask the average lay individual what greatly influences the transformation to an effective school, and they would first mention a school district's budget, and then probably suggest more time for test prepping.

The surprising truth is, "successful schools typically have no greater amounts of time or resources, the difference is how time, focus, and structure are used; how staff development, school improvement, personnel evaluation, and classroom assistance are used together; and how instructional leadership is defined and employed" (Glickman, 2002, p. 2).

This seeming contradiction of what truly constitutes a successful school baffles many, but to the *great* leader - - and that will be you, by the way - - it is an intricate ballet that requires a grand balancing act of your various roles on a day-to-day basis.

One Word

Throughout this book I will use one word I request that you associate with the end result you should be seeking to achieve in school - - and that word is **_great_**. Think *great teachers* and *great pedagogy* resulting in *great opportunities* for students by creating and sustaining pedagogical *greatness* via teacher growth. I am certainly not interested in sustaining poor-quality teaching or even settling for just effective teaching. *Effective teaching is like kissing your sister!*

What I always strived for was to witness *great* teaching, and everything presented in this book will be focused on steps toward achieving, supporting, and sustaining *great* teaching within classrooms.

Will you miss the mark? Yes, you will, and will probably miss more often than not, at least initially in your career. However, you need to acquire the tools to support *greatness* and the tools to allow educators to achieve *greatness*, because developing an awareness of the stages of each teacher's growth is one of your initial steps. And if you fall a little short every now and then, you fall back to *effective* teaching, and that really isn't so bad. After all, your sister is probably a nice person!

I will settle for effectiveness while in the pipeline toward achieving greatness. However, effective teaching is where the line in the sand is drawn, and nothing below that line is acceptable!

Role Play

It would be difficult to overstate the momentous role a building administrator plays in establishing the quality and scope of teaching within in a school.

Through a concentrated effort focused on teacher growth, you set the *expectation for the quality of instruction*, and from there all things emanate. A building filled with *great* teachers is the foundation of a highly successful school that prepares its students well for whatever comes next in their lives.

Nothing remotely close to this goal can occur without the commitment and ongoing efforts of a *great* principal and his or her cadre of building-level administrators, all of whom understand and can implement a collaborative process of teacher growth - - what I refer to as a **Teacher Growth Trajectory** or **TGT**.

You will seek to maintain this upward continuum for *every* teacher. This feat can only be successfully accomplished if the ethos of the school is one where *change through growth* is the highly acceptable norm. That culture originates with you and how you interact with people - - the people who see you as their pedagogical collaborator, from whom their comfort zone in the school is derived. They also see you influencing their professional life, which requires a clear understanding of who you are and what you expect from yourself and from others.

And if who you are is a *collaborator*, and you are willing to *deeply, intentionally, and purposefully* listen to colleagues, and your focus is on students and their learning, you stand a better chance of winning their hearts, and subsequently their minds and energies.

Enumerating the qualities that make for *great* instruction is one thing, but seeing to it that your cadre of teachers achieves an understanding of them collectively is another. It is through the supervision of instruction that you take on the hard work and heavy lifting that will advance the school from its core.

While a collective understanding of your bottom line goal is important, the individual and personalized teacher-by-teacher buy-in and subsequent application is the only way to achieve that goal. A brick wall is not constructed instantaneously; it is built one brick at a time. In order to create and maintain a cohort of *great* teachers, you must engage *each educator* in a sustained and productive program of teacher growth with the buy-in and cooperation of the teacher being critically important for success.

Understand that you are seeking to construct and align the observation process as a means of presenting to a teacher a track toward pedagogical growth, and a process for purposeful reflection on their own practice.

Its effectiveness far surpasses Professional Learning Communities, or the myriad of in-service workshops, group professional development seminars, or conferences that seek to enhance instruction. What other opportunity will you have for a one-on-one, prescribed, and focused exchange of ideas, concepts and pedagogical practices with _each_ teacher _individually_?

Make the observation process less of a formality, and bring it to the level of _the_ most important teacher growth _opportunity_ that you will have with the teacher.

May I Assume

My assumption is that teachers are, in fact, trying their best!

Having that mind-set, you are now in the position to accept their efforts _and their deficiencies,_ not to label them as being recalcitrant if their results are not good, but rather to discover more closely, and in greater detail, their _degree of deficiency or need._

You should not see the word deficient as meaning anything more than a teacher who needs support in order to grow pedagogically. How they react to your comments (never, _ever_ using the word _deficient_ with them), and how you address their need to grow, will make all the difference.

Your job will be to help teachers grow by measured steps that will be reflected in their personalized Teacher Growth Trajectory.

If they are _unwilling_ to work to become the best possible version of themselves, I look to send them on their way to somewhere else - - any-where that their current mind-set and lack of teaching attributes will be appreciated - - or either to early retirement, not granting continuation of probation, or by a move to terminate.

Many people are held back from doing better because they fear what the path toward getting there might look like. If they try something new or different, they might fail and look foolish. To do better, they might have to learn something new, which would mean admitting they didn't know something in the first place.

David Greer, in his article _"Doing Their Best"_ (2017), paints an incredible vision of what it will look and feel like when a person achieves their next level of performance.

He makes sure that person knows he believes in them and in their ca-pabilities. He lets them know he truly believes they can reach the next level. And while he is building them up, he still holds them accountable for delivering the very best performance they can while stretching them-selves into their future capability.

This is the mind-set you as a professional must acquire, and one you must make transparent to all teachers.

How Do You Perceive Yourself?

Successful school leaders understand that achieving their goals will not be unproblematic. Instead, it will require perseverance to create and maintain a community of teacher-learners - - all hell-bent on their own Teacher Growth Trajectory.

One major issue that needs to be addressed initially is the question of how and where do you see *yourself* within this process?

- Do you see yourself and/or portray yourself as the be-all and end-all of pedagogical knowledge?
- Do you see yourself as the principal learner in the school? When there are things you don't know, do you skim over them and move on abruptly, or
- Do you roll up your sleeves and jump in to learn all you can?

The picture you portray will be critically important! If you want others to learn, you must be seen as a learner.

Whenever we adopted a new math, reading, social studies, science, or any curriculum series, I always sat right alongside the teachers during all the in-service workshops from the publisher to bring us up to speed on the new resource. I wasn't there to see if the teachers were paying attention, I was there to learn with them, and I made sure I was viewed in that light via my words and deeds.

You can never ask others to admit or accept their need to grow professionally, and to subsequently jump on the TGT growth train, when you admit nothing, and/or portray total knowledge and understanding while waving to others from the station while their growth train whizzes past.

You must be on board, and, frankly, you must be the first one to jump on board! In doing so, you encourage others to fill vital connective learning roles within the school.

The pride of a leader that leads them to believe they are omnipotent, and that they alone are the main reason for the success of the organization, has been the downfall of many leaders throughout history. Myopic vision is a terrible affliction, brought on by a feeling of power and omnipotence simply because someone hired you to be principal!

Please always remember to bring others into your canoe, provide them each with a paddle, and then ask their opinions. One sure cure for myopic vision brought on by your sense of or desire for omnipotence will be you standing in the unemployment line.

It's Plato, Not Play-Doh

For all the good that can come from unity, with everyone sitting in the same canoe and paddling in the same direction, it is ultimately how you mold, model, and critique the vision that will allow members of the teaching staff to find success. In essence, you hold the keys with which they may open the doors to their professional growth.

They will be as important in developing their highly functional Teacher Growth Trajectory, as you will be. For, absent your requirement for a well-thought-out and almost completely self-directed growth trajectory, many will wallow in place, thinking they have already reached the highest of echelons of pedagogy, and/or their current level of expertise is fine because no one has said anything different, or challenged them to grow even further.

Never before has Plato's statement, *know thyself* rung truer than when it is correlated to the role of a principal.

To change others for selfish, self-serving reasons is a road easily taken by the ineffective leader, since it comes from a yearning to fill a void they have within themselves. These leaders truly do not know who or what they stand for and, unfortunately, are blinded by this lack of knowledge.

In contrast, the *great* principal has the ability to see others for their attributes, and to understand what they are truly capable of and how they can influence the greater good.

I was an art teacher, not a psychologist or academic educator, and I think that made me who I became professionally, and the Greenleaf-type (Robert Greenleaf) servant leader I developed into. I knew I needed others more pedagogically gifted and astute than I was to convey our school to a highly productive level.

That understanding is the glue that holds together a community of learners to seek "…a cause beyond oneself" (Glickman & Gordon, 2014, p. 35).

If successful, you will be a voice of reason, leadership, confidence, and perspective, and you will ultimately achieve *greatness*. And as self-serving as it may seem, you want *greatness!* Why? Because what comes with the position of *greatness* will be the perception, if not the sheer fact, that you know what you are doing! This perception will serve you well with existing faculty, both in the school and in the school district at large.

It also gains you automatic compliance from teachers new to the school. Think about what that new teacher must be thinking as they enter the school where the ethos of *greatness* exists. It would be like me entering a Porsche dealership!

Evaluate Your Personal Leadership Style

The study of leadership leads down many roads, and many times these roads intersect.

A theory may focus on charisma, or authority models, traits or style, but each one offers only a glimpse into the reasons why a leader is not only needed, but requires willing followers to be successful. Certainly personality is a valuable commodity for leadership, but force of personality alone, and without the benefit of intelligence, does not a leader make!

Peter Drucker, management expert and author, wrote, "Leadership is not magnetic personality that can just as well be a glib tongue. Leadership is not making friends and influencing people, that is flattery" (Drucker, 1924, p. 1).

I have described myself many times as being as charismatic as a bowl of vanilla ice cream on a radiator in the middle of a January blizzard! I have seen and worked with many, many *charismatic*, Ben and Jerry's Cherry Garcia-type people. However, charisma can only get you so far. I am not so sure they have accomplished anything more than I have during their careers - - although maybe their retirement dinner was better attended than mine!

The incidentals of leadership move beyond the effects of charisma, or the abilities of a detailed organizer. According to Richard Hughes, Robert Ginnett, and Gordon Curphy (2009), leaders can develop employees through positive interactions, as well as make difficult decisions, but still accomplish results. Drucker summarized these facts when he wrote, "Leadership is lifting a person's vision to higher sights, the raising of a person's performance to a higher standard, the building of a personality beyond its normal limitations" (Drucker, 1924, p. 18).

Principals who only appear in classrooms to perform observations enforce the assumption that the observation process is obligatory at best and probably punitive at worst. Principals who do not seek out *listening opportunities* through collaborative teacher-principal dialogues on an individual basis encourage a hierarchical approach to teacher growth. This might lead to teachers emulating this in the classroom through lecture-based, cookie-cutter lessons instead of individualized, student-based ones.

Principals who do not encourage, support, and model self-reflection and peer collaboration will not find it in their school. They will most likely see teachers who come to work, perform the least that is required of them and work on a vacation-to-vacation-based (VACA) mentality.

Being in the Room Where It Happens

On the most primitive level, most administrators will note the objective of classroom observation is to improve teacher practice in a variety of areas. At best, the supervisor (I hate the word "supervisor" and never use it, and I also abhor the word "subordinate") will use the observations to help guide teachers to enhance their planning, instruction, classroom environment, and possibly even their professionalism -- their *professional maturity*.

Please allow me to move all of these thoughts to a subset level and note that while these may, in fact, be the results of your efforts, the main act of an observation is to simply get your butt into the classroom! Once there -- and by there, I mean on a regular basis -- you now have the entrée for discourse about what is taking place. Absent your face-in-the-place, how can you acquire the credibility to address both the positive and not-so-positive events that transpire in the room? You need to be "…in the room where it happens" (Hamilton [the musical], 2014).

This renders the three-times-per-year formal observation and nothing else a useless and almost embarrassing exercise on your part. How can you speak with any conviction or knowledge, or even be seen as an authority, without your presence -- *your regular presence* -- in the classroom?

The Following is a Test!

If, when you walk into a classroom, the teacher stops what he or she is doing and asks, "Is everything all right?" then it clearly indicates you were not in that classroom often enough!

Classroom Presence

Please do not paint yourself into the proverbial corner by not being a regular presence in a teacher's classroom, and subsequently routinely judging him or her based only on limited visits. Teacher effectiveness and prowess must be viewed within a context of your regular presence so there is a broad scope of experiences being analyzed on the basis of more than sporadic visits.

Your presence is part of the interactions you are having with the teacher. Initially you will be looking less at the results of those efforts than you will be the imbuing of them. Your regular presence allows you to see and subsequently ask:
1) What have you tried?
2) What has worked, and to what degree?
3) What has not come to positive fruition, and why do you think it didn't?
4) And, most important, what are you trying next?

This is important, because you will not accept complacency - - as in, "I've tried everything..." and/or the teacher giving up on a student -- even if it is June 1st!

There are numerous reasons to be a regular presence in classrooms. One HUGE reason is that you are learning what *great* pedagogy looks like, smells like, feels like, tastes like, and sounds like! No one is born with all the answers, but you can be taught most of them.

I was a presence, and as I walked around I watched, listened with purpose and intent, and mentally recorded what I was witnessing (the *great* and the not-so-great). I subsequently utilized what I witnessed and applied the knowledge going forward, for and with other teachers, and it became part of my toolbox of suggestions. I became a well-trained expert, regurgitating what I experienced and adding it to the teachers' pedagogical toolbox.

A Little Closure

There can never be an effective and long-lasting dialogue if you are not a regular presence in the classroom.

You will not be taken seriously, and your efforts, regardless of how well-founded and well-intended, will fall significantly and miserably short.

If your immediate reaction is that you do not have time to devote to being in the classroom, then please allow me to refer you back for your career consideration to the concept of putting your hands into the mouths of strangers. You will be doing very little to improve the quality of instruction in school unless you spend significant time in classrooms, and the dental profession is a noble endeavor - - unless, of course, you are an "anti-dentite" (Seinfeld, on 10/13/2006)!

Being a principal is not about having all the answers. It is about assisting teachers in *finding the answers,* and it can only be logically achieved via your firsthand knowledge of what takes place in the classroom.

So, how does one get started rolling this ball up the hill?

Teacher Growth Trajectory (TGT)

Chapter 1
Developing a Teacher Growth Trajectory (TGT) to Improve Pedagogy, and Its Subsequent Impact on Student Outcomes

Begin with the end in mind. ~ Stephen Covey

Leadership Style for Optimum Teacher Growth

Leadership style is a broad term that attempts to explain the relationship between task and outcomes rather than focusing on behaviors (Northouse, 2013).

The primary use of research on leadership styles is to help others assess their focus and understand the effect of both tasks performed and the relationships that need to be managed (Northouse, 2013). This area of research highlights the actual behaviors of leaders in various situations.

Rachel Farrell (2011) conducted a survey of leaders and discovered that central traits of *great* leaders begin and end with honesty, integrity, and other traits that develop trust and loyalty among subordinates (her word, not mine). These important traits involve empathy and the ability to empower others to accomplish tasks, achieve goals, and develop future leaders (Raja & Palanichamy, 2011; Holt & Margues, 2012). Empathy, humility, and other traits also elicit loyalty (Raja & Palanichamy, 2011; Holt & Margues, 2012).

The next major theme in Farrell's study was the concept of dependability, reliability, and the ability to demonstrate task-minded success. More than the ability to accomplish goals and ensure productivity, leadership involves the ability to transform a person while also influencing them to succeed (Raja & Palanichamy, 2011). By the same token, empathy is required to develop the influence necessary to cause people to act outside their comfort zone to further develop professional skills (Holt & Margues, 2012). Unless you are able to do so, your Teacher Growth Trajectory (TGT) effort will be as effective as a lead balloon.

Regardless of the leader's traits, intelligence, or style, common decency demands integrity, a concern for others, and also the ability to complete tasks. Without them, you have an ice cream cone sans any ice cream.

Your job, and a foundational component of success, will be your ability to convey this to the faculty, and subsequently encourage a drive toward professional growth trajectories in your most successful teachers (let's not forget them), and your most needy teachers (and you will never be able to forget them, because they will constantly remind you of their presence through their daily actions and inabilities).

Got a Minute?

Empathy is an action as much as a value, but, personality aside, you must choose at the very least to be courteous to colleagues. Doesn't it sound silly to write that, because it is so basic a humanistic concept?

However, sometimes during the pace of your day, courtesy can take a back seat to short-term efficiency. You are heading down the hallway, already four minutes late for a meeting, and a teacher approaches you with a question. "Got a minute, Don?" Well, hell no, I don't. But obviously you cannot say that!

Whatever you say and do, that teacher must not be pushed aside (metaphorically), but you must also keep heading to the meeting you are already late for. What you say and do in that instant will have an impact on the person asking you a question, and consequently the people who have now been waiting five minutes for you to show up!

Leadership is a delicate balance of empathy, strong but positive self-confidence, and awareness -- a total awareness of what is occurring around you at all times, and how it impacts staff. This balance requires positive personality traits and the intelligence to act in the manner appropriate for the situation, always remembering the impact of your actions and inactions (both physical and verbal).

If teachers are going to embrace and fully commit themselves to a TGT and attainment of a new level of pedagogical success, they must feel personally supported, and they must *trust* you. If strong relationships and trust are not palpable, teachers are not going to feel as though they have the courage (yes, I wrote courage) necessary to embark on and follow through with a TGT. You not only have a responsibility to the faculty to foster professional growth, but you also have the responsibility to be a support during this process. Because teachers will be looking for you, and they need to see you as a *support service*, not someone who is making judgments or simply being reactionary.

To influence positive results requires both intelligence and an open personality. The key word here is *influence*. You can probably get people to do things you want because you are the boss. However, influencing them to *want* to do something requires a different dynamic, and, I would suggest, increasingly better results.

You have their minds because you're the boss; however, it's their hearts you want!

Connected

Your establishment of an ethos with regard to TGTs can take three directions, only one of which will be highly productive.

The first one is where you are seen as the person in control. Yes, you are the principal, and you are in control, but don't remind anyone of that unless it is absolutely necessary. If you are leading effectively, it will never be necessary - - OK, almost never! Most people feel controlled when they perceive that there is an autocratic leader and/or they feel too micro-managed.

The second would be you establishing by your actions, deeds and/or words, a culture of indifference, where teachers feel that the people they work with don't care about the work they do with kids. *Our only focus as educators should be on kids*, and when you don't acknowledge a teacher's work with their students, it is extremely disheartening for them!

Both cultures of control and cultures of indifference make teachers feel unsupported, left out, and lonely.

The best ethos you can establish for teachers is one of *feeling connected*. In this type of culture, teachers feel connected to their colleagues, their school, and their student and parent populations - - and, yes, let me go out on a limb here - - *connected to you!*

When people experience this connection, they feel valued, and they will thrive. Reginald Green (2017) writes, "To obtain commitment, trust must exist between leaders and followers, and that trust has to be developed in a reciprocal manner" (p.2).

3

The Process

Experienced principals already know, and as a neophyte you will soon learn, that there is no way on G-d's green earth you will be able to do everything that needs to be accomplished within a school by yourself.

I would have accomplished very little during my tenure as principal if I hadn't had a faculty who led the way while I spent most days running to catch up with them. However, you need to create the dynamic that grows into this kind of ethos.

A faculty is a cadre of professionals who are highly opinionated and fiercely protective of their independence within the confines of their classroom. These are the people you want to turn into deeply interdependent cohorts.

But do not make the mistake of trying to create the co-dependency en masse and all at once. The process is a one-teacher-at-a-time endeavor, and the vehicle is the Teacher Growth Trajectory (TGT) via the observation process. The observation process is a natural way to create success in the school, because its roots are embedded in a one-on-one relationship.

As the initial step, you need to know where you are going and how you want to get there, and the teachers are the individuals who will assist you in propelling students to the highest achievement possible.

Knowing how to ask the right questions is essential to sorting through options, clarifying objectives, and making the best decisions possible. Be patient, and think out and through a process that formulates and asks appropriate questions *to assist each teacher in finding the solution, best practice, and/or to start on the right path toward their professional growth through purposeful self-reflection.*

"Learners attain understanding only through regular reflection, self-assessment, and self-adjustment as they apply prior learning to new situations and tasks through assessments that demand reflection and transfer" (Cordeiro & Cunningham, 2013, p. 220). You must develop a strategy and practice of skillfully asking purposeful questions - - ones that result in teacher self-reflection and subsequent growth.

The timing of when those questions are asked can also be significant. Your role is to be directional and purposeful in guiding the path of the questions and conversations, *and guiding is not dictating.* Be open to alternative options for concrete steps toward the goal.

It is not my way or the highway - - yet! Remember, you are seeking to move from *concept with discussions* to *results* and subsequent *positive outcomes for the students.*

May the *Force* Be with You!

The observation process *forces* both teacher and administrator to interact. It *forces* you to be in the classroom. The ensuing observation *forces* discussions that center on kids and their accomplishments as a direct result of teacher pedagogy. It *forces* the two of you to talk about classroom activities. It *forces* a conversation at least a minimum number of times per year. (The word *minimum*, however, is never an acceptable word, or a word that invokes satisfaction and the sense that you're doing a *great* job.)

However, in order for any component of your process to work, and subsequently increase student success via creating a highly accountable and successful cohort of teachers, the word *force* must not be even hinted at. It must be removed from the narrative, and one would hope that eventually it ceases to be even a thought in teachers' minds.

Force is the sword of Damocles in this process. What you are ultimately going for is a process that is seen by the teacher as enhancing their pedagogy via a TGT, which is based on *ongoing collaborative discussions between the teacher and you*, with the altruistic outcome of exceptional student learning (that was a mouthful)!

Root Canal

The dichotomy here is that the observation process for most teachers is about as welcome as having a root canal.

Teachers assume they are being *measured* and judged during the observation, and sometimes paranoia takes over, leaving them with the feeling that the observation will be used *against* them.

The actual bottom line is that, even in the age of APPR, a teacher being removed from their position due to incompetency within the classroom is highly unlikely. Incompetency in the classroom is extremely hard to prove, even in the face of an extended period of poor performance and your extensive and detailed write-ups. Most boards of education are hesitant to even head in the direction of removal of a tenured teacher because of the time and considerable expense it incurs.

Tenure provides a job for life, and it is extremely rare that someone loses her or his job based upon classroom incompetence. There are many who should, but regrettably, removal doesn't occur to anywhere near the degree it should.

The teacher unions are well equipped, and armed with attorneys who make sure it doesn't happen *to anyone*. Teacher union representatives don't care about a teacher's degree of proficiency. They will readily admit it is not their job. Their job is to protect the weakest link (weakest teacher) in the chain. By providing this protection, they subsequently protect everyone with skill levels above the weakest teacher.

The union will insist on strict adherence to due process and the contract, and question whether you followed the contract to the letter! They will also try to make the case that not enough was done by you to assist and support the teacher. In the worst-case scenario for you, they may even try to indicate you are capricious or, even worse, discriminatory or incompetent. Union leadership will try anything to keep their dues-paying members employed. They have no interest in whether or not the employee is proficient. They will not help you, and will look at any and every place you might have technically slipped up.

Bottom Line

In light of this, you must be wondering whether what I am suggesting to you in terms of utilizing observations to sustain teacher growth is simply an act of a madman or a trivial pursuit? Or will you just be spinning your wheels in the mud at a monster truck rally?

My response is yes, no, maybe, possibly, sometimes, and/or upon occasion! The fact of the matter is, if you don't approach the process of teacher observation as an opportunity to assist teachers in their pedagogical growth, then all of the above is more than likely true.

Therefore, if you don't look at the process as an evaluation, and instead look at it as an opportunity to discuss with the teacher their growth trajectory, predicated upon classroom performance, supported by the **evidence** collected - - with no subjectivity, ambiguity or partialities - - then the meetings (pre- and post-observation conferences, as well as others [and there will be and should be lots of other meetings]), coupled with the subsequent dialogues, take on a different profile.

This is what you are trying to accomplish, and it is rendered down to your ability to work with people - - putting them at ease, establishing your trust credentials, and together creating a Teacher Growth Trajectory (TGT) through your process of feeding-back, feeding-forward and feeding-up.

Let's do this!

Pet Peeve

I am going to ask you to join in on a small, yet highly significant pet peeve of mine.

I will ask you to join me in *discarding* from your vocabulary two words.

Your sacred vow to me is to never use either of them in connection with teacher observation and/or the TGT process. It will, at first, seem minimal and petty, and almost counterintuitive, yet I will have accomplished my mission if, by the end of this book, you feel the same as I do and follow my lead.

I have never thought, spoken, written or in any other way used the words *teacher improvement*. The words *teacher improvement* carries with them a negative connotation. The word *improvement* carries with it the stigma that something is not right and needs to be *improved*.

Since most teachers already view the observation process in somewhat of a negative light, teacher *growth* has a less threatening and more positive sound, feel, and connotation, and one I want to perpetuate in all my conversations with teachers.

I humbly submit to you that the label of *teacher growth* should be the words that dominate your thoughts, actions, and conversations with colleagues. Telling someone we will be working on *growth*, instead of using the word *improvement*, has a psychological ramification. The subliminal message is profound and can, in turn, become a real asset.

And please, don't get me started on the term *weakness*. Weakness is a word that also should never even enter your mind, much less be written or spoken.

Three Times Six, Carry the Two, and Divide by Your Weight

One cannot assume that teachers in your school are all extraordinary professionals. As in every profession, there are exemplary practitioners as well as those who are apathetic and ineffective. My estimate is that between nine and eleven percent of the teachers in any school in America are incompetent or bordering on incompetence.

Don't believe me? Quickly, think of all the teachers within *your school* who you would not want teaching your own child! Take that number, and the total number of teachers in your school, and apply the mathematical practice that would give you a percentage (I was an art teacher, not a math teacher, and now you know why). What is the percentage? Also, now factor in how upset you will be with that principal for giving your child that particular teacher!!!

Due to tenure laws in many states, you are permanently joined at the hip with those nine- to eleven-percenters who have been granted tenure by some asleep-at-the-wheel principal!

However, if any of the current teachers in your school do not have the potential to be *great* and are non-tenured - - well, you know what to do with them - - cut bait with them in June!

The only moral issue in this regard is a question you must ask yourself; *have I done everything I can as a principal to enhance the professional growth of these teacher?*

Without that effort, you are not fulfilling your own job responsibilities!

I once had a superintendent who boldly stated that it was not his job when he was a principal to train teachers. At whatever level of proficiency they came to him, he would determine their effectiveness and subsequently act accordingly. It was thumbs-up or thumbs–down! He had no intention of devoting hours of effort to support and/or pursue growth in each teacher's pedagogical ability.

At first blush that might seem fine. Seek out only the most qualified, give them a chance, and measure with a thumbs-up or thumbs-down at an appropriate yard-marker during their first and second year of teaching. Cut! Dry! Simple! Effective?

No, not effective at all, because there are so many individual components of a faculty that go unnoticed and underdeveloped, and the wrong people can be left questioning their own effectiveness.

This superintendent also advocated leaving the effective and *great* teachers alone. "Hey, why bother? There were no phone calls from parents or complaining students, and annual growth rates for each child were acceptable."

If you are inclined to think the way my former superintendent did, then this would probably be the best time to try to get your money back where you purchased this book, since at this point the spine of the book isn't significantly creased. In the immortal words of Meat Loaf, "Stop right there, before you go any further…" (Steinman, 1977).

Take a Walk with Me

There is but one great resource for teachers that can create a constant and steady stream of teacher growth, and it is their fellow teachers. And this calls for the removal of the traditional method of teacher growth and replacing it with a teacher-centric model.

Take a walk with me, and imagine that within every teacher's schedule there are times, maybe once during the week, for him or her to sit in and watch a colleague teach! This would be followed up with a before-school or after-school, 30-minute *faculty touch-base* between the two of them once every three weeks. This process would be rotated every five months with a new team working together.

Now throw into this mix you meeting with the teachers and asking about their experiences with colleagues and how they influenced their pedagogy going forward.

<u>Nirvana</u>!

Same Thing, but a Different Year

Continued growth and development should be the mantra of every teacher, but too often tenured teachers lack the incentive to continue growing as professionals.

This is not because they are lazy, or steeped in the ironclad notion that with tenure comes invincibility. For most, it is because <u>no one has ever asked them about what they do</u>, asked them to think about, to purposefully reflect upon, to assess themselves and the results of their pedagogical methods. No one has taken anything but a mere cursory and functional interest in his or her efforts within the classroom.

Teachers are locked into the notion and drink the Kool-Aid that, regardless of whether they are a poor-quality teacher or a teacher at the height of excellence, tenure allows for isolation as well as a sense of being impervious to change or alteration.

There is a sense among many that once they pass over the threshold of tenure, they have been through the gauntlet, passed the exam, and been anointed as OK. They now can go on with the remainder of their career in lockstep with what they believe got them tenure. <u>They think what earned them tenure must have been acceptable, so they will just continue to do the same until their retirement dinner</u>.

Never underestimate the allure of the status quo!

You want to work purposefully with teachers so they can grow professionally, using the only measurable and acceptable results of student advancement and success.

There is an important rationale for identifying what part of a teacher's practice needs growth. According to Andres Ericsson and Robert Pool in their book, <u>Peak</u>, "...once a person reaches that level of acceptable performance and automaticity, the additional years of practice don't lead to improvement."

If anything, the doctor or cab driver who's been at it for twenty years is likely to be a bit worse than the one who's been doing it for only five, and the reason is that these automated abilities gradually deteriorate in the absence of deliberate efforts to improve" (2016, p. 13).

Sleeping Giant

As a principal, you cannot let those effective and *great* teachers meander through their careers under-supported, under-supervised, and under-appreciated.

Carl Glickman, Stephen Gordon and Jovita Ross-Gordon (2014) suggested that we ought to shift toward a collegial model, "...characterized by purposeful adult interactions about improving school wide teaching and learning" (p. 6). Your role will be to make these effective and *great* individuals even better by getting them to assist you in bringing all pedagogical practitioners in the school to a higher level - - because you will never be able to accomplish the task alone. My growth as an educator and as a leader of educators was enhanced tenfold every time I sat down and reviewed best practices with *great* teachers who were employing their best practices right before my eyes. I knew what I was seeing, and was smart enough to take heed, mine that gold, and take mental notes for use at a later date. And boy, did they make me look really, really smart going forward!

Your role will be to resist overlooking or looking over your outstanding veteran staff members. For too long it was too easy for a principal to ignore the professional growth of their highest-performing teachers. After all, they were already performing at an exceptional level, and their students demonstrated proficiency. What more could a principal want?

In theory, the job of a principal is proportionally easier in direct ratio to the number of *great* teachers on their staff - - or at least it would seem that way. But the second you allow it to be your mind-set is the second you and the staff start moving backwards, downhill, and to the detriment of the students within the school.

School ethos is about how much teachers (and your cadre of building-level administrators) are engaged and valued through school-wide dialogues. The culture of the school is what dictates how something will happen.

If the culture within the school is more about rule-following than risk-taking, based upon extended years of complacency - - even complacency at a high level of performance - - a school-wide Teacher Growth Trajectory program will be hard to develop.

Angela Duckworth defines complacency through these quotes: "I can't learn anymore." "I am what I am." "This is how I do things" (2016, p.185).

However, if you support a Teacher Growth Trajectory program because you understand the value for students and can successfully convey that to the teachers, they will support your plan; because they understand the growth that could result from the process will produce long-term value for the kids.

Mayonnaise

In reality, it is most likely that the *great* teachers in school are *starving in silence*. Starving for attention! Starving for recognition! Starving for conversations about what they are doing in their classrooms! And, starving for growth opportunities to raise their pedagogy to an even higher level!

Some of the best conversations I ever had as an administrator were with *great* teachers talking about their craft and the application of their expertise on behalf of student growth. Add into this mix that these are the colleagues you want as role models for teachers in need of a support system, with you as the person pointing a finger toward these *great* teachers and saying to other teachers, "...emulate what they are doing and aspire to their level of effectiveness."

This is a concept alien to our profession, the noting of one teacher who is better at their craft than another. The reality is that teacher unions homogenize their members, not allowing or recognizing that some stand taller than others, and many, many times principals do so as well! Think mayonnaise, and now think salsa! You want salsa's bright, outstanding colors, textures, and flavors (bright, outstanding teachers whose pedagogy stands out as exemplary).

There are many principals who cannot differentiate between what they consider the mundane and mandated necessity portion of their job - - to evaluate teacher performance in a perfunctory fashion - - and the moral obligation to enhance instruction through teacher growth. At times these can seem to be mutually exclusive, with the latter being way down the rung because of massive time constraints.

Ironically, one of the major time constraints is the time committed to creating the paper trail of *proving* you observed teachers. Many principals are unable to make the connection between the observation system and the goal to improve student learning through teacher growth because the time-consuming paperwork, *mandated* paperwork, gets in the way! *They, unfortunately, see professional development and its use to guide teacher growth and the teacher observation system as two separate entities.*

Mass-generated and -consumed district-wide professional development many times is vanilla generic learning that relies on imported talking heads to deliver information.

The Teacher Growth Trajectory evolves to create relevant and sustained growth *specifically* developed for each individual teacher. A TGT will not work if it doesn't connect to *specific* and personalized needs. The observation system is your front door, and the threshold that must be crossed toward teacher growth through TGTs.

Extra Help

You need to create the process of teacher growth outside the label of district-wide professional development. Professional development, quite frankly, rarely comes under the auspices of the building principal, and is more likely to be under the direction of the assistant superintendent for instruction (and is performed on a district-wide level). Therefore, professional development is generic.

TGTs, on the other hand, have the specificity associated with them to develop teacher growth by the administrator in the building, who knows their teachers the best! The assistant superintendent probably doesn't even know the names of the teachers or what they teach, and you know *everything* about them. Given that concept, whom do you want in charge of teacher growth, and what system and/or process do you think will produce the best results for your kids?

If a student was not performing well in an academic area, the teacher will (or should) sit with the student and offer suggestions for growth. The teacher also works with the student during extra help sessions, and then assesses whether or not there has been any growth. The teacher would not wait for the student to fail the next quiz or a cumulative exam before intervening.

You need to apply this same concept with teachers. Instead of waiting until the next formal observation to see if there has been any growth, you need to work with the teacher in a continuing fashion to find avenues that will lead to and subsequently sustain growth. The assessment of progress needs to be continual and ongoing, just as a teacher would do for a student.

This is why allowing the next district-wide PD session to be your standard for teacher growth is ridiculous, and highlights the importance, need for, and merits of the observation component being married to developing teacher growth trajectories.

Pass the Mayo

To further indicate the closed-minded, myopic vision of the majority of central office administrators, I once requested that during one of our district's professional development sessions, our Superintendent's Conference Day, that I be allowed to maintain the faculty of the school in the building for the day. I forwarded to the assistant superintendent detailed and specific components of what we would be working on, and also what I would give to her at the end of the day to validate/prove what we accomplished.

The response to my request was "no, we could not do that." I was told candidly that when the remainder of the district faculty did not see us at the district-wide sessions, there would be "...too much conversation and push-back..." as to what we were doing. It would subsequently be "...too difficult to explain this to the other teachers, other administrators, and the board of education as to why you were by yourselves." According to the assistant superintendent, we all needed to be doing the same thing, on the same day and at the same time - - regardless of need. Pass the mayo!

OK, I'll Take One

The observation system has been tainted by the experiences of teachers and/or experiences they have heard about. There is a huge elephant in the room (although the words huge and elephant in this sentence are clearly redundant).

Yes, formal and informal observation is a tool that can be utilized to exit teachers from the profession. Believe it or not, there are some people who, when questioned, identify themselves as educators, when the reality is they stink at what they do! They graduated from college with a teaching degree, and the state in which the college is located granted them a teaching license, *not based upon their ability to teach*, but because the university they graduated from indicated that they graduated by passing at least the minimum number of courses.

There is no indicator that they are potentially a *great* teacher, or even a competent teacher, or even that they possess the skill sets for teaching. You're only told that they graduated - - passed courses, and possibly even failed a couple - - and yet they were hired.

Oh, yes, the state issuing the certification to teachers relies on the university for granting certifications. Never mind that their student teaching experience could have been with a crappy teacher who just wanted the money associated with being a supervising teacher. Or the supervisory teacher could be someone who wanted the college credits offered by the university so they can take additional courses toward their master's degree. Now, are those the criteria you want for people training and certifying new teachers? Supervising teachers are not necessarily *great teachers*. They are volunteers who simply want a student teacher.

Less than 1% of teachers throughout the nation are fired for incompetence. Wow, that means the universities granting degrees, the states that certified them, and the principal who hired them are all darn near perfect!

I know I asked this before, but now I want to add an increased degree of difficulty. *Quick,* name three (3) teachers within your school that you would <u>never</u> want your own child to have as a teacher. No, I said only three! Please stop at three - - and so much for the concept of learning your craft in college, perfection in hiring, and the granting of tenure only to the best!

Moral Obligation

I insisted that you stop at three only because I want you to keep reading and I don't want you to become depressed.

Fact número uno: *<u>The only reason there is a poor-quality teacher (or teachers) in school is because of a poorly performing principal</u>*! Assuming that you will be a reasonably capable administrator, and you will have someone who you think will be an outstanding teacher, your responsibility within the first two years of this teacher's employment is to determine his or her strength and potential. Absent strengths and a *strong* potential - - fire them! Do not ask them back.

The reason you would do this is twofold, one morally based and the other practically based.

1)   You have a moral obligation to put only the best in front of the students in your school.

2) The poorer the quality of that teacher, the more time you will need to commit to their growth, not to mention fielding complaints from parents and students!

As a Result of the Interview, Does the Best Teacher Get the Job? Or the Best Interviewee?

During my 35-year tenure as a principal, I let 11 people go after their second year. I did not grant them continuation of probation. I, in reality, fired them!

I looked at each incident as _my failure_ during the interview process, and self-reflected heavily about why I offered him or her the job in the first place. However, at the end of the second year when I told them they would not be asked back, I went home that night, put my head on my pillow and slept the sleep of the righteous and the just.

This was possible because I knew in my mind and heart that I helped each of them, and supported each of them in their attempts to become an effective teacher (potential _greatness_ would have possibly come later). While I felt I failed during the hiring process, I did not carry that thought through to the firing. I did the best I could with what was presented to me in the classroom, and it simply did not come to fruition based upon the teacher's marginal ability and/or their inability to grow. Their thought was to _make it to tenure_, and my thought was they did not _grow into tenure_.

The last person, #11 that I had to let go, was during my final year prior to my retirement. I guess I could have let her slip by. After all, it would eventually become my successor's problem. However, I was consumed by the thought that my successor would think less of me and, even more important, I did not want my colleagues, the faculty, to think less of me!

The Ones That Got by Me +2

And yes, three teachers did get by me during those 35 years. I thought they would be _great_, but they turned out to be terrible - - _terrible!_ I would have accepted bad, but they went beyond bad, all the way to terrible.

Every day, when I either walked by their classrooms or walked in, I kicked myself in the butt and asked myself why didn't I see it coming? They were the albatross around my neck!

However, I learned from them, since their hiring came early in my career. Their self-reflection was nonexistent, because they saw themselves as good teachers, despite my documentation pointing in a 179-degree opposite direction. I continually *fed*-them-back, *fed*-them-forward and *fed*-them-up. However, their response to my feedback efforts of support was to believe I was doing it because I did not like them.

Nothing worked - - ever. However, I never got *fed up* and quit on them!

Then there were the two I was forced to hire who turned out to be terrible as well. The precursor to this was that I was told to hire them by the superintendent, based upon the robust system of nepotism and cronyism in the district. The TGT concept also did not work for the two of them either because they felt invincible.

That is five (5) out of approximately 47 classroom teachers. *Quick*, do the math for me!

A Nuance

There is an interesting nuance of meaning between desire for growth and the demand for compliance. I may have misused the word *nuance*, because in the eyes and minds of some teachers, there is an inappropriate link between the two.

Some teachers will look at your efforts as their need to *comply* because, after all, you're the boss! This is the avenue you want to avoid going down, and the mind-set you want to banish from the teacher's mind quickly and completely.

This is also where the trust you have established with the teacher will come in handy. *Your initial job will be to create a desire for professional growth*. Getting someone to comply is mental; you are the boss and they will do what they are told. This, however, is not the foundational underpinning or mantra that will provide the teacher with the most effective growth potential.

What you first need to establish are *collaborative initiatives rather than directed behaviors*. When a principal embarks on collaborative growth trajectories, he or she shares the growth process *with* the teacher in a *joint effort* to grow.

When utilizing a more directed approach - - which usually is the forerunner to only obtaining compliance - - you give (orders) suggestions for instructional growth, and you merely hope the teacher will integrate the changes/suggestions/orders from headquarters. This leads to haphazard outcomes, and almost never results in a positive influence on teacher growth.

When you create a more collegial ethos, one with purposeful self-reflection as a foundational tenet, teachers can feel inherently motivated to enhance their practice. What you will be doing is developing a mutual sense of empowerment and collaboration. The ship needs to be steered by the teacher, but the map/the GPS of the voyage must be outlined or, at minimum, significantly influenced by you.

When people feel empowered they are more inclined to dedicate themselves to a pattern of sustained introspection and subsequent growth. John Maxwell talks about leaders becoming *great,* not because of their power, but because of their ability to empower others. They use their position, relationships, and productivity to invest in their followers and develop them until those followers become leaders in their own right. Please look at TGTs as making an investment.

Now You Know, What Will You Do with the Information?

One of the strongest tenets of the education profession is the concept of a job for life, or tenure. The pros and cons of tenure will not be explored here. They are not germane to our focus, except for the concept of tenure equaling your marriage to that teacher for their professional life.

Confer tenure wisely, because you will look foolish if you give it to undeserving people. However, the concept of losing one's job is enough to scare anyone in any profession. Confiding in your boss about the areas where you feel you might not be doing well, and/or even agreeing with him or her that there are areas in need of growth, can be counterintuitive, even in positions where tenure exists.

So let's take tenure and make it work for us! A teacher has tenure, and unless they commit a felony, or are convicted of touching a child inappropriately, they are not going anywhere.

With that being postulated, how do you develop in your teachers the attitude that purposeful self-reflection is an important growth tool? Provide the teachers with two reasons:

1) It provides an opportunity for personalized growth in pedagogical techniques, and

2) It provides a foundation of understanding and professional awareness of what is actually occurring in the classroom, and its subsequent impact on students.

It is possible that neither of these reasons will be of any significance to those teachers who are convinced they are already Socrates, or those who are counting down to the end of the school year with a large red X marked on each calendar day, with a huge smiley face on the first day of the next VACA.

However, stay on them, and never give up, because these two concepts are nonthreatening, and cut to heart of why most teachers are in school. Approach the concepts without personal bias, without prejudice, without a condescending or pompous tone. Instead, present them as a discussion of why we are here, and what they will be held accountable for.

And you can also add for some teachers, "…because I care about you, I bought you a new red magic marker, because the one you've been using for years appears to be running a little dry!"

Prior to feeding-back, feeding-forward, and feeding-up, make sure to remind yourself why you are doing it.

The purpose is to *support teacher growth*.

You won't accomplish this if you're harsh, critical, or offensive. That's not to say you must always be positive. There is a role for negativity (and red X-ers did bring that out in me), and even controlled disappointment, if someone isn't paying sufficient attention to your requests. A recalcitrant educator is the same as recalcitrant child.

However, it should be used sparingly. You'll usually get much more from people when your approach is positive, with the purpose for their growth stated clearly and emphatically.

Run It Up the Flagpole and See Who Salutes

Please allow me to interject this horrible concept, and one I am sure will diminish me in your eyes, if the preceding pages have not accomplished it already. I am not advocating that a teacher has to be hung by their heels from the flagpole outside the main entrance to the school in order to get the attention of the other teachers, as in, I mean business and teacher growth trajectory is important to our students!

However, having postulated that statement, *teacher growth is key*.

And trust me, after you have denied continuation of probation or denied tenure (the proverbial hoist up on the flagpole by their heels) to anyone incapable of, or unwilling to reaching a highly effective status through developing a TGT, you will, from that point forward, have the full attention of the remainder of your teachers!

I don't want to be next is a powerful motivator, so make it work toward the advantage of the students.

Please allow me to soften this, if I may. Everyone in the school knows who the ineffective teachers are, and if it is a newly hired, non-tenured teacher - - well, your colleagues will be standing around waiting to see what you do about it. *Trust me, you increase your credibility and your position on TGTs when you let an ineffective teacher go.*

And remember this: *not one great teacher I ever worked with wanted a poor-quality teacher in their cohort.*

Your House (House #1)

Your job will be to cultivate and develop the attitude that you are there to create a highly positive and motivating ethos centered around building the skills necessary to becoming a *great* teacher.

How do you cultivate this? How do you make a teacher feel supported and part of the collaboration that is taking place in the school?

There are two distinct *houses* that you and the teachers will live in as you provide a roadmap toward pedagogical growth through feeding-back, feeding-forward, and feeding-up.

I define *your house* (House #1) as the relationship you develop with *each* specific teacher. One of the first major ideas to focus on in pursuit of a successful and *great* school is building relationships. Human nature dictates if someone is not working with you, they are working against you - - and in my eyes, against *my kids!*

Fostering and establishing relationships of mutual respect and collegiality is foundational. Your observations, both formal and informal, and the resulting conversations that take place prior to and following the observation, will dictate and establish the landscape of that dialogue, the unwritten and yet very real music to your dance with the teacher. It will be those formal and informal discussions about pedagogy within the classroom that create the dialogue.

You are two research physicians discussing your latest work in finding a cure for a disease. You are an actor and a director who mutually respect each other and are not seen by either of you as one having more power over the other, and therefore, discussing how to create a *great* performance - - as equals, as collaborators, as members of the same team, and as mutually dependent upon each other. You are Fred Astaire and Ginger Rogers, or Cyd Charisse and Gene Kelly (I have just dated myself!

Millennials, Google and YouTube these people, and then watch them collaborate!).

In this *house* - - your house - - discussions with individual teachers ensue around quality, growth, mutual respect, and a desire to assist students. From the outset, you must determine what is the teacher's attitude toward growth and working one-on-one with you. Once you have established this, from their comments and/or deeds, you must ask yourself: *What have I done to establish the desired mutual respect and confidence? What additional efforts should I make to partner successfully with this teacher?*

Your Bed and Breakfast (House #2)

There is another and equally important house, and this one goes beyond an individual relationship.

In your bed and breakfast (House #2), it is the relationship you have with *the faculty as a whole,* and how you create a collaborative team of growth seekers who depend on and support each other's growth. You cannot have a successful bed and breakfast until you have sold this premise to the individuals who will eventually take up residency there.

While visiting this bed and breakfast, you are each in separate rooms, and you will each go your own way at certain times. However, there are times when, for example at breakfast, you are all sitting at the same table - - *sharing,* family-style. Picture, if you will, this Currier and Ives moment, passing the warm waffles, rolls, eggs, blueberry scones, pastries, French toast, and other goodies, from person to person around a shared table, prior to parting for your individual events of the day. (At this point, I will understand if you put the book down and run out to your local Panera for an elephant ear or cinnamon bun. I make myself hungry every time I read this passage. I mentioned Panera only because I am hoping for a product placement residual).

The foundational questions crucial to developing *your house* (House #1) are basically the same for the bed and breakfast (House #2). What must the attitude be of the faculty sharing the B&B table and, most important, how do you create it?

People will look at your ability to create this attitude where there was none. They will also look toward creating this attitude where the pre-established attitude you inherited from prior building administration - - and someone, of course, who never read this book - - is somewhat negative.

So, regardless of your current working location (in your house or in the B&B), the attitude of teachers must be one based almost exclusively on *trust.*

- Can they trust you?
- Can they open up to you about where they feel they need to grow professionally?
- Can they trust you enough to be candid about their areas of pedagogy that need support, reinforcement, or growth, and/or their fears about not being able to grow professionally?

Their basic question, what they will be waiting to see develop is: what will you do with the information garnered from the observation process and from the conversations that lead toward the collaborative planning of a TGT?

Therefore, again, let's take tenure and make it work for us. A teacher has tenure and is not going anywhere. How do you develop the attitude that I want to grow professionally (even when I don't have to in order to retain my job [now there is a scary thought]), and I want you (building administrator) to assist me?

Remember, these are educators with tenure who don't have to do a darn thing except show up for work.

Now you are going to ask them to explore their strengths and face their pedagogical growth needs! Until you win them over with the TGT concept, they will internalize this as a battle between their professional strengths and weaknesses (their word, not mine). And they see themselves winning if there are more strengths than weaknesses. Sounds like work to me, especially when they don't have to do it.

So, how are you going to convince them to do it?

Navigating

Winning over the attitude of an *entire faculty* is a significant task that will keep you busy well into your fifth year in a building, and quite probably well beyond. The problem may feel like the challenge is too large to address, and it might appear best to let everything ride rather than upset people who have been in the school for possibly decades.

However, if the past teacher support and growth effort (which was the past administration's effort) is not what you want, or teachers are not meeting minimal standards of proficiency based upon student outcomes, or complacency has taken a foothold - - then it is time to head to the drawing board.

The longer you let lack of teacher growth continue after you have taken on the mantle of leadership in the building, the more it appears unimportant to you, and as a result, the harder it will be to reverse course or stem the tide.

It takes over six miles for a cruise ship to make a 180-degree turn at sea. Think of your school as a cruise ship, and the Herculean effort it will require to alter course when you have taken over from a captain whose purpose and direction associated with faculty growth was on autopilot for a few years. It will be harder to reverse course than it will be to steer a new course.

Tackle a challenge like this head-on, but with strength of conviction and the knowledge that it doesn't have to be completed by Tuesday. I always knew I wanted to be a principal in just one building for my entire career. Being an assistant superintendent, superintendent, and so on, was never a draw for me, because I would be too far from the kids, and too far from the action and the potential of making a real hands-on, long-term positive difference for kids.

With my goals clear, I had the advantage of time on my side.

If being a principal is a stepping-stone to other places - - which is not a bad thing if it's *your* thing - - just know that bringing the concepts unfolding here to fruition will be a little more frantic on your part.

We once had a principal in the district who swore to the staff that he would be there forever, which was well received since he was the third principal in the building in the last seven years. The faculty had heard too many unfulfilled promises from previous principals, and they offered their hearts and minds to them, only to feel rejected when the principal left. Not surprisingly, they felt they had been used as stepping-stones when the two former principals went on to be assistant superintendents.

When the new principal arrived and made grandiose statements - - and his natural charisma carried him a long way - - the teachers again swallowed the bait. Two years later he became the assistant superintendent for curriculum and instruction in the district, and none of the staff in his former school would give him the time of day. He was dead to them!

Rule #1, don't make promises you have no intention of keeping!

Everyone prefers consistency and things they're familiar with. For instance, I never throw out jeans or flannel shirts. The longer I wear them, the more comfortable they are. My old jeans and shirts are never discarded; they simply disintegrate off me over time. By now you're probably imagining someone walking around in raggedy, disheveled clothes - - not a pretty picture! Your school and the pedagogical skills of your faculty cannot be allowed to reach an equivalent state. In your mind, and through your deeds, imagine the school as Brooks Brothers or Neiman Marcus, not the Salvation Army Thrift Store!

Growth Train, Not the Blame Train

The word *growth* here is the optimal word, and must dominate your discussions with teachers. What is most important to you is their growth. It is not the ferreting-out of poor teaching practices (which may, in fact, exist), but rather their pedagogical enhancement.

Because you are learning how to wield the TGT tool, you are indeed heading in the same direction with what you hope will be the same result: teacher growth.

But never forget you are on the _growth train_, not the _blame train_ for this journey. This is not a journey that points fingers at inconsistencies or inabilities. Those inconsistencies and inabilities are there, and they form the basis of the teacher's downward spiral that has been unfortunately nurtured by inappropriate and apathetic administration that inadvertently or consciously supports the status quo.

However, once you have established in your mind where the first steps are located for each teacher, and can work with each teacher to *see their growth potential*, it renders down to a well-planned and collaborative Teacher Growth Trajectory.

Purposeful Self-Reflection

An important initial step in this process is for the faculty to see you as a contemplative promoter of growth through *purposeful self-reflection*. Teachers should see the self-reflection process as having no tangible down side.

Remember, you are building trust at this stage. Inviting teacher growth through ongoing reflective inquiry serves as the antithesis of the traditional hierarchical observation relationship between teachers and a principal that probably was prevalent in the school prior to your arrival.

And while self-reflection seems at first as an individualistic endeavor - - and it is for the most part - - I humbly suggest that as the building principal you must continuously engage with and even measure the amount of purposeful self-reflection taking place.

Your device for measuring *great* self-reflection is a focused, continual, and linear discourse between you and the teacher with you *listening deeply and purposefully* and *with intent!* You want to be able to hear the first stages of teacher growth during the dialogues and, of course, subsequently by seeing it in the classroom.

I know your question now will be: *How do you measure purposeful self-reflection?*

Well, first you measure results.

1) Has the teacher grown in his or her ability to illustrate their teaching techniques and boots-on-the-ground pedagogical practices for you, as well as provide you with logical and well-thought-out explanations?

2) Can the teacher demonstrate a relationship between these techniques and practices and student growth, as well as the value they add to each student's growth?

3) Can the teacher see all of this in the context of delivery of effective instruction to students?

4) Does the teacher recognize areas in need of further and/or sustained growth?

Secondly,

1) Has student ability increased?

2) Have students learned more, and are they better able to apply what they have learned?

3) Does the teacher employ accurate and varied assessment devices?

Teacher growth and student growth are the *only two areas that count.*

Yes, you will hear back from teachers: *"Oh, I feel so much better about myself now I am self-reflecting. I feel in control. I enjoy teaching more now that I have this perspective."* <u>Never</u> accept these responses, and be leery when you hear them, because someone is feeding you a bunch of bull - - unless you see it via the seven (7) questions noted above!

During the TGT planning process and the ongoing meetings intertwined with the process, a teacher might indicate that they are trying the best they can. This will be accompanied by a forlorn look of exhaustion, frustration, and/or "I can't do any more" (think Bambi right after her mother is killed).

This is subterfuge! You cannot accept this as a response to a TGT. This is not the focus, attitude, or degree of commitment that should be invested in the TGT. *The only thing that matters is results - - not effort!*

Your vision cannot be based upon teacher effort but rather student outcomes. The only question requiring an answer is: Have student outcomes improved based upon the results of the teacher's pedagogy in the classroom? Effort toward that goal, while commendable, is not the fruition you require.

How much more frankly can I say it? If a teacher cannot improve student outcomes, then they should not be a teacher! *What other profession will permit the retention of employees who cannot do their job?* This is the curse that surrounds our profession.

David Brooks (2015) writes in his book, <u>The Road to Character</u> that, "Humility is an awareness that your individual talents alone are inadequate to the tasks that have been assigned to you." That is all well and good. However, humility should not be a prerequisite for the profession of teaching, or an excuse for ineffective teaching in the school where you are principal.

I suggest that determination and perseverance (Angela Duckworth's <u>Grit</u>, 2016) applied to a TGT is the antidote to humility.

If this sounds harsh to your ears and mind-set, I cannot apologize. What I will say is, get back to me after you have been a principal for eight years.

Never Accept an Epiphany

Purposeful self-reflection is meant to produce results, not some personal epiphany regarding the teacher's place within the structure of education.

Specific conversations regarding *specific* classroom pedagogical-based issues that result in tangible change that can be seen and subsequently measured are the only results you are looking for as a result of purposeful self-reflection as applied to a TGT.

<u>"Here is what I was doing yesterday, and this is what I did today and here are the results, and, based on these results, tomorrow I will...</u>" is really the only thing I am deeply and intentionally listening for and want to hear! This mind-set comes as a result of constructive, forward-thinking and positive dialogues between professionals who view each other as equals in this process.

The area of purposeful self-reflection is not grandiose or all-encompassing, but rather is a laser beam focus on one pimple on the posterior of the elephant - - this time. Your subsequent conversations with the teacher will always, at some point down the road, end with questions like:

What is next?

What have you been thinking about?

What are you less than pleased with?

What, in your heart, do you want to do better?

How have you assisted the strongest performing student in your class this week?

How have you assisted the most academically needy student in your class this week?

How have you assisted the average-performing student in your class this week?

What was the last pedagogical-based question that you discussed with colleague?

What area are you still looking to drill down into? (Notice, I never use the word weakness.)

What are you most pleased with?

….and also add,

Now you have purposefully reflected, what question(s) do you have for me and, most important, **how do you feel I can I assist you?**

And now you await a potentially fascinating and fulfilling juncture! At some point in this ongoing continuum of developing a TGT, what you want to hear from a teacher is something like: *"I'm good,"* and *"I got this."*

The teacher gets it! Your work with him or her on building their TGT has gotten to where you want it to be: the teacher getting it, doing it, reflecting and growing as a result - - *and* being in charge of their TGT continuum.

You have ridden the growth train into the station, the result of which is purposeful *self*-reflection, *self*-assessment, *self*-confidence and *self*-directed growth. This teacher still requires your support and visibility, but little else. This person becomes your emissary to others, spreading the gospel of the TGT! Can I hear an *Amen*?

It has been less about you pointing out deficiencies than it has been about you *asking the right questions* that then elicits the purposeful self-reflective process that then leads to growth results.

This shared process and decision-making is consistent with Fred Lunenburg and Allan Ornstein's (2013) discussion of Ouchi's Theory Z organizations that feature higher productivity and satisfaction because people have participated in shaping their goals and objectives and have not simply been instructed on what to do now (or next).

Understanding the Intent Up Front

We have been informed since the writings of Carol Ann Tomlinson first hit our educational literature bookshelves that one size does not fit all, and your approach to feedback shouldn't be the same either.

In the book <u>Mentoring Matters: A practical guide to learning-focused relationships</u> (2003), Laura Lipton writes of three alternative stances that can help frame a productive conversation: *consulting, collaborating, and coaching.* According to Lipton (2003), "Skilled mentors must operate across a continuous continuum of interaction to support learning for their colleagues" (p 21).

Conversations with a teacher who demonstrates highly effective practices, and who is striving to grow, is going to be different from a conversation with a teacher highlighting their ineffective practices.

Decide your approach up front: are you going to explore a topic together, ask clarifying questions, and collaborate on new ways to support their instructional practice? Or does the time need to be spent more prescriptively by communicating pedagogical concerns? The guiding factor in any of this will always be their proximity to pedagogical *greatness* and *their willingness to grow pedagogically.*

I submit that your approach to the teacher will have significant impact on their acceptance of a collaborative TGT. Selecting the appropriate stance - - though each is still built on trust - - will have an impact on the productivity of the meeting.

Please do not be so entrenched that you are not deeply and purposefully listening and thus cannot be convinced otherwise concerning the best initial step on their TGT path.

A Little Chapter Closure

In an effort to maintain the focus, it is important for you to project where the conversation is hopefully going to end before it begins and plan how to redirect any conversation initiated by the teacher that may be headed off task.

This does not mean you cannot or should not be influenced off your predetermined path if and when the teacher makes viable points. In fact, you will likely feel comforted or rewarded (or even thrilled) when the teacher does begin to suggest her or his own initiatives. At that point, back off somewhat, even if one or two of your key points have not been established at that particular meeting. You made a major breakthrough if the teacher is attempting to *self*-propel his or her own growth trajectory.

"If you want to build a ship, don't herd people together to collect wood, and don't be so rigid to assign tasks and work, but rather teach them to long for the immensity of the sea" (Antoine de Saint-Exupery, The Little Prince, 1942).

Once you understand this passage, you will understand what establishing a Teacher Growth Trajectory is all about.

Chapter 2
Taking a Leadership Role in
Developing a Teacher Growth Trajectory (TGT)

Former President Ronald Reagan said, "The greatest leader is not necessarily the one who does the greatest things. He [sorry for the gender bias on Ronnie's part] is the one that gets the people to do the greatest things."

You Give a Little to Get a Lot

The job of school principal is transforming rapidly, and for those who do not accept the new reality, and do not seek ways to embrace the change, potentially there will be dire consequences.

The smorgasbord of a principal's responsibilities is constantly being added to, and each new responsibility placed upon a principal's desk has the potential to move you further and further from contact with students and teachers.

There is no stronger impact area indicating this kind of erosion than in the area of your involvement in teacher growth. The all-important emphasis on pedagogical growth can have less time devoted to it due to an increasing and overwhelming array of responsibilities placed upon a principal. Your development and use of collegial power to support and fortify your goals for your school will be the key to success, given the hand you are being dealt.

The mantra of an exemplary leader is "I can't do it alone," and for good reason. You simply cannot get extraordinary things accomplished by yourself.

Collaboration is the master skill that enables teams, partnerships, and other alliances to function effectively. Please note that I wrote collaboration, *not delegation!* Many new administrators get caught up in the concept that a *great* administrator is a *great* delegator. I take strong exception to that concept. Be a collaborator, not an excessive delegator! Delegation says, "Here, do this." Collaboration says, "Let's do this together."

"Collaboration can be sustained only when leaders promote a sense of mutual reliance - - the feeling that we are all in this together" (Kouzes & Posner, 2002, p.265).

Stephen Covey references the importance of synergy. He defines synergy as the state in which the whole is more than the sum of the parts.

Collaboration and communication with various stakeholders is essential when acting as an educational leader. When you involve people in decision-making, policies, and procedures that guide the culture of the building, everyone feels a sense of ownership. Using synergy as the model for your leadership demeanor empowers the staff, and the sum always equals something far greater than any single piece. This overall gestalt permeates into TGTs, making them less of a new initiative and more like business as usual.

Principals tend to focus on how they can push information out to their teachers. But often the best learning comes when information is drawn from the teacher through dialogue. Socrates believed that all learning happens through dialogue. He knew that knowledge was *not transferred* from the head of the teacher to the head of a student like water moving between vessels, but rather *is built* within the mind of the student, by the student, through reflection and response.

It is important to remember one fundamental principle of improving instruction. It is not simply a transfer of knowledge from the head of the principal to the head of the faculty member. It is not like transferring data between two databases, where a perfect copy of the first one is made in the second one. Basically, the principal sends prompts to the teacher in written and/or spoken form. The teacher sees those cues, combines them with a lot of other prompts, and creates knowledge in their own head as a result.

This means that what teachers hear is filtered by a number of different things. It's filtered by their past experiences, by their expectations, by their fears, by their state of mind, and by their emotions - - and let's not forget filtered by the degree of trust that they have in you!.

This entire context goes into interpreting the communication, and if you could see directly into the mind of the person you are speaking to, you'd probably be shocked at how very different what they hear and internalize is from what you are trying to communicate. If you have or had teenaged children, you will know exactly what I mean!

Hoe, Hoe, Hoe

In that sense, when you think about it, teacher growth via your feedback to teachers is similar to gardening.

Now, I'm a terrible gardener. I kill all my plants within a couple of weeks. I simply water them every day, and after a couple of weeks they die. People say to me, "Well, you're overwatering them. You have to test the soil; you have to see if it's too wet. If it's too wet, you pull back. If it's too dry, you add more water. What about the sun? Are you giving them too much sun or too little sun? What about nutrients, and what about all of these other things?" In other words, there are a lot of different factors that go into growing a plant, and a *great* gardener is able to read those factors and make adjustments.

This is analogous to seeking teacher growth through acquisition of knowledge and the subsequent increased awareness of present capabilities. There are a lot of different factors that go into how a principal develops a working knowledge of teachers, and her or his ability to read those factors, to see where the teacher is and be able to quantify what the teacher requires to grow.

It's not simply pushing out the same content to every teacher; it's reading what the teacher needs in order to cultivate their growth.

Overwatering

When things aren't working out, you obviously need to do something different. You can't be like me and just keep adding more and more water, to the point where you simply drown the plant. If things aren't working out, and if the teacher isn't getting the message, you have to try a different approach, because something is preventing the message from getting through.

In seeking to not drown teachers by overwatering them, I am about to plunge into yet another metaphor. In the medical profession, there is very often a question of whether the patient truly understands their medical condition. In these cases, one good technique is for the doctor, instead of explaining the condition to the patient, to start by asking the patient to explain their condition to the doctor. Then the doctor can evaluate whether the patient truly understands it.

The Collaborative Principle and the Principal

Carrie Tucker (2008) wrote, "Principals committed to building successful collaborative school cultures recognize the need to behave more like a facilitator and less like a boss" (p. 8). Her research is complimented by Kathleen Foord and Jean Haar's (2009) findings that emphasize the need for "ongoing leader involvement, not as a director but as a monitor and coach" (p. 22).

Peter Northouse, in his book Leadership, Theory and Practice (2013), points out the many perspectives used to define leadership, but finally settles on the definition of leadership as a process whereby an individual influences a group of individuals to achieve a common goal. James Kouzes and Barry Posner (2012) wrote, "Leadership is a relationship between those who aspire to lead and those who choose to follow. It's the quality of this relationship that matters most..." (p.87).

It is that influence upon others, as they self-select whom in their hearts and minds to follow, which will further support your efforts as an administrator to achieve pedagogical *greatness* within the school.

Within the context of a school system, where principals have an increasing array of job responsibilities, is it any wonder that constantly adding new layers of responsibility is starting to become the proverbial straw on the camel's (and principal's) back sans a collaborative ethos?

From Instructional *Leader* to Instructional *Manager*

Very little will be removed from the table of responsibility set before every school administrator. As previously noted, one place where the drain of time based upon increased responsibility is being felt is in the area of teacher growth. *How can a principal maintain a highly effective teacher growth initiative and still address the multitude of responsibilities that, at times, can stand in the way of fulfilling that goal/responsibility?* While you should never fully abdicate your instructional leadership responsibility, a smart leader realizes that creating an ethos and practice where *teachers take on the mantle of instructional leaders* serves everyone.

My suggestion is that you alter your perspective and practice and transform your role from instructional *leader* to instructional *manager*. Please share responsibilities with *great* educators who view their growth trajectory as an important component of their pedagogical responsibility. Become an inclusive leader who understands and recognizes that the best gains in teacher growth are made within the walls of a collaborative school, and not necessarily solely emanating from the principal's office.

You are attempting to reduce the discrepancy between where the teacher is currently - - in terms of effectiveness in the classroom - - and the performance goals and level of attainment that hopefully you have collaboratively established.

This can only be accomplished via supportive delivery and a mutual understanding of descriptive information about how the teacher was doing a few months ago, is doing now, and where both of you want to be next month, in two months, by the end of the school year, and beyond. You are never going into the classroom simply to do an observation in isolation. You are going into the teacher's classroom to observe growth that is on a continuum. Grant Wiggins wrote, "Effective feedback requires that a person has a goal, takes action to achieve that goal, and receives goal-related information about her or his actions on a continuing basis" (2012, p.13).

The successful leader has the ability to observe and mentor *great* and not-so-great teaching. You must effectively make observations, and as a result of them, scaffold teacher growth. By holding teachers accountable for their teaching, you can develop a unique organizational ethos that aspires to support all staff and therefore all students.

Through collaboration and one-on-one decision-making with *each* teacher, you strive to transform the school organization into a community of professional learners - - teachers who serve to illustrate one of my favorite terms, *professional maturity!* This is truly what constitutes a successful school. And your influence, abilities, and work ethic, fixed on the end result of teacher-sustained growth via a TGT, ultimately decides the organization's fate and, by extension, the academic fate of the students.

Professional Maturity

I have already written about inherent motivation and its importance to the process of TGTs. The definition of the word inherent is clear to everyone, but I submit that it is important for you to find an all-encompassing term that encapsulates what you are trying to elicit from the faculty. A term that defines the ethos you are constructing. For me, that catch phrase is *professional maturity*.

Your movement from instructional leader to instructional manager can only be fully and successfully accomplished if the staff demonstrates professional maturity. This means they have fundamentally accepted their own growth potential, and the collective ambiance of everyone in the school is to grow both collaboratively and pedagogically.

I never indicated to the faculty that I was looking for, or that they must develop, professional maturity. I think mentioning it would be a disaster, since some would be insulted or offended if I did. However, in verbal and written communications to all who could read and to all who could listen, I referred to the outstanding *professional maturity* of the faculty and the subsequent cornucopia of results achieved by them. I sneak in the back door!

Teachers should "...implement forms of teaching and learning appropriate and effective for the populations they serve, and be willing to become pliable and malleable to successfully fulfill the needs of all levels of ability in their students" (Leithwood & Riehl, 2003, p. 3). This essential flexibility cannot be directly built into teacher's growth trajectory, but it surely must be a result of it! It comes to fruition when you create an environment where teachers ask themselves, "Am I reaching every one of my students?" And once a response to the question is rendered, they must take on the necessary growth challenges with confidence because they know that <u>standing alongside them</u> in a collaborative posture will be - - *you!*

The huge shift from instructional *leader* to instructional *manager* will take courage! William Treasurer, in his book <u>Courageous Leadership</u> (2009), outlines the importance of courage within a leader. He, in fact, points out that a courageous leader has a strong belief system and pursues goals with values and passion for the good of the students. It will take courage to admit and assume the position of being an instructional *manager* and not the instructional *leader*. But as the reservoir of your time is drained based upon a myriad of responsibilities requiring attention, this becomes an adjustment well worth the effort.

For the *leader* to *manager* shift to be successful, a leader must be able to inspire leadership roles in others. I am not indicating or prescribing those teachers should constantly stand up and lead groups of other teachers, but rather that they are in a position to serve as *definitive pedagogical models*. These models can be in areas of new concept introduction, assessment, transitioning, developing relevant homework, differentiation, fostering classroom discussions, test and quiz development, curriculum enhancement and parent communications.

What you must do is find best pedagogical practices emerging from leaders *within the faculty* who can and will embrace the role of instructional mentor, either within their grade level and/or department. You should muster courage and recognize faculty leaders (they are already in your cohort of teachers, but in many cases they are dormant), as curriculum and/or pedagogical specialists, and as experts who could assist colleagues in their TGT fulfillment. Absent this sharing of the pedagogical-based torch, you will find it increasingly more difficult to find time to serve as the sole guide of professional growth.

Who Best?

I have always been confident and comfortable in knowing that many curriculum development functions and outstanding pedagogical practices, once exclusively housed in my canoe, are being successfully handled by *great* teachers with a passion for creating and including into classrooms vibrant and exciting experiences for students. Their enthusiasm embraces the entire school environment, and they are willing to share their expertise. Who better than classroom teachers to engage in these efforts and create vibrant and productive environments responsible for teacher growth?

My years of being a principal don't go back to chisels and stone tablets, or even to quills and inkwells. However, I was present when the first SMART Boards were being installed in classrooms. One sign that the TGT was working in school, and that teachers had, in fact, become leaders in pedagogy enhancement from classroom to classroom, was when one of the teachers presented a lesson to me utilizing the SMART Board.

At our post-observation conference, she noted that this was the same lesson/concept that was used by one of her colleagues on the same grade level, but that the teacher originating the lesson reflected on the process and outcomes and wanted to see how the application of a revised model would work. She subsequently shared the lesson and her modifications with this teacher, who presented the lesson (and it just happened to be during a formal observation). What an outstanding experience! I don't recall the lesson, nor do I remember the strength of the lesson and/or presentation, *but I do remember* that collaboration was taking place outside of my vision and earshot.

The only question I asked was, "Did you go back to the teacher and discuss the lesson and its impact?" She said, "Yes," and I said, "that is fantastic! I cannot thank the two of you enough. *Great* job!" I noted introduction of this breakthrough on each of their end-of-year evaluations and praised it to the sky. And, my friends, word gets around, because teachers talk to each other! I remember being as happy as a pig in... - - well, you know what!

As time commitments become more compressed by the anvil-like pressures, it is imperative that your mind-set should not be that you could still deliver everything by yourself. Rather, you must now engage and seek how can you get the same results - - and, I submit to you, even better results - - by using time and professional resources (including, most pointedly, human capital) more effectively.

In essence, you are not giving away power or authority; you are adjusting responsibilities and moving areas of certain responsibilities to *great* teachers who are inherently close to the process, and are in the position to create the best results.

You must have the courage to realize that you do not have all the time in the world, and an app has yet to be developed that creates a 25-hour day. However, there are highly capable colleagues within schools who can accomplish a component of your job better than you can!

It is a strong and courageous principal who realizes collaboration is sometimes their most powerful action tool.

Emergent Leaders

Leaders need to know, according to James Kouzes and Barry Posner (2012):

- How to model the behavior that they want their followers to do
- How to create a vision and inspire others to realize that vision
- How to challenge processes rather than remaining stagnant
- How to enable others to do things
- How to encourage others to do their best
- How to instill in a faculty a sense of professionalism (what I allude to as professional maturity)

There are emergent leaders within every faculty. The foundational question becomes, how can you harness and utilize the talents of those educators and create a cohesive cadre of change agents - - your new instructional leaders - - who drive professional growth opportunities?

Pamela Mendels (2007) writes, in an article focusing on the Wallace Foundation in New York City, about highlighting and cultivating leadership in others and its subsequent importance for the ethos and productivity of a school:

This process of letting go by the principal instills confidence, trust, and respect to each and every teacher imbedded within the change process. The principal must develop an institution that embraces change on the level that it is not something new, but rather something regularly performed within the school to improve and benefit students. Who better than pivotal and knowledgeable teachers to make this occur?

In addition, the claw-back of time gained by you and the trust and respect that will be reciprocated between you and the teachers becomes enormous. By encouraging staff members to analyze pedagogical issues within the school, determine what needs growth, *and lead in the development of that growth*, teachers will be more likely to fully participate in the steps toward their own growth. When teachers have a vested interest in the process, they will certainly do everything possible to get the job done because they *own the process.*

There are two separate but nevertheless equally beneficial outcomes of this process. The first focuses on helping individual teachers reach their potential, and the second focuses on student acquisition of knowledge and enhanced ability.

This leads to the concept that, as the available time a building leader has becomes more constrained, you must first and foremost focus on the ethos you build in the school.

You must build an atmosphere where individuals feel they are a part of the bigger picture, and committed to each other and, therefore, the school. You and the teachers must believe that you are better as a team than you are as outstanding individuals. When educators are supported in improving their craft, feel their expertise is valued, and serve as instructional leaders, the culture of the school and the movement forward allow you to lead from the middle of the cohort (as a collaborator) and not necessarily always from the front.

Driving Dr. Don

You and the faculty will be unsuccessful if you allow members of the school (you and the teachers) to remain stagnant in terms of growth.

This statement is not meant to place blame, although it does require that a principal have a specific type of mentality to get the job accomplished, and to do it correctly. A passion, drive and commitment are foundational!

I created an excellent working relationship with all (OK, most) of my colleagues who were principals of schools within the district and those in surrounding school districts as well. *Great* people in *great* schools, who were very nice, dedicated professionals.

Nonetheless, I wanted the school where I was principal to be the best by whatever measurement was applied. I was passionate about being the best! The concept fueled me! It made me arrogant! It made me demanding! It made me unsympathetic to those teachers living from VACA to VACA and used their vocation - - and *my kids* - - as the vehicle to get from VACA to VACA. I had teachers request transfers out of the school to other schools in the district. One was even a Physical Education teacher!

Good-gravy-Marie, even a PE teacher wanted out of the school where I was principal! I had teachers retire just a little earlier than they thought they would because of me. And I also had teachers who cried when they were involuntarily transferred out of the school because of district need based on fluctuations in enrollment.

Our school was recognized as a New York State Blue Ribbon School of Excellence!

The United States Department of Education School recognized our school for Overall Excellence!

Redbook Magazine recognized our school as one the 72 Best Elementary Schools in America!

I was recognized as the New York State Elementary School Principal of the Year!

Why all these recognitions? It was because of the teachers and their continual growth and focus, and the *professional maturity* ethos created within the school.

By the way, the key word here is *our*. I never saw the school as anything other than *our* school - - all of us, the entire team. I always saw myself as just one member of the team who, upon occasion, got to stand up front, as in being recognized as principal of the year and/or representing the school faculty and staff on two trips to the White House because of the awards.

Recall, if you will, that I wrote in the introduction about achieving *greatness* and how it can work for you! Imagine the team in our collective canoe receiving these recognitions. Imagine what they did for intrinsic motivation and supporting the concept of *professional maturity!*

Now, again take it a step further and put yourself in the place of a new teacher coming into the building and what he or she must be thinking! How hard would the TGT concept be for them to accept? Like water off a duck's back!

A Little Principal Reflection

One of the initial questions you need to ask yourself is what you feel you need to know/learn and/or experience to prepare yourself for the role of observer of pedagogical practices.

Then, what will you need to know/learn and/or experience to be able to work collaboratively with teachers to chart a course of sustainable teacher growth with you as a guide on the side, not as someone pushing the teacher up a hill?

Being able to cull out from your experiences and your innate abilities the thing or things you feel might be an obstacle or obstacles to this endeavor will provide you with some precursors to consider and a potential direction.

You will need to figure out where *your own* professional growth trajectory needs to be long before ever trying a TGT plan on someone else. The problem is that you have a short window of opportunity - - less than four years for your new teacher - - and a steep learning curve if you are presently not well prepared to undertake this endeavor.

Brussels Sprouts

There is an odious tendency that rears its ugly head during the observation process, and it occurs when principals (administrators) turn it into *let's just get it done*. A principal may tell him or herself, "I have X number to do this year, and it is simply a matter of putting them on the weekly conveyer belt of school-related business that must be completed, and as the list is diminished, my sense of accomplishment grows proportionally. I am close to getting finished with this task; therefore, I am doing well."

Sort of reminds me of my childhood dinner plate and the Brussels sprouts I was told to finish. Steamed, overly salted - - *and* without butter! I pushed them around my plate with my fork while I wondered how many more florets I had to eat until I was considered finished. I didn't appreciate them until I started preparing them myself as an adult, split and braised in virgin olive oil, garlic, and small pieces of bacon, with red pepper flakes and topped with grated Parmesan and Romano cheese.

What you will be creating through a TGT is a process that is more effective and palatable (olive oil, bacon, garlic, Parmesan, and Romano cheese), and less stagnant (boiled and salted). Yes, it will be more work making the Brussels sprouts the new way, but it will also be better accepted, even if it takes time to bear fruit while teachers further develop their *professional maturity.*

Authentic Leadership

Maya Angelou wrote, "I've learned that people will forget what you said, people will forget what you did, but people will never forget how you made them feel."

Biplab Datta (2015) wrote about one word commonly associated with excellent leadership, and that word is *authenticity*. Many people simply think of authenticity as being genuine or being true to themselves. However, the reality of *authentic leadership* is more rigorous and complex.

You must work to achieve authenticity, because it generates significant results. Research indicates that "…authentic leadership leads to various dimensions of managerial effectiveness including organizational performance, satisfaction of follower needs, and improvement in the quality of work life. Authentic leadership leads to a decrease in negative attitudes and behavior of followers like absenteeism, dissatisfaction and hostility. It conversely leads to enhancement in positive group attitudes and behavior" (Datta, 2015, p. 70).

The first step to authenticity is *awareness*. However, instead of using the term self-awareness, Karrissa Thacker (2016) uses "…selves-awareness…" in reference to the idea that "there is no one single version of any of us to behold. We show different sides of ourselves in different contexts all the time" (p. 73).

This means that through intense personal and professional reflection and reflection on others' perception of us, we must identify our own strengths, weaknesses, values, mores, and motivations. Additionally, a crucial part of *awareness* is having a clear vision of the kind of leader you want to be.

Thacker (2016) goes on to write, "The leadership development task is to keep reminding yourself of your ideal self and to remain cognizant of your current self at the same time" (p. 83). In this regard, even if your actions occasionally fall short due to circumstances, they are always authentic *as long as they are aligned with your pursuit of the vision.* The ends do justify the means. However, you can't be too Machiavellian, because the *means* are highly important, and do require care and deliberate planning. Be forewarned that a misuse of the path to the goal can erode the trust factor.

Authentic leaders must also recognize the importance of *transparency*. Thatcher (2016) wrote, "You cannot be an authentic leader without having the courage to be transparent and have honest conversations at the right time" (p. 104).

There is that word again - - *courage!* This is in regard to both your personal and professional lives. While leaders must be very cautious regarding what is and is not appropriate, being emotionally transparent and vulnerable can deepen the relationship you have with your followers (Thacker, 2016). Professionally, *strategic transparency* is necessary for the growth of individuals and organizations as a whole. "Alan Mulally, leader of Ford Motor Company's transformation noted, you can't manage a secret" (Thacker, 2016, p. 105).

In order for teams to come together to conquer a problem, they must first understand the reality of what they are up against. While leaders should be transparent with problems, they must also present followers with a plan of action and the belief that together and through hard work, they will solve them. This is where your presentation toehold of a TGT concept originates.

Favorites

An established colleague of mine once offered this sage advice as I was beginning my administrative career. She told me not to have favorites and/or show favoritism! "Don't show the faculty that you favor anyone, be consistent and be fair and stay in the middle of the road," she said.

While I accept fair and consistent, staying in the middle of the road will only get you run over. I did have favorites! I made my favorites known to everyone by my actions and deeds throughout the building and throughout the years. These favorites, however, were not the people who sucked up to me!

My favorites were *great* teachers, or those working diligently at becoming a *great* teacher.

My favorites were those who didn't always agree with me, and eventually showed me a better way because I was willing to listen, and *they were willing and felt comfortable enough with me* to share.

My favorites were teachers who put kids first, second, _and_ third!

My favorites were those who took pedagogical chances. Some worked and some failed, but we tried it, and together we all grew from all the experiences.

My favorites were those who did not have a red magic marker.

My favorites were those who displayed - - yes, you guessed it - - *professional maturity*.

Those were the people who were my favorites, and I beamed when I was with them. I pushed them into the spotlight, giving them all the credit, and I did proclaim them as *great* teachers and better than the others. As previously noted, this is one of the major problems with our profession, the idea that no particular one teacher is better than the others. Remember mayonnaise, and that you want salsa!

Why can't we point out better performers?

Why can't we show others who should be emulated?

Why can't we point toward a particular teacher and say, "*...do what he does or she does*"?

Why can't we label certain teachers as *great* teachers?

Well, why not? I always did!

(The only issue is the need for this to be covert, strictly internal building dynamics. Publicly announcing the best teachers will create a mess for you at student placement time. What parent wants anything less than the best teacher for their child?)

Once Upon a Time

Once, very early in my career, I nominated a teacher to be recognized by the Walt Disney Outstanding Teacher Recognition program. The teacher was initially a little reluctant because she was shy and didn't think she deserved the honor. However, she eventually acquiesced and allowed me to recommend her.

The paperwork involved required a written recommendation from the teachers' union president. The union president refused!

I remember Lou meeting with me, the Disney recommendation form rolled up in his hand -- like a handle of an axe -- and stating he would not distinguish one of his teachers from the rest. He boasted, "All the teachers in the school district deserve this award." The guy was a mouth breathing, freakin' Neanderthal!

The teacher backed out, and I withdrew her name to maintain labor peace with the union president. But upon reflection, I decided he was right. This was too public. However, he did not move me off course from noting teacher *greatness* to our colleagues internally.

First

During my first meeting with teachers new to the school, I point to a teacher on their grade level and say, "For this entire school year, do what he/she does, when he/she does it and how he/she does it! I know you have wanted to be a teacher all your life, and that you are excited about starting your first teaching position and utilizing all the lessons and activities you have been dreaming and planning to do for years. That's all fine, and I look forward to seeing every one of them. However, for this first year, I want you to mimic, follow, emulate, and copycat (Mr. or Ms.) _____."

Of course I asked that specific teacher beforehand if they would take the new teacher under their wing (this was outside of or in addition to whomever the district assigned to the teacher as their formal mentor). The veteran teachers knew what I was talking about, because years earlier I had placed each of them under someone else's wing!

It was an ethos, a collaborative effort, a system, and a process inherent in the culture of our school and its induction process. And no, I was not building Stepford-Teachers (although I was accused of doing just that by colleagues outside the building but within the district).

Building such an essential climate for success can only be achieved through commitment from the faculty. It was very slow going at first, very much like building a beach one grain of sand at a time. I also asked the second- and third-year teachers who I had developed confidence in to eyeball the new kid on the block, and provide her or him with the perspective that only a relatively newer teacher would have.

Can you create a school ethos built on collaboration and shared decision-making among all levels of staff members, including administration, department heads, teachers, curriculum coaches, and other staff members, *and* bring the new teacher into the collaborative mix as quickly as possible?

Collaboration within an academic setting is essential, because it builds upon a sense of belonging and importance for included members - - especially for the new kid on the block. It helps new teachers feel like they belong to the organization. It also fosters an atmosphere of understanding school-wide goals and motivates him or her to be part of the process toward professional and organizational greatness. Your untenured teacher cannot be brought into this realm quickly enough.

Induction

Another way to positively impact the environment of the school and build a TGT mind-set is by providing a strong induction program that highlights the degree of professional growth through commitment that you expect.

The induction program should note what the teacher new to the building can expect from you as the building principal involving their professional teacher growth trajectory. While these are certainly individualized and personalized discussions, a comment about growth trajectories at the first general meeting reinforces the concept.

Delivered at induction, this highlights the prominent position it holds in your mind, and creates the ethos that this is a regular and expected part of the teaching assignment at your particular school. TGT is not an add-on presented in October, but rather an integral component of daily life in school that is discussed in August. Making use of the experts within the school environment can help teachers new to the school with immediate and personalized support. You have the teachers focused on TGT starting at "hello!"

You are not retraining or re-indoctrinating established faculty. You are presenting this concept and practice from the first day a teacher begins in the school. Now, fast-forward to you being in one school for a couple of decades, and imagine what you will eventually have as a cadre of educators!

My professional life grew more wonderful each and every year!

Invite Them Into the Canoe

An administration based on fear, control, secrecy, or an agenda with only one person as the author is in complete opposition to the kind of growth mind-set you want your teachers to expect.

An administrator who uses these types of powers will not be able to build trust with staff, and will instead lead people to avoid risk-taking and focus only on the status quo, simply to appease you. The status quo is a known commodity and extremely comfortable, like your oldest pair of jeans. Teachers in such a system may never know what your goals are, and since they have not been invited to participate (join you in the canoe) via their own growth trajectory, they will have no idea in which direction to grow (or row).

MUSTabating

MUSTabating is thinking that something *must be done*, with you granting no quarter. The TGT concept presented at new teacher induction creates the idea that it is one of the processes that *must be done*.

There will be many MUSTabatings: arriving at school, student supervision, and class on time, reaching out to parents, providing extra help for students, and so on. They are all preconditions of a successful employment and continuation of employment, as well as the foundational structure of this particular school. MUSTabating issues are the parts that have a tremendous positive impact building toward a *great* school. You clearly *must* place TGT on the list as one of those *musts, beginning with* the induction meeting.

Having an Opponent is Not as Good as Having an Ally

Even when everything meets expectations, there are still many opportunities for teacher growth, and you should strive to offer suggestions for continued enhancement of pedagogy.

Obviously, when a lesson does not meet standards, you must be prepared to present the information in a manner that does not alienate the teacher. After all, *having an opponent is not as good as having an ally*.

Effective feeding-back, feeding-forward and feeding-up are the keys to quality growth that is focused in the correct and most beneficial direction! It is important to remember that you cannot and should not comment on every issue or concern you may have after viewing the teacher. Select the most critically important, relevant, useful points for growth for the teacher, and communicate them as clearly and concisely as possible.

Resist the temptation to share too many "...this is what I did in *my* class..." So much of teaching is personal preference that it will likely not be helpful to recommend that the teacher use your preferred method. The irony here is that while personal preference will be understood by you, and to some extent accommodated, it must be tempered by adding the concept that it must be an *effective* personal preference!

Also, it is best to approach your recommendations from a student perspective, and in a collegial tone. Avoid recommendations that appear arrogant and that set you up as the expert. You are, but don't flaunt it, because it's vital to maintain a collegial atmosphere.

How Do You Get to Carnegie Hall?

Practice, practice, practice is what is required to develop your ability to *deeply and intentionally listen,* to think about what you are seeing, and then process all the information. Time certainly grants you the ability to get better, and all the on-the-job practice will turn you into a speedy recorder of what you are witnessing, and a proficient gatherer of **evidence**.

One way that I found helpful, and a fun way to practice delineating what you are watching during a formal observation, is to take your tablet (not the one with the 10 Commandments chiseled on it), and while you are watching television, try to type what one character is saying and doing in a television show, or even try doing it during a commercial. You will become adept at noting what is being said and done, and you will develop your keyboard skills at the same time (I'd stay away from doing this while watching GoT, because I still don't know what the heck is going on there).

Courage (There's That Word Again)

> I am convinced that courage is the most important of all the virtues. Because without courage, you cannot practice any other virtue consistently.
> ~ Maya Angelou

It will require courage to care less about being liked and more about creating a team of educators always focused on a pursuit of professional pedagogical growth.

Members of the faculty who are not accustomed to engaging in dialogues with the building principal and/or with colleagues about growth of their pedagogy might look at you and your effort as boat-rocking. *"We've always done it this way…"* is probably the most potentially damaging fixed mind-set that faculty members can have, because they are *not* moving forward, they are marching in place - - and they are complacent and even happy, thrilled, and somewhat proud of that complacency. *We have already reached the pinnacle* will be their mantra!

(However, if you think you have reached the peak, do you realize in which direction your next step will take you?)

Please Like Me

The desire to be liked will be hard to resist. It's human nature to want to be liked. Your decision is this: do you want to be *liked* because you have maintained the status quo (translation - - left people alone), or do you want to be *respected* because you have created an environment and culture of high expectations and a blueprint for continual faculty growth? This is your decision, and your call, and do not let it become clouded. Also, do not let me know if you choose the former instead of the latter.

Unfortunately, what may often be the best thing to do for students may also trigger knee-jerk disapproval from colleagues. Teachers are often resistant to change, and your efforts may make people *uncomfortable*, which result in them becoming resistant, many times in an almost recalcitrant fashion. This needs to be avoided at all costs!

So how does one move forward with pushing an agenda of professional growth as an outgrowth of the observation process? What might appear as overwhelming at first is doable if you use all the tools you have at your disposal. The most important tools in your toolbox are *time* and *commitment.* If you commit long-term to a school, you are in a position to slowly instill in people a growth mind-set that is neither threatening nor debilitating!

And please allow me to respectfully remind you - - and this will be so obvious that I feel I must apologize in advance - - that the new people you hire will be loyal to you! You have given them something they have dreamed about, probably for years. Do not underestimate that power! Don't abuse it but also don't underuse it. As previously written, it will also not hurt when they hear about the teachers you let go after two years because they were not meeting the standards of providing exemplary pedagogy to the students.

The power of the throne is scary, and it sounds ominous. But remember to maintain it in check, although "...it is good to be king" (Mel Brooks, *History of the World Part 1*, 1981) - - and please allow me to equally add, "or queen."

O Captain! My Captain!

Great schools are the result of *great* leadership. James Collins (2001) portrayed a leader as an individual who displays a balance between humility and will. Leaders transform theory into practice through their ability to create *disciplined* employees, *disciplined* thinking, *disciplined* behaviors and *disciplined* actions (Collins, 2001). When organization members display *discipline* (what I call professional maturity), leaders do not have to keep a strict chain of oversight.

The working environment is developed under friendly and respectful conditions, and your actions show consistency because your communications, intentions, and actions are reliable, which creates teacher buy-in.

Preston Pysh, in his book <u>The Diary of a West Point Cadet</u> (2011), lays out what he believes to be the twelve most important lessons for any leader:

1) Leaders listen
2) Leaders build effective teams
3) Leaders are detail-oriented
4) Leaders speak up
5) Leaders are truthful at all times
6) Leaders are mentally tough
7) Leaders are creative
8) Leaders take charge and lead by example
9) Leaders learn from their mistakes
10) Leaders are competitive and use foresight to plan and win
11) Leaders network with people they admire
12) Leaders work hard and possess patience

While Captain Pysh was referring to his service at the United States Military Academy at West Point, it occurred to me as I read his points that each and every one is clearly applicable to your role as a principal.

Pysh further writes, "Subordinates (his choice of words, not mine) have a strong potential to provide great input - - when a leader doesn't give his (Pysh wrote this in 2011, but he is still disrespectfully gender-specific - - Army mentality) subordinates the appropriate respect and venue to provide their input, frustration and information sharing is inhibited from the bottom up. If subordinates perceive disrespect, their desire to continue helping the leader diminishes rapidly" (p. 24).

There is nothing in his concept that doesn't speak loud and clear to the relationship you want to have with the teachers you will be working with - - of course with exclusion of the word subordinates - - to assist in establishing their individualized TGT.

Pysh further asserts, "The failure of many leaders is their inability to cohesively utilize an individual's attributes for the success of the group - - when a leader takes charge of a group, he immediately needs to understand that every team member has positive attributes that can be extracted and applied to the team's success" (p. 40).

The implications of this statement for an educational leader are huge! You *must* know your teachers. You *must* know their strengths and growth needs and realize that just about *everyone can be used to strengthen other members of the school.*

This is the same knowledge leaders must pay heed to when forming Professional Learning Communities (PLCs), or grouping teachers for other tasks like curriculum committee work. Additionally, you must be willing to admit that you aren't the solitary keeper of knowledge. There are others within the organization who know as much, maybe more, about certain topics, and their expertise and input must be recognized and valued.

This concept is an easy one, and one you *must* embrace to construct a *great* school. The best teacher growth facilitator is another teacher!

Community of Inquiry (CoI)

Please allow me to now de-emphasize the Professional Learning Community (PLC) concept as has been delineated during many years in our profession. A professional learning community (PLC) is a group of educators who meet frequently, exchange knowledge, and work together to improve the performance of the students in the school. "A PLC is a group of collegial faculty and staff joined together through their dedication to student learning" (Gray, Kruze, & Tarter, 2015, p. 23).

In its place, please seek to develop a *Community of Inquiry*. At its foundation, a *Community of Inquiry* (CoI) is built around each *individual* teacher's TGT and your desire to establish a standard of growth within the school that is built upon the premise that individual TGTs create a collaborative growth mind-set within the culture of a school.

Three (3) types of *components* are subsumed within a CoI, and are its fabric. Frankly, a deep and sustained TGT process built within the ethos of a school is only possible through *cognitive, social* and *teaching* presence.

The *cognitive presence* within a *Community of Inquiry* is the purposeful, reflective process to gather relevant and informative insights into each teacher's sustained growth. What are the areas targeted for growth that provide integration to support the areas of growth and the resolution of applying new and/or enhanced processes?

The *social presence* within a *Community of Inquiry* supports the sharing of expertise, concepts, ideas, perceptions, theory and best practices within the faculty. It represents an open communication built on and sustained by trust among specific teachers and you. You are developing and allowing to occur a group cohesion interacting around the common thread of pedagogical growth through *individual* TGTs. While the specific goals will be different for each teacher, the concept CoI creates a global growth initiative where everyone brings something to the banquet to share with others while they are growing individually.

The *teaching presence* within a *Community of Inquiry* supports the discourse that shapes and renders growth through change. Your feeding-back, feeding-forward, and feeding-up are the structural keys to this component. It is the design of the organization through maneuvering the parts rather than seeking to alter the faculty as a whole. This component addresses specific and direct pedagogical needs toward universal attainment of *great* teaching.

But I Have My Master's Degree

Many veteran teachers believe their advanced degrees and their years of experience are enough, and don't believe they require a growth trajectory. They might feel somewhat belittled if you do not recognizing their skill level based upon their time in the trenches. The problem for many is that they are in a trench they have dug for themselves based upon the very years of repetitive pedagogy that translates *to them* as growth and professional achievement.

However, in most cases it isn't growth as much as it is repetition. *A TGT serves as the ladder out of the trench.* And it is not the teacher's fault. An administrator who lets teachers alone in their classrooms, and is not a regular presence in the classroom, and doesn't engage teachers in purposeful reflection, is saying to the teacher by his or her absence that everything is fine -- I don't need to see you; you are doing fine! Please define *fine* for me and is *fine* acceptable to you? If it is, please start looking for the receipt for this book.

Initially, there may exist a strong misconception among the teachers about the development of TGTs. The more veteran teachers may imagine (and/or want to believe) that TGTs should only be focused on weak and unproven teachers.

However, the reality is that a *great*, well-developed, and effectively focused and delivered growth trajectory will work for *everyone*. What doesn't help is when you and your cadre of building-level administrators are not prepared to work with strong classroom teachers, and you subsequently offer them limited feedback.

Actually, these are the educators who are able to benefit most from feeding-forward and feeding-up. Additionally, you support this misperception of growth trajectories being only for weak teachers when you only develop growth trajectories for teachers believed to be weak. *TGTs are for everyone in the school.* When teachers look to the left, when they look to the right, when they look straight ahead, and when they look to the rear, they must see everyone purposefully engaged in a TGT.

Think of Oprah and her past holiday giveaway television shows, "...and you get a TGT, and you get a TGT, and you get one, and you and you - - everyone gets a TGT!"

A Little Metacog Never Hurt Anyone

Without trying to be too theoretically based (which has never been my forte) let's define metacognition as active monitoring and regulation of one's cognitive (thinking) processes.

The TGT process in many ways seeks to kick-start the metacognitive process in teachers. I equate most teachers' normal mind-set to the drive from Los Angeles to Las Vegas, a long stretch of open road that requires nothing more than mindless repeating of the driving process, never stopping to smell the roses along the roadside (there are no roses along the roadside - - it is a desert - - but I was stuck with what to write to give you an idea that teaching is not mindless repetition of what was previously done - - mile after mile, day after day, and school year after school year). Where is the growth?

Metacognition is thinking about one's thinking! It is an awareness of how you think and the application of the metacog process. It is conscious thought, and an awareness of your mental process that promotes purposeful reflection, control, assessment and subsequent growth as it is applied to the learning process. It allows one to problem-solve, estimate performance, and self-determine how much was learned.

Metacognition simply allows teachers to take control of their own pedagogical growth in the TGT atmosphere that you are developing. Finally, and most important, it involves purposeful, self-reflective mental activities that raise learning awareness and bring attention to one's role in the activity. Metacognition leads to self-confidence and indirectly to student success based upon teacher's pedagogical growth.

You are not in any manner leaving the teacher to grow autonomously. Ultimately, you certainly are looking for them to plan, organize, control and assess their own TGT. They will experience higher levels of success because they have growth through an internal process, not one mandated by you.

<u>The irony is not lost on me, and should not be lost on you, that what you are doing is providing for teachers the same thing you want them to provide for their students: time, and an environment to maximize learning and growth via learning strategies that fit their own learning style</u>!

The metacognition process allows teachers to take charge of their own learning. It involves awareness of how they learn, an evaluation of their learning needs, generating strategies to meet these needs, and then implementing the strategies (Hacker, 2009).

Ugly

Please take another walk with me to a place where things can get a little ugly, especially if you have a teacher who is not up for the challenge of *purposeful* self-reflection and/or growth based upon collaboration.

And, I will admit, I was a little fanatical and dogmatic when this occurred, and I may have stepped *just slightly* over the line. However, I would do it again in a New York minute!

I had a *great* teacher announce in September that she would be retiring at the end of the school year. The last thing I wanted was for her to *only* pack up on her last day and parcel out her physical teaching materials (supplies, equipment, lesson plans, and so on) to those left behind. What I *really* wanted her to leave behind was her talent, skill sets and academic mind-set: her sense of continued growth for herself and her students, her pedagogical prowess, and her *greatness* as a teacher.

I asked her if, during the course of the school year, I could send in colleagues to watch her teach. She was embarrassed and at first indicated some degree of discomfort with the thought. I simply said that her walking out the door with her physical teaching materials dispersed to others would be fine, but leaving when her pedagogical skill sets hadn't been disseminated or, at the very least, exposed to others would be a sin.

She eventually agreed and had a steady stream of visitors during the school year. However, one teacher I *invited* to see her didn't want to go (remember earlier I mentioned two teachers who were hired based upon nepotism? Want to make an educated guess here?).

I indicated to the teacher in question how powerful a teacher Diane was, and that I wanted Diane to leave some of that knowledge and ability behind for everyone else. This particular teacher felt she did not require the visits because she was already an outstanding educator. She then made a huge error! She asked me if, when she was set to retire, I would do the same and have others come in and view her (self-described) exceptional skills in the classroom. In a heartbeat I said calmly, "Never, because you are not a *great* teacher!" The teacher was stunned!

Now there will be times when inadvertently your stock will rise based upon something you have done (and, to be totally candid with you, there will be times when your stock can drop like a rock because of something you did).

This teacher, the stunned one, verbally complained about what I had said to her to all who had auditory perceptiveness in the Faculty Room. How terrible it was for me to say this to her, and how dare I not think of her as a *great* teacher!

Bottom line: everyone in the school knew how she got her job (it was who she was related to), and that she was not a *great* teacher by any stretch of the imagination. Now, how do you think I looked in the minds of the teachers?

The teachers' union eventually got involved, wanting to pump the brakes on any initiative to stratify their members (just let the teachers' union get involved, and you will see it is *one for all and all for the weakest one!*). The union position was that they did not want me telling teachers what to do during their prep time.

OK, I agreed that I should not dictate to teachers how to spend their preparation periods. I subsequently assigned teachers to the visit during their teaching day, and I went in and covered their class while they visited Diane. Not every teacher wanted it that way, and most went during their prep period. However, in every faculty there will be union-runners (as I call them), and my research and experience has indicated that in many cases there is a direct correlation between the weaker the teacher and the faster they run to the bosom of the teachers' union.

By the way, because I know you are curious, the teacher who wanted me to anoint her as a *great* teacher upon her retirement never went to see Diane teach! So, in her end-of-year evaluation I wrote about the "...missed opportunity..." when she did not avail herself of the opportunity to see a colleague demonstrate highly effective pedagogy. I noted that it would have "...served her well, based upon my past observations..." (and I specifically added the dates of the observations I thought would have been impacted, and specifically enumerated the areas that were targeted by me for growth that aligned with the specific areas of the retiring teacher's strengths).

OK, I am vindictive! I am an _____! I was really, really _____ that she would not take advantage of this opportunity! But I knew she believed, given her link to district hierarchy, she was untouchable. She thought she was hired because she was a *great* teacher and not because of whom she knew. I was forced to hire this person in the first place and it made me mad! It embarrassed me that she was in our teaching cohort.

So, I wrote what I wrote. And, if you are thinking it had an impact - - well, it had zero, zilch, nada, nil, null, zip, naught and none.

But what the hell, *I* felt better!

Never Give Up

I will *never* give up on the naysayers. I will *never* give up on the union-runners. I will *never* give up on trying to improve the quality of education for the students in school, especially when someone is short-changing them by their *unwillingness* to grow.

I am a dog with a favorite bone. I report on what I see, and do not placate anyone trying to force my silence. During my second-to-last year prior to my retirement, I was still working on teacher growth with one of the poorest teachers in the school. Personally, I think she got tired of me relentlessly, year after year, working with her in developing a growth trajectory that she never bought into.

During that year, she sued me via her union for age discrimination. I was targeting her because of her age, she claimed. She did not prevail in her suit because, a) I could show that I hired teachers older than she was, and b) I had a trail of observation reports and archived efforts to improve her pedagogy documented for many, many years prior to her becoming, as she claimed, old. Having lost her case, she subsequently retired.

Who won? *The kids did!* <u>Never give up</u>!

A Little Secret

We had a little secret that bonded our school cohort together. It buoyed our already incredibly high sense of accomplishment as a *teaching team,* and really bonded us as a group. The school district (superintendent and board of education) decided it was time for a new formal reading series, and a process was set in motion to review formats from publishers, followed by a committee making a decision about what series we would purchase as a district-wide initiative.

Every elementary school had representatives on the committee. Reports back from the reps from our school were less than enthusiastic about everything under review. However, a district-wide final decision was made and the district formally adopted one of the series reviewed by the committee.

That spring and into the fall we were in-serviced on the series and how to best utilize the books, workbooks, computer software and Teacher Editions we were all given.

While it was unanimous that this was the best of the reading series that had been up for review and adoption, the teachers in our school felt it was significantly short of the methods we were currently using in our school.

Remember, a textbook series is not designed specifically for your student population, but rather for a national mass market. The publishers' goal is to make one edition fit all. Publishers want to sell the same books in New York, Wisconsin, California, Alabama, Texas, and so on, so the series was homogenized, pasteurized, middle-of-the-road, and we were way beyond it. The teachers in our school were extremely upset about the district-wide mandate to use the series, because we viewed textbooks as resources, not as a curriculum.

So, as a faculty, we swore allegiance to the series, opened the boxes of fresh new books when they were delivered, and placed them on the shelves in the classrooms.

Now, please remember and take into the *strongest of considerations* that I had already worked in the district as principal for more than two decades, and our school had won numerous awards and recognitions that were proudly displayed in our hallway.

So I DO NOT recommend you do what I did - - at least during your first twenty years or so.

At a September faculty meeting, I announced that "…our district-approved reading series is ____ & ____ (the one the district purchased), and we were all trained, and the materials and supplies are in our classrooms." And then I said, "I have great confidence in you, and your ability to select the most appropriate learning materials for each student in your classroom, and you must select appropriately for the advancement of each student, and use an eclectic approach to teaching reading and writing from the vast amount of support materials you have at your disposal."

One faculty member raised her hand and asked, "…then do we have to use ____ & ____?"

I picked up my notecard and read with deep conviction and a firm voice, "*…our district-approved reading series is ____ & ____, and we were all trained, and the materials and supplies are in our classrooms. I have great confidence in you and your ability to select the appropriate learning materials for each student in your classroom, and you must select appropriately for the advancement of each student, and select an eclectic approach to teaching reading and writing from the vast number of support materials you have at your disposal.*"

"Do I need to read this again?" I asked in an extremely pleasant and frilly voice. "Please trust me. I only want what is best for our kids, and YOU and YOUR academic decisions are what are best for our kids."

Cocky? Too powerful? Too self-assured? Too out-there? Nope! Nope! Nope! Nope!

We had already demonstrated our abilities, and everyone in central office knew how *great* we were, and they had always left us alone. Besides, the only time our superintendent came to our school was for a photo op for the district newsletter, and the assistant superintendent for curriculum and instruction was there even less. Truth be told, I only saw the two of them when I was in central office for cabinet meetings.

So, this wasn't as much bravado as it might appear on the surface. I trusted the amount of human capital I had with the teachers, and I also counted on the human capital I had established with administration in district office. I always had in the back of my mind this goofy thought that they were afraid to come to our school! And boy, did this bond us as a cadre of teachers!!

Hippo

Let me address the hippopotamus in the room (just so tired of always seeing elephants or 800-pound gorillas; they're so big, how did they even get in the room?) for just about every school, and for just about every school leader.

As previously addressed, the desire to be liked by one's own staff can cloud judgment and make it difficult to do what is best in any situation.

Unfortunately, what may be construed as being the best for a teacher (by the teacher) may not equate to what is best for the kids. When you follow through on what is best for the students, you may/will receive disapproval from that teacher. People are often resistant to change, and the change that leaders have to push forward will often make these same people fight back simply because they do not want to move out of their own comfort zone.

The only people who like change are babies with wet diapers. Therefore, maintaining one's integrity - - translation, your focus is on what is best for the students, always - - is extremely important. And always remember, it is *impossible* to please everyone.

"If they like you because you're fair, consistent, empathetic, or a positive person, that's great. But if they like you only because you provide them with everything they want and no degree of discomfort, what have you gained" (Cottrell, 2002, p. 20)?

This concept is especially essential for new school building leaders who may have been a teacher in the same building or district, or even as you enter a new facility where no one knows you. The reality here is that *it is important to be liked or disliked for the right reasons* (It is always most comforting to me to be disliked for the right reasons.)

You will be able to accept being disliked if the academic goals for your students are being met. And the reality is that once those who dislike you see the end result, their opinion of you will inevitably change. You may have forced them to alter practices that were not leading to positive outcomes, and, once viewed within the proper context of *we are here for kids*, opinions will change. You must always do what is right and avoid the gray areas.

> To know what is right and not do it is the worst cowardice.
> ~ Confucius

Porsche

In my youth I worked at a soft-serve ice cream drive-in (Carvel, for those of you familiar with this regional confection). My boss would constantly observe the exact number of swirls I put on a small cone and the exact number I would add to the large cone. For him, each swirl cost him money, and his profit was based upon the prescribed amount of ice cream allocated for each cone.

He would tell me, "Never ask if the customer wants a sugar cone versus a waffle cone..." and "...always serve the waffle cone unless the customer asked for the sugar cone."

Why? Obviously, the sugar cone cost him more, and his profit was less each time a sugar cone went out of the store.

We're talking about factions of a penny, but in his mind and in his practice, *it all added up*. Who knew important life lessons could be hidden in swirls of ice cream? It was the end result of the addition or subtraction of all the components that created the impact. I also had all the proof I needed as I saw him drive to and from work in his black Porsche 911 Targa (my dream car).

Apply the same principle to the Teacher Growth Trajectory (TGT) process. It is in many ways the small components of what a teacher does or does not do that are significant in the long run. And, of most importance and subsequent consequence in a school building where we had students for six years (kindergarten through fifth grade), I had the luxury of time with them so the little pieces certainly did add up. The small components added to a teacher's pedagogical practices built up over time and helped to create a more effective teacher for the wide range of student capabilities that walked through the main entrance of our school.

Given the scope of time I had with *my kids*, and the length of time I would have with the teachers, measured in terms of a career, I could look at feedback as a conversation opener, the beginning of a dialogue, the first step into the dialogue of a growth trajectory. Rarely was there the "...you must stop that now and do this other thing immediately."

Reverse Engineering is Impossible

Reverse engineering is impossible, and while only a fool trips over what is behind them, one's reputation as a teacher is solidified in short order - - two or three years at the most - - and in the school district, it follows him or her - - *and you* - - forever.

So, while I will assert that you need to address all the issues that relate to underperformance by faculty members, and support your neophyte teachers (and I just wrote that time is on your side) it is crucial to their success and yours that the process of teacher growth trajectories begin in short order.

In many ways, <u>perception is reality, especially in the eyes and minds of those with little information</u>. Therefore, and unfortunately, what parents hear about a teacher sets their reputation early, quickly, and in rapidly drying concrete. The imperative is to get to know the pedagogical prowess of your new teacher(s) quickly. This doesn't mean that you make quick decisions; it does mean, however, that you begin immediately, and your focus needs to be targeted.

Lug Nuts

Glickman et al. (2014) argue that we ought to shift toward a collegial model, "characterized by purposeful adult interactions about improving school wide teaching and learning" (p. 6).

This is certainly an excellent concept, and one that can prove to be highly successful. However, the antithesis is when teachers are rated either numerically or otherwise based upon the results of their efforts, categorized by a rating system that serves to rank-order teachers based upon a myriad of factors.

Most certainly, there are professions where results are obvious. The General Motors assembly line worker whose job it is to place lug nuts on a newly assembled car as it rolls down the assembly line and, subsequently the tire that he/she is assigned to fasten with lug nuts regularly falls off, can be clearly seen as incompetent. The worker is observed and evaluated, followed by a professional development intervention so he or she can do her or his job efficiently. If the wheel stays on, he/she keeps his or her job. However, if the wheels keep falling off after intervention, there will come a time when he/she will be fired. "Fired," "let go", "terminated," all words that signify an inability to perform one's job effectively, and, therefore, the person has her or his job taken away.

Please allow me ask you a few simple questions:

1) How many teachers have you worked with who have lug nut issues (they are not very good), to the point, and based upon your first-hand knowledge of their ability, that you would not want to place your own flesh-and-blood child in their classroom?

2) During the course of your career, how many of the above-referenced teachers have you seen "fired," "let go", or "terminated"?

3) How many times have you been aware of leaders (principals, assistant principals, department chairpersons and others) attempting to work with these teachers to improve their pedagogy?

4) How many times have you seen these kinds of teachers ignored and/or allowed to continue in their incompetent manner, given easier courses/classes to teach, easier kids to teach, moved from grade level to grade level or course to course, or building to building, hoping to closet them away from the spotlight?

How did this make you feel? Would you define any of the above as *great* administration? The reality is that:

Number 1 occurs a great deal (as previously noted, between nine to eleven percent of any faculty is either incompetent or bordering on incompetence).

Number 2 never happens (how many people do you know who were fired from their teaching job based upon incompetence in the classroom), and

Number 3 initially occurs but rarely continues, which leads to Number 4.

In all honesty, my dumping grounds for recalcitrant and ineffective teachers were second and fifth grade. Sorry! While I certainly had some outstanding teachers on those grade levels, if I had to place someone who wasn't performing well, and the district administration was unwilling to process and go through the considerable expense of moving to dismiss a teacher based upon incompetence in the classroom (as reflected in my numerous and expertly chronicled and archived observation reports), those were the closets I tried to hide them in.

Just so you know, incompetence is incompetence, and they were equally as incompetent in my attempt to hide them, but at the very least they were where they could do less damage. (And just so you know, *my kids* coming out of that second-grade class *always* had a *great* teacher the subsequent school year - - ***always!***)

One of the damning features of our profession, and the one enlightened parents know and understand only too well, is that tenure for a teacher provides a job for life, and the teacher's ability after earning tenure has nothing to do with whether they are going to continue being employed. The guarantee of a job for life is alien pretty much to everyone who works for a living and who gets evaluated. It is archaic, disruptive to the profession and to students - - and yes, I, too, had a job for life based upon tenure.

Let's Get Personal

Interpersonal skills are extremely important to develop and refine. When working to sustain a positive relationship with a colleague, it is integral to relate to them in a way that displays calm and confidence. The stronger your interpersonal skills are, the more appealing you become. Interpersonal skills such as verbal and non-verbal social communication and interaction, attentive and deep, purposeful listening, attitude, assertiveness, and inclusive methods of decision-making, all play a role in the way relationships are fostered. You must be constantly conscious of the way people interact with others.

Having said that, I ask you to please realize that <u>communication is what is *heard*, not what is *said*.</u>

So getting a teacher to accept your feedback requires that it be delivered within a context that makes the teacher receptive to it. You have to assume that teachers don't want to perform poorly. After all, they are enormously invested in their practice (we would hope), and they feel a sense of pride and accomplishment (we would also hope). So when feedback to a teacher does not work, it is often due to the context in which the feedback was given.

Strong and positive communication, and deep, active, and intentional listening are a large part of being a leader. People like to feel as though they are heard, and that their comments or concerns matter. Your interpersonal skills factor into this belief. When there are barriers in communication, one's interpersonal skills may be hindered. If a leader uses overcomplicated or unfamiliar terms, if there is lack of attention, or if there are language, emotional, or cultural barriers, then one's interpersonal skills may appear to be negative.

You can best create a productive and professional environment when you are cognizant of the fact that the performance of the teachers in the school is the core of the success of the students. In reading Frederick Herzberg (1966 - - yes, this is a long time ago, but it is still relevant. I graduated from high school in 1966 *and* I am *still* relevant) about job enrichment or motivation-hygiene theory, he points to several of the facets that people need to have fulfilled in order to work well. "One side deals with fundamental needs such as safety, nourishment, and other basic drives. The other side of human nature has a compelling urge to be successful..." (p.57).

Prove Me Wrong

Herzberg's quotation is important, because after you are able to satisfy the basic needs of teachers to whatever degree possible, you need to adhere to *the assumption* that all professionals wish to learn and enhance their practice. If you buy into this, but with a realist's perspective, you may also be facing a somewhat self-defeating prophesy of attempting to develop those who you feel cannot and do not want to grow. It may not be valid that all teachers have *professional maturity* and wish to educate children and/or develop their own pedagogy. You will encounter those who, unfortunately, prove you wrong. Think large red Xs on a calendar. *When you give up on these people, then they win, and your students lose.* Stay on their case regularly and often, but not in harassment mode, but rather one that demands fulfillment of your parameters for quality learning experiences for *all* students. *Demand attention be paid and due diligence applied.* Call it out when you don't see it. And never, *ever* give the teacher what he or she wants, if that is to be left alone in classrooms, an island unto themselves.

In such cases, I frankly and also covertly show them I do not respect them! No quality prep times either the first or last period of the day, no prep either directly before or after lunch, and cafeteria supervision in the loudest and most difficult session. I once transferred a highly recalcitrant fifth grade teacher to teach kindergarten. Do what it takes to get them to retire in their first year of eligibility!

Do I sound like a baby? Do I sound like an _ _ _ again? I do! However, these people are taking money under false pretenses, and are subverting the potential lives of children. If they don't like kids and don't like teaching, they should get out! It's an easy life if and when the boss (you) isn't looking and doesn't request and expect anything from them.

It will not be, however, the life I will create for them.

In the Final Analysis, What Makes People Tick, Tick, Tick...?

In my experience, encouraging and motivating factors are different for different people. Some people are encouraged by public displays and recognition for a job well done, others are content with a quiet pat on the back, and others are inherently motivated and do not need extrinsic rewards. Figuring out what encourages individuals is helpful when trying to empower staff members. Also, for those others, figure out what gets to them. I did not feel bad being viewed as vindictive toward those who were not in sync with the ethos of professional educators doing *great* things for *my kids*.

Knowing what makes staff members tick is beneficial when using staff to take on additional roles and responsibilities. I have noticed that most of the time teachers tend to be helpful and devote additional time to hosting workshops, mentoring, and so on when asked, coupled with encouragement and appreciation. People like to feel they are viewed as competent and that what they are doing matters.

According to William Glasser (1998), "boss-managers who firmly believe that people can only be motivated from the outside fail to understand that all of our motivation comes from within ourselves" (p. 41).

Benchmark

In utilizing a benchmark to evaluate yourself, one of the criteria to consider is whether the faculty is growing as a result of self-satisfaction within the school. In other words, are they academically healthier and wiser (Johnson, 2013)? There are five distinct concepts that define a servant leader according to Paul Johnson, who has expanded upon Greenleaf. They include:
1) Stewardship

1) Obligation
2) Partnership
3) Emotional healing
4) Elevating purpose

Stewardship is defined as being supportive of your employees. It also aligns with taking on the responsibility to protect and nurture the group members while also ensuring that the organizational goals are being addressed (Johnson, 2013).

Another theory of distinguishing oneself as a servant leader involves partnership. While it is typically expected for leaders to provide a clear vision and motivate others, there are limitations to a leader's talents (Moxley, 2002). Unlike other types of leaders, servant leaders do not view employees as subordinates but rather as partners (Johnson, 2013).

It is the goal of servant leaders to allocate power equitably. Some of the approaches to empowering partners include sharing information, entrusting partners to carry out important tasks, and urging partners to develop and strengthen their talents. However, servant leaders must be aware that serving others "...must be combined with careful reasoning" (Johnson, 2013, p. 241) to avoid the perception that servant leaders are weak when needing to make the tough decisions. It is possible to be a servant leader yet make the hard calls organizations depend on to achieve their missions.

A crucial component of servant leadership is emotional healing. This is the ability to listen deeply and perceive the needs of others (Zisa, 2013). Servant leaders come to respect and value the art of intentional, deep listening, which allows an increase of their knowledge and the ability to empathize with others' viewpoints (Zisa, 2013).

An elevating purpose is one of the unique characteristics of servant leadership, and is not only its servant focus but also its spiritual foundation (Boyum, 2012). Servant leadership evolved into an innovative paradigm to solidify relationships and to care for and serve others (Boyum, 2012).

I know I am starting to get a little too kumbaya-ish. Sorry! I will pull myself back. However, I firmly believe the normative servant leadership theories described above allow you to be the most helpful while creating the foundational tenets of a TGT.

Relevance

As a leader, one of the components of an effective lesson that you will be looking for as you observe teachers is the degree of relevance for *all* students in the class. To be effective, areas of learning should:

- Apply to all students, regardless of their place on the developmental continuum, and
- Define a wide range of performance expectations; therefore, accommodating learning goals for all students in the classroom.

As you think about your own teaching and that of others whom you have observed in a formal or informal setting, you need to establish in your mind what are the indicators that the component of *relevance* is present.

A good mind game to play would be to think of the scenario where all tests were abolished. Now, what mechanism would be used to measure student learning? What would be the limitations of that assessment process, or those processes, and what conversely would be the advantages? Finally, how would you be able to tell if these measurements were accurate? A huge part of the **evidence** you will be gathering is the use of other measurement devices rather than relying solely on assessments via written tests. You will need to justify these selected measurements to the teacher if he or she is stuck in the cycle of teach, practice, test; teach, practice, test; teach, practice, test.

So in general, as you reflect on assessment and its impact on how you will focus your attention, what assessment methods would you use to assist in determining teaching success and, subsequently, student growth?

Rank Order

Think of a teacher within your school that you consider to be a *great* teacher and write down three (3) things that teacher does in the classroom that made you think of this particular teacher.

1)
2)
3)

louNow, think of a teacher you are less than enthusiastic about and make a list of traits you found undesirable.

1)

2)

3)

What you need to do is think how you would consume, analyze, synthesize and spit back out to another teacher the components and pedagogy that made a particular teacher *great*. The concept must not be content/curriculum-dependent. You need to look beyond *what* was being taught to the *how* it was taught!

How do you apply those components to the teacher and address some of the issues on the least favorable list? Developing the list based upon your observation(s) is easy. The hard part is the sell to the teacher who thinks they are *great* and believes they do not require pedagogical growth because they're already so good!!!!!!!

Speedboats, Sailboats, Barges, and Rowboats with One Oar

Please forget about 'HEDI.' Cataloging each member of your faculty in terms of Highly Effective, Effective, Developing, and Ineffective does not present a realistic picture of your certificated staff members.

I submit to you that you can break down your staff into the following more relevant and realistic categories: *speedboats, sailboats, barges,* and *rowboats with one oar.* You know which teacher belongs in each boat, and can create a definition of each category as well as I can.

Also, for purposes of clarity, it might be good to break down your teachers into three compartments in terms of their style of teaching: authoritarian, democratic, and laissez-faire.

The authoritarian educator would direct all classroom activities, and the laissez-faire style teacher would be the polar opposite. Neither on its own is conducive to *great* teaching. I have used both these terms when I processed how I would address teaching styles.

Obviously the more democratic teacher would promote the participation and involvement of all students. However, it's possible to be too democratic.

My belief is that both democratic and authoritarian styles can be effective, given the right circumstances and the personality of the teacher, *and* the learning styles of the students.

A laissez-faire style teacher would be considered ineffective due to the lack of structure, goals, and directions. Most students would be lost in this type of setting, and their learning would be severely impeded.

Identifying a teaching style and determining its appropriateness in the given circumstances would be a good way to identify an effective teaching style and the teacher's appropriate watercraft.

Human Capital

One of the most interesting concepts that I repeatedly tried to develop, improve, create, and support was the value of human capital within the school. I was smart enough from the get-go to realize that I was not smart enough to effectively coordinate all the operations of a school and still have a positive and productive influence on student outcomes.

While one might think or believe, or want to think and believe, that there is a direct correlation between the two (coordinating school operations and student outcomes), there isn't. And the forest is so dense with trees that getting from one end of it to the other - - well, that path through the woods to grandma's house is not direct, and not easy or even possible for one person - - even one with blue spandex tights, red boots, a red cape, and large S on their chest.

Therefore, development of human capital within the school is imperative! Who currently are, or whom do you want to develop as, teacher-leaders? How do you instill in and empower the teachers - - the ones who have surfaced as masters of their profession through growth - - with abilities far beyond those of mortal teachers?

Your power increases tenfold or more, the more power you give away! You develop human capital by providing important and relevant tasks. These tasks influence the direction and outcomes for students.

The presence of teacher-leaders acknowledges the reality that teachers are fundamental lynchpins in student learning outcomes, and therefore is important to the achievement of sustained outcomes and growth.

Effective teacher-leaders build capacity for the collaborative innovation and creativity necessary to realize educational growth and goals for increased student academic achievement (Barth, 2001).

Give the practice of teacher-leader to those members of the school's cadre who want that mantle, can wear the responsibility well, are seen by others as authoritative in their chosen capacity, and who also can and want to empower others. You have empowered them, and used the school's human capital to create positive outcomes.

Yes, there will those standing on the sidelines. Yes, there will be those sticking a foot out as others run by, and yes, there will be those disagreeing with the selected path. To them you simply say, "Please join us or get out of our way!"

Sharpen Your Axe

As previously noted, I have been developing an app that will extend every day by one (1) hour to a 25-hour day. It is still in beta testing, so for now you're still stuck within the confines of the prehistoric 24-hour day.

From the perspective of relating most of what I do on a daily basis to cooking, something I love to do, prior to starting to cook for family and/or friends, I always sharpen my knives. Abraham Lincoln, when asked about how he chopped down trees, said, "It takes three hours, the first two of which I spend sharpening my axe."

In all honesty, when was the last time you sharpened your axe? When was the last time the teachers sharpened their axes? Exactly my point! It's normally something you take for granted. The axe was sharp when you last sharpened it, and therefore, it will always be sharp!

Well, no. It will not!

A Little Chapter Closure

Now take a leap with me and replace "axe" with the word *teacher*. A teacher's practice needs to be honed and sharpened from time to time, and not just once a year or once a decade!

Teachers in a school will work at optimal efficiency if their skills and pedagogical abilities are regularly honed and sharpened. This comes from their guided and purposeful reflective practice that you facilitate, and a practice that you expect from each of them.

It is presented to them, not as an indicator that you are displeased with their performance or the results of the efforts (let's not forget *my kids* in this scenario), but rather with your emphasis on their growth coupled with their honest self-reflection. Good teachers often plateau professionally because they are not offered the resources, support, and professional guidance necessary to help them develop into *great* teachers, and that my friend, is *your* j-o-b!

Chapter 3
Intentional Listening

*Courage is what it takes to stand up and speak; courage is also
what it takes to sit down and listen.*
~ Winston Churchill

Leadership is a principle-based process of working together that produces trust, integrity, and breakthrough results by building true consensus, ownership, and alignment in all aspects of the organization (Marshall, 1995). Warren Bennis (2004) attributed the success of a leader to his or her ability to not only relate to people, but also to engage people so they are motivated. People are invited into engagement when they are listened to with purpose, an open mind, and high intentions.

Intentionally Listen with Your Eyes

Periodically, take the pulse of a teacher by asking how everything is going, and is he or she comfortable in the TGT process and the steps to be taken.

At that point, it is good to do what I always did, *listen with your eyes!* You will *see* how he or she feels about what is happening. The art of listening with your eyes is a skill that you will need to develop. It is most important to the continuation of the teacher's growth, and your work with him or her, that you recognize the progress that has been made. Remember to have a sense of humor that will lighten the entire experience. But be cautious that the teacher doesn't see your light humor as being disparaging to them or at their expense.

Deep Listening

Amy Jen Su and Christine Riordan describe the deep listening mind-set using six concepts that can help leaders be good listeners (Stibitz, 2015):

- Make it a priority. Determine that you are not going to interrupt or judge and *just listen*. Plan ahead to listen thoroughly.
- Know thyself. Figure out whether you are a good listener. You can ask people who will tell you the truth.
- Remove distractions. Put down the phone or other distractions and focus on the person speaking. Give him or her your full attention.
- Add nonverbal clues that you are listening, such as a smile, or a nod.
- Control your reactions. Don't react with negative emotions or interrupt people too soon. Don't get overly excited and become a distraction either. However, it is good to exhibit some nonverbal or verbal enthusiasm when positive information is presented.
- Validate and verify. Good listeners paraphrase and ask if it is what the speaker meant. They don't prejudge or make assumptions.
- Good listeners talk *with* and not *at* people.

William Isaacs is the founder and president of Dialogos. Dialogos is a company that offers educational programs for transformational leadership. These programs focus on dialogue. Interestingly, Isaacs (1999) refers to debate as "...unproductive defensiveness" (p.3). This limits teacher empowerment. Unfortunately, debate "in which each participant argues her or his position against the others' position" (Glover, 2007, p.2) is all too common.

People who listen to others only to poke holes in their arguments, or people who listen only to prepare a response are using a non-productive starter and will not be able to effectively commence the development of a TGT.

The problem with *listening just to respond* is this: "Progress is seldom made and the conversation ends where it begins" (Glover, 2007, p.2).

As someone who set out to change the world through education, to recognize this in myself was heartbreaking. While heartbreaking, it was also eye-opening and transformational. It provided me with a more laser-like focus in my communications with others.

Isaacs goes on to write that when people engage in a conversation, they unconsciously choose whether to debate, dialog, or openly discuss. As noted above, debate isn't often productive. Become more conscious of the choices you make during communications, and choose to *engage more* in dialogue based upon productive listening and open discussion.

These concepts and practices are "...much more likely to generate the teacher leadership that is essential for creating changes in schools" (Glover, 2007, p.13). This is because constructive change happens through open conversation.

Isaacs suggests four conversational practices that contribute to dialogue and discussion. They are:
1) Deep listening
2) Respecting others
3) Suspending assumptions
4) Voicing personal truths

He asserts that "...by infusing these practices into conversations, a leader can bring out the best in others and coax out leadership potential" (Isaacs, 1999, p.2). The idea of deep listening is to "...actively try to understand how a speaker views and understands the topic under discussion" (Glover, 2007, p.3).

The idea behind this is to *listen to understand* in order to gain another perspective. If you are only listening to respond, what you are really listening for are ideas that agree with yours. If you are only listening to respond, you are not listening to questions that could build ideas. The foundational tenets of a productive TGT are built around your ability to listen, logically respond, and not prejudge.

If you are not listening deeply, you are listening for concerns and/or fears. If you are listening for concerns and fears, then teachers don't feel secure. As I noted in my book <u>The Principal: Traversing the Hire Wire with No Net Below</u>, "Sometimes all a teacher, student or a parent of a child wants is to be heard. Teachers need to feel they are a participant in the decision-making of the school via your ears, heart, and mind" (Sternberg, 2012, p.3). When teachers feel listened to, not only do they feel more secure, and safe enough to take risks, but they also are more productive, successful and satisfied.

Eric Glover (2007) writes that as he listened deeply, he "...learned to respect teachers [sic] views as legitimate so that he could listen to the sense in what they were saying and recognize their words as expressions of their understanding of the truth; to set my opinions and assumptions aside so they would not interfere with my truly hearing what teachers were saying" (p.22).

Listening deeply begins with understanding that the opinions of teachers are real perspectives because they are what they see as truth. By setting aside assumptions, you will be able to gain the perspectives of others and collaboration leads to the best ideas.

Subjective Truths

Glover (2007) also recommends that when presenting ideas, leaders present them as *subjective truths* rather than objective facts. Think pre- and post-observation conferences as foundational input for a TGT. In my mind, this goes along with putting aside opinions, not an easy thing to do. Subjective truths are to say/think/and attest to, but are nevertheless very difficult for most of us unless we really, really, *really* work at it.

When you begin to *listen deeply*, you are able *to see* the truth in the statements of others, which leads to valuable shifts in your perspective.

Being part of shared decision-making in terms of growth allows others to know that you value their thoughts and perspectives. I have written a great deal about empowering teachers, and time and time again, the idea of collaboration and shared decision-making has been mentioned as constructive in making teachers feel empowered.

Empowered teachers feel satisfied and safe. They look at themselves from the inside out, and consciously reflect on their growth trajectory as a positive enhancement of their skill sets. They grow professionally. They produce quality instruction. Their students learn. The cumulative result is that they feel *great* about themselves.

Kristy Costello (2014), an educational administrator, asserts that educational leaders should do three things: Listen, Care, and Try. She writes, "While a big part of our job is talking, an even bigger part is listening to the concerns, criticisms and suggestions of our faculty, staff, and students" (p.12).

When we listen to these concerns, criticisms and fears, we validate teachers, but we can also assist them to realize where changes need to be made? Thomas Hoerr (2013), in his article *Principal Connection: Can You Listen Too Well?*, reminds us, "Hearing is only the first step in listening. An important aspect of leadership is stepping back and understanding the perspectives that people bring to a situation. Why do they see things this way? Leaders need to understand the perceptions that inform what people are saying" (p.86).

And that is <u>listening to understand instead of listening to respond</u>. It is listening in order to hear beliefs and values. When educational leaders are able to do this, they are truly able to understand. When we understand, we can empower. When we empower, we help to create dynamic environments that support teacher growth through a TGT, and the result is that we move kids forward. When we move kids forward, we change the world - - and, after all, isn't that why we chose this profession? I'm sure it wasn't for the pay!

Gracious Space

The term *gracious space* is a wonderful pair of words that frankly I fell in love with - - second only to *professional maturity* - - and I offer these words to you so you might affectionately adopt them as well. Owning the term allows people to have transparent conversations about issues that matter to them. It is an honest dialogue, where people can voice different perspectives and generate creative solutions and influence their work in innovative ways.

Gracious space focuses on intention, setting, process, openness, and learning. "When people in an organization practice the philosophy of *gracious space*, they come together in a setting that encourages deeper listening and concentration in a setting that is free from distractions and conducive to meaningful conversation" (Dufresne & McKenzie, 2009, p.38).

The participants are open to listening and respecting diverse viewpoints. They embrace the idea of <u>letting go of knowing all the answers and being right all the time, and it can lead them to not needing to, and also to a fuller understanding that there is something to be learned from everyone</u>. Deeper listening through the practice of affording others *gracious space* is a practice to employ on a daily basis!

A Little Chapter Closure

The one thing we do most often when we are not sleeping is listening, the concept and skill set that I would ask you to hone most sharply in your professional career, and one that requires perfecting if your ability to be seen by others as a deep and purposeful listener!

Early in my career it was the one thing I did poorly and the one thing that required the most attention and effort on my part.

Please do not underestimate the importance of this practice.

Chapter 4
How Does a Teacher Growth Trajectory (TGT) Work?

Before you are a leader, success is all about growing yourself.
When you become a leader, success is all about growing others.
~ Jack Welch

An effective Teacher Growth Trajectory must start by answering two basic questions:

- What steps/actions/resources should be focused on specific areas in need of growth based upon evidence gathered from observed pedagogical practices?
- What should a teacher be able to do when they walk into their classroom the next day, next week, next month and next year?

Winnie the Pooh Would Be Proud Of...

All I ever wanted to do was to make my little corner of the Hundred Acre Wood *perfect*. If what the faculty and I were able to accomplish spread elsewhere, so be it. If not, our 875+ students were getting a quality educational experience based upon the fact that teachers were growing professionally and applying their highly honed pedagogical skills toward a positive outcome for each of their students.

We picked up an award/recognition or two along the way, but the very next day we were back in the building, still perfecting our craft. The complexity of that singular job focus and responsibility allowed little time to try and change the academic world elsewhere, so we hunkered down and did what we could in our corner of the Hundred Acre Wood. It required innovative leadership at times, but mostly just an application of some good old common sense. But the bottom line was that whatever we did we did as a team; our focus was *always* on the betterment of our kids.

Neophyte Teachers

Unfortunately, what tends to happen with most untenured teachers is that your approach tends to be more conventional. There is a tendency to establish less of a sense of collaboration and more of a feeling of *I am watching you* - - and certainly that is what the teacher feels regardless of your attempts at building collegiality.

This is probably intrinsic to everyone, especially to new teachers, who are made to feel this way by colleagues and onward up the hierarchy to members of the district office. In many ways this belief is also somewhat self-imposed, but it is not necessarily paranoia, because many times principals do not spend enough time talking *with* the neophyte teacher, and *deeply and intentionally listening* to them talk about how they *work* their classrooms. Your use of a TGT will serve to eradicate the lack of focused dialogue, and hopefully relieve some of the new teacher's anxiety.

Collaboration with new teachers is reflected in time spent together to discuss educational goals, progress toward goals, and, if issues arise, areas in need of growth and possible solutions. It is spent listening to the educator discuss how they develop questions for their students, and how they create an environment where spoon-fed learning gives way to acquisition of skills based upon the inquisitive nature of the students.

Lest you forget, while everyone is looking at this new teacher with the thought of "what is he or she bringing to the table?", the teachers are also *looking at you,* because you hired this person and placed your initial stamp of approval on them.

As I point out to each new teacher who enters my corner of the Wood, *"...your success is my success."*

I know I just added a ton more pressure on their shoulders, but my intent and meaning is to convey that *I am here for you, to support and locate available resources - - be they human or material - - so you can succeed.*

When you explain it that way, and they learn about Teacher Growth Trajectories within the school, they will feel better and more comfortable (add a smiley-face emoji be appropriate here).

Setting the Foundation for TGT

Leadership takes place with people, involves the use of influence, and is used to attain goals (Datta, 2016). A leader is a person who has a special degree of power to create the conditions for followers, where the conditions can either be productive and harmonious or toxic (Johnson, 2013).

It all depends on the leader's emotional intelligence, integrity and resilience. It is important to note that a successful leader possesses emotional intelligence, makes ethical decisions, and has resilience.

Emotional intelligence has been defined as the capacity for recognizing and analyzing one's own feelings and those of others, for motivating ourselves, and for managing the emotional will in us and in our relationships (Maulding, Peters, Roberts, Leonard & Sparkman, 2012).

An ineffective TGT comes from *not* being able to say yes to the following questions:

- Is the TGT plan actionable? Does it articulate what teachers will be working toward and subsequently able to do?
- Is it evaluable? Will you be able to easily evaluate whether teachers have accomplished the TGT objective(s)? What evidence will you have that teachers are growing pedagogically?
- Is it feasible? Can you accomplish this objective in a reasonable amount of time?

Bottom Line

To put it as simply and bluntly as possible, in most cases a Teacher Growth Trajectory is a process to address what is missing from a teacher's pedagogical practice, and what, if added, would place that teacher on a trajectory toward pedagogical *greatness!*

The foundation of the TGT is to provide the teacher with **evidence** acquired during your observation, or from other times, of the missing component(s) and then developing a growth plan (a TGT) to address the gap.

Your ability to positively influence colleagues to reach *greatness* is directly related to your leadership ability. It will be imperative for the success of your students that you establish an ethos and conditions within the school that allow for TGTs to be accepted as a foundational component of everyday school life - - as accepted as a teacher's dedicated space in the school parking lot.

It will be important to have a Teacher Growth Trajectory plan (see Appendix D). You cannot enter into the teacher growth phase of your responsibility without a well-developed, directional, and specific plan.

It isn't, by the way, strictly *your plan*, but rather one that, while the parameters were initially developed by you, it is well known to the teacher that you are flexible enough to ebb and flow as needed.

Imagine the plan as a conglomeration of the ideas and the best practices of many. It is the starting point leading toward your desired outcome, but the journey has still to be mapped out in a collaborative fashion. The variations (ebb and flow) rely on the needs of the students and the teacher and, while the basic structure is in place, it nevertheless adjusts as needed.

Cornerstone

The first element that is the cornerstone of a Teacher Growth Trajectory is the preparation stage, as it impacts all subsequent aspects of the instructional process.

Great teachers are those who dedicate a significant amount of time to planning and developing comprehensive units that align with state standards, as well as assessments that are varied in terms of design and effectiveness. These educators also consider the learning styles of the students they work with, and prepare lessons and student activities to promote the strengths of their students through individualization, differentiation, and personalization.

The grain of salt that must be taken here is the possibility, probability, and difficulty of achieving these three within a class of twenty-seven or more students. While you will need to be demanding, at the same time *be cognizant and understanding* of the parameters in which teachers work.

This process is a journey, not a race. The willingness of the teachers to accept a journey is dependent upon how you introduce and monitor the TGT, and how deeply you have listened and subsequently reacted via your support.

Fear Not the TGT

As previously noted, many people are held back from attempting to do better through developing a formal growth trajectory because they fear what the path toward growth might look like. If they try something new, they might fail, or at least look foolish - - or so they believe. To do better, they might have to learn something new, which would mean admitting they don't know something in the first place, regardless of how many years they have been teaching. That pill is not sugarcoated for many people!

Being challenged to grow through fear can be a stormy place for most people. Picture yourself learning how to surf. You are out there, trying to ride the waves, and you think everyone on the beach has nothing better to do than watch you fall off repeatedly.

You accept that you will fall off many times while you are learning; however, the reality is that no one on the beach is watching you! They are all too self-absorbed, baking in the sun, developing the conditions that will inevitably lead to a carcinoma twenty years later. In essence, the principal is the only one watching.

Another hill to climb on the way to a TGT is that teachers have always had all the answers. They know things that others do not, and people (kids and parents) go to them for answers! Now, inexplicably, a TGT implies to them that *no, you do not have all the answers, and you need to grow further!* A very difficult situation for some teachers to accept when, by nature of the beast, teachers has always been seen as having *all* the answers.

Fail Safely

Let teachers know you believe in them by your actions and deeds, not just your words.

Perhaps a teacher has never had someone believe in his or her potential. Let him or her know that you truly believe they can reach their next level. However, this is not all milk, honey, and Ben and Jerry's Cherry Garcia ice cream! Hold them accountable for both delivering the very best performance they can and stretching themselves into their future capability.

There will be happy accidents and well as learning from failures. The huge issue here is let them *fail safely.* People can and should have the ability to *fail in order to learn. The issue here is also how often, as well as how serious, the failure is.* If you were to dissect someone's growth, it will be composed of many small steps along the way prior to the overall accomplishment, and some steps will be less firm than others. This is the type of compassion and understanding that must be inbred in your leadership of growth through a Teacher Growth Trajectory.
Relationships

When teachers are motivated and feel a part of the school team, they establish what they have witnessed others establishing within the ethos of the building:

1) Ownership of their own teaching
2) Ownership of their own growth
3) A willingness to relate goals to their own experience, even if it is a lack of extensive experience because this is, in fact, their first rodeo within this particular school, even if they are a veteran of decades of teaching.

The relationship between collaboration and shared decision-making is an ideal model for a school. I want you to take shared decision-making to a more micro level. We are all familiar with the concept as it is used in school governance. However, shared decision-making is exactly the kind of model, concept, and foundation that you want to instill in your one-on-one discussions with teachers about their TGT.

Patty and Walking the Walk

Is it very easy to say you are a principal who acknowledges and respects a teacher's opinion and the sanctity of their classroom in terms of their ability to create a successful learning environment.

One of the more highly regarded teachers who long ago established in my mind her credibility and strength as a *great* educator once inadvertently taught me a huge lesson! It is to me the definitive example of acknowledging that *great teachers know best,* and one of your strengths as an educational leader will be to recognize and practice this obvious and easily stated mantra. However, when push comes to shove, can you walk the *great-teachers-know-best* walk?

As I was walking around and visiting classrooms on no particular mission other than to get my butt out of the office, I walked into Patty's room (3rd grade) and started to head to the rear of the classroom. On the chalkboard was a large chalk outline of a clock with the numbers 12, 3, 6, and 9 in the proper locations, and with the clock divided into four quarters, with a line through the 12 and going down through the center and stopping at the 6. There was another line running from the 9 and going through the center and stopping at the 3. In each of the quarters formed by the bisecting lines was a large paper replica of a quarter (a 25-cent coin). Patty was teaching quarter-past-the-hour and quarter-to-the-hour, and using the quarters to help the students understand the concept.

This struck me as odd since there are 15 minutes in each quarter hour, not 25 minutes! I said nothing. Just hung in the room for a few more minutes and eventually left as quietly as I had entered, as was my custom. The use of the twenty-five cent pieces to represent the quarter hour bugged me all day and night, because I was convinced the students would think that there were 25 minutes within a quarter hour.

Finally, as I was walking around the next day, I found Patty alone in her classroom. "Patty, could you explain something to me that has been bothering me all night?" I asked. She immediately responded, "It's the quarters, isn't it?" "Yes", I said.

Patty knew me well enough and read my face perfectly during the time I was in her room for the now infamous, Quarter Lesson! I simply suggested that I was confused why she used the quarters when there are 15 minutes in a quarter hour.

"Doesn't that confuse the students?" I asked. In my mind I heard Mr. Spock saying, "...but captain, that is highly illogical!"

Her simple explanation was that she had no idea why it worked as well as it did. However, over the years she has come to realize that the kids just get it. She continues the practice because it has always worked.

Now a principal who wants it their way, and doesn't trust their teacher enough to accept their method and response, would have insisted that they not use the quarters because he or she believed it would confuse the children.

I smiled, thanked her, and left the room. It didn't matter to me that *I* didn't get it, or that *I* felt the kids wouldn't get it, or conclude that because *I* didn't like the method Patty should change. Her comment to me that the kids "get it" was enough for me because of the trust factor.

Trust your teacher, and you will trust her or his expertise. My suggestion is to trust your feelings a lot less than you trust the knowledge base of *great* teachers, no matter what logic might or might not be telling you. What do you think Patty's reaction would have been if I had told her I didn't like the method and I wanted her to stop using it?

Paradox

David Novak wrote in his book, <u>Taking People with You</u>, "Identify what you want to change, make a plan for improving yourself and your skills, set deadlines and benchmarks, and seek out feedback and help" (2012, p.219).

The way you conduct yourself and represent your ideas to teachers plays a key role in the development of a school team and the ideals that they hold close.

He goes on to point out that this idea, "...requires living with a paradox: to inspire as a leader, you need to know your stuff, but also be able to admit when you don't know your stuff. You need to be both confident and vulnerable at the same time" (Novak, 2012, p. 31).

Novak believes *great* leaders should have conviction, know their stuff, know their environment, build self-awareness, be open and honest about what they don't know, use positive self-talk and positive thought, and get out of their comfort zone. He believes that, taken together, these qualities can help keep leaders grounded.

Once leaders have established who they are, and the staff has a solid understanding of who they are and what they stand for, they can begin to work on helping others remember to be themselves as well (Novak, 2013).

As noted previously by Datta, Novak also teaches his readers the importance of what he refers to as "extraordinary authenticity." He defines extraordinary authenticity as "having the ability to be yourself in even the toughest situations" (Novak, 2012, p.31).

Leadership Traits for Teacher Growth: How Teacher-Leaders Influence TGTs

One important element of every TGT is the involvement of teacher-leaders within the faculty. One method to help determine teacher-leaders is to identify leadership traits. These traits are best compared to a person's character, because traits are actions over time that defines a person's behavior (Northouse, 2013). Thus, teacher-leaders are products of their behavior, and trait research demonstrates the stability of the teacher-leader's character over time, while also highlighting the strengths of each leader's qualities.

When looking for that teacher-leader, it is less about *their desire* to be one and more about *their potential* to be one. I wanted to be a professional baseball player and be a second baseman for the Boston Red Sox: a) I really, really wanted to do it; however, b) I had no *potential* ability to be a second baseman.

You must be keenly aware of the differences between *desire* and *ability*. Having the ambition to assist others is an important criterion; however, it is a far-off second. When assessing a potential teacher-leader's ability to help, ask yourself these questions:

Reality is:

1) Does the potential teacher-leader engage others in a positive manner?
2) Can you depend on this person to accomplish goals or tasks?
3) How does the person you are considering to be a teacher-leader respond to stress, change, or emotional retorts?
4) Is the person open to new ideas? Are they able to *deeply and intentionally listen* to ideas that may not have been their first thought, and yet turn out to be well developed and worthwhile, even if it wasn't their idea/suggestion?
5) Can the person be influenced to consider or accept an idea or practice other than the one he or she brings to the table, because the teacher they are supporting has a better approach?
6) How flexible is the person?
7) Will they think wearing the mantle of teacher-leader makes them omnipotent? If yes, find someone else, because if they were truly omnipotent they would have seen that coming and never said they were omnipotent!

Along with the traits addressed as positives, you should also avoid or overcome negative traits that inhibit success. According to Peter Northouse (2013), these traits include emotional instability, indecision, laziness, narcissistic tendencies, and other behaviors that destroy team building, innovation, and productivity. These are traits that will certainly not be helpful in the teacher growth process, where trust will be a huge issue.

TGT Marker: Factor in Intelligent Design

Robert Sternberg (unfortunately, no relation but I may check out Ancestery.com on this one to be sure) does not shy away from criticism of intelligence testing when he writes, "I did poorly on the tests and so, in the first three years of school, I had teachers who thought I was stupid and when people think you're stupid, they have low expectations for you" (Sternberg, 2014, p. 1).

Sternberg's insights offer more than a commentary on the treatment of people depending on perceived intelligence. Sternberg's research changed the values of basic intelligence tests to include measuring the methods a person uses to address a problem (Hughes, Ginnett & Curphy, 2009).

The measurements are divided into three core concepts, beginning with analytic intelligence (Hughes, Ginnett & Curphy, 2009). Analytic intelligence includes the rate of learning, the ability to make decisions, and the ability to reach accurate inferences (Hughes, Ginnett & Curphy, 2009).

The next measure is practical intelligence, which can be compared to common sense or the ability to recognize problems and develop solutions (Hughes, Ginnett & Curphy, 2009).

The last measure is creative intelligence, the ability to develop practical and realistic solutions, which expands on innovation (Hughes, Ginnett & Curphy, 2009).

Square One

While there is no expectation that you need a degree in psychology to be a *great* principal, it obviously can't hurt to understand peoples' psyches. Absent that degree, you must approach TGT sessions in a somewhat analytical fashion, and develop a sense of what it will take to move and motivate each teacher off Square One and get them leaning and moving forward, upward, and onward by investing in their TGT!

Look at Square One as a teacher's entrenchment in self-centered notions that all is well because they have never heard otherwise! Nor have they ever entered into a *purposefully self-reflective posture* relative to what they are doing and how it affects the outcomes for *my kids*. And, can their students do better if they are better? The bottom line is that, while all may be well, would you accept "doing well enough" as the standard for your own children? "Well" is never good enough, and entrenchment on Square One is not growth!

EI

As previously mentioned, a person's emotional intelligence (EI) plays a major role in guiding emotions into positive results (Hughes, Ginnett & Curphy, 2009). For instance, the ability to perceive and manage the emotions of others helps a leader assess each employee and assist in managing contentious issues.

Another factor is the ability to use emotion to motivate others, adapt to stressful situations, and remain flexible in changing conditions (Hughes, Ginnett & Curphy, 2009).

Northouse (2013) defines leadership as "...a process whereby an individual influences a group of individuals to achieve a common goal" (p.5).

How well you control your emotions and attempt to work within and understand the emotions of others will influence your effectiveness as a leader. A leader with emotional intelligence will be more effective at exerting influence over their staff to achieve positive outcomes for the team. Peter Miller (2012) lists the primary aspects of emotional intelligence as "self-awareness, self-regulation, motivation, empathy and social skills" (p.9).

James Kouzes and Barry Posner want you to *animate the vision* by doing more than simply describing it. It implies the ability to express emotions and arouse others to join a cause by appealing to their ideals.

In short, if you animate a vision, you have the ability to breathe life into it. "To enlist others you have to help them *see* and *feel* how their own interests and aspirations are aligned with the vision. You have to paint a compelling picture of the future, one that enables constituents to experience viscerally what it would be like to actually live and work in an exciting and uplifting future" (Kouzes, Posner, 2012, p.141).

It is important to realize that a lack of communication and clarity can derail any TGT initiative, might cause you to be frustrated, and ultimately can impact commitment. You need to be mindful of the emotional base of individual teachers, their interactions within their spheres of influence, and how communication skills, strategies, and techniques can enhance clarity and direction while improving relationships among those you lead.

To build the collective capacity and human capital, you need to understand the interconnectivity of relationships, psychology, sociology, and communication dynamics within the building as a means to further enhance the growth performance of the teachers, and, as a result, all the students.

Finally, the ability to understand emotions is the backbone of modern leadership by using "...empathy and other skills to influence, motivate, and develop trust among subordinates" (Hughes, Ginnett & Curphy, 2009; Holt & Margues, 2012). Success depends on using personality combined with intelligence to influence people to accomplish goals, tasks, and remain motivated over long periods (Raja & Palanichamy, 2011).

Intriguingly, the concept is applicable for you as a school leader, as well as the teachers you strategically place as teacher-leaders, as well as with other teachers, and affects how they work with the students in their classroom.

When you and your teacher-leaders understand these concepts, they should have an extremely positive influence on your approach to other teachers as you present the concept of the TGT model to each.

TGT Marker: Allocate 25% of Your Time to TGTs

As previously noted, the demands on school leaders are greater than ever, leaving less time for observations and high-quality feedback and follow-up with teachers - - if you allow the time drain to impact those areas.

In <u>Leverage Leadership</u>, Paul Bambrick-Santoyo (2012) suggests that school leaders spend 25% of their time on observation and varying degrees of feedback. Though research shows this is ideal, it can feel unrealistic and overwhelming for school leaders without the right support.

For example, you may lack the content-area expertise needed to provide relevant, practical feedback to some teachers based upon the specific content courses they teach. An observer with a background in English, for example, is not likely prepared and able to provide meaningful content feedback to a statistics teacher.

On the middle and high school levels, department chairpersons and/or directors can assist with content priorities.

Elementary leaders need to be masters of all things academic, and that is why and where deployment of teacher-leaders is so critical at this level.

Greenleaf - - Servant Leadership

I previously touched upon Greenleaf. Robert Greenleaf was a theorist who first proposed the servant-leadership theory in 1970. His theory was that a leader's primary role is that of motivation and service to others.

He created a style of leadership that would give people a reason to pause for thought, and to challenge any long-standing assumptions about the relationship between leaders and followers in an organization.

Greenleaf suggested that servant-leadership begins in a leader when he or she assumes the position of servant in their interactions with followers. He believed that authentic leadership arises out of a fundamental desire to help others. His concept of servant-leadership was that of motivation and purpose that should encourage greatness in others, and also believed that organizational success was derived from his servant-leadership theory.

It is now up to you to transfer these principles through your interactions with and reactions to staff at a point of offering support and suggestions for growth, and the blueprint is a TGT!

The servant-leader is a person who has reached a high level of emotional maturity. They transcend their own desire for power and recognition. They have come to a desire to serve others, and this conscious choice puts them in position where they are naturally chosen to lead, not of their own volition, but by the unconscious choice of the group being led.

Yes, you are the principal, and people will follow you because of the title on your door. However, <u>you want them to follow because they want to follow you</u>. In this way, the servant-leader is not a will-to-power leader. They naturally lead due to knowing where the real decision-making should be based, and that is upon the pedagogical ability of those who follow them. The concept, while not difficult to understand, is at times difficult to master.

Think of it this way: The more power you give away, the more power you will ultimately have!

Litmus Test

The servant-leader's desire is to make sure the needs of other people are being met. The litmus test of a servant-leader is whether *the people being served grow as individuals by becoming stronger in their practices, and are happy being more autonomous*, therefore developing and fulfilling their growth trajectory potential.

Teaching and mentoring are major requirements of servant-leadership. If you are a list-maker, you should find Greenleaf's (1991) ten characters of servant-leadership very helpful:
- Listening
- Empathy
- Healing
- Awareness
- Persuasion
- Conceptualization
- Foresight
- Stewardship
- Commitment to the growth of others
- Building community

You establish long-term relationships based on respect, and having the faculty view the trust that they have in you as being based upon how they are treated professionally. You will be more strongly supported by your cadre of teachers and you will accomplish more together because you embrace the concept of shared, distributed leadership.

By empowering others to perform at their maximum potential through taking charge of their own growth, you are able to motivate, inspire, and ultimately gain buy-in. Instead of viewing leadership in the literal sense of having others follow every directive without wavering, your mantra should be a *shared journey of success*. Leaders like this think with a collective _we_ mind-set versus the _I_ mind-set.

According to Global Leadership and Organizational Behavior Effectiveness (GLOBE, 2013; Johnson, 2013), successful leaders are associated with the following traits:

- Motive initiator
- Insightful
- Inspiring
- Communicative
- Reliable
- Dynamic
- Positive
- Confidence builder

One other trait that leaders display is a high level of integrity, which elevates the trust and commitment of employees, thereby promoting a heightened level of loyalty (Singh, 2011).

A Sinek Attack: Attention Teachers, You May Now Be Exiting Your Comfort Zone

One reason why teachers may not be able to take advantage of your efforts of feeding-back, feeding-forward, and feeding-up is because they aren't ready!

The parameters and prerequisites for commencing a Teacher Growth Trajectory are many times the most important component of the process. Once you have created the foundation and the teacher buy-in for the process, your path and that of the teacher become easier.

You can understand pedagogy inside and out, and the application of nuances; however, if you are unable to define *why* someone should do something different in their practice, all your knowledge can ultimately be wasted.

The *why* must not be based upon your desire or preference. Remember the quarter-past and quarter-to concept from Patti? Teachers will accept a piece of **evidence** long before they will accept something that appears to be capricious or subjective and not **evidence**-based. The difficult part will be showing the teacher something they do not believe is happening, and that is where your **evidence** gathering is critically important (as well as the process you use to approach the teacher with the **evidence**).

Your role is to help transform the unclear and possibly invisible occurrences into something clear and visible to the teacher.

Please always remember to explain *why* what the teacher did *may not* be the best for their students and *may not* have the desired outcome. Many times it isn't a question of what they wanted to do but rather what was not brought to positive fruition. Your responsibility is to collaborate with the teacher to accomplish the path that will be best for kids.

How do you get people to leave their comfort zone and buy into new ideas? How do you get them to tap into their fundamental motivations rather than manipulating them into action?

According to Simon Sinek, you achieve it by convincing colleagues that what you are proposing is the right thing to do and they are a natural fit with the ethos of the school. In his book <u>Start with Why</u>, Sinek (2011) suggests starting by explaining <u>*why*</u> you want or need to make changes or, in this case, suggestions for the components of a TGT.

Why should anyone spend their time listening, let alone following, if they don't know *why?* The *why* catches people's attention, and hopefully their minds, and that's when you can move to the *how*. You must have the attention of all those who will be influenced by change, and if they know both the *why* they need to do something, and also *how* to go about it, and then they will feel supported in *what* that needs to be accomplished.

Sinek's model for influencing people can be the means whereby you become an effective transformational school leader. You become a leader who seeks to be a facilitator of change that constantly improves the school via teacher growth, thus providing the best educational experiences for students.

Sinek says that *great* leaders "...inspire people to act..." (p. 7), meaning that change is not driven by one individual (you) but by members of the cohort of educators being led. The way *great* leaders inspire is by being able to clearly articulate *why* they hold the beliefs they do, and *why* what they suggest would be to the benefit of the kids.

<u>The *why* gets to the fundamentals of a vision that should be shared and brought to life through the participation of all stakeholders.</u>

Simon Says...

In a review of the research and literature of author Simon Sinek, I discovered his explanation of a critical component to successful leadership that he refers to as the Golden Circle. The Golden Circle is a diagram that involves three questions all organizations should address in developing a theory or idea to strengthen their organization:

What?

How?

Why?

A great way to move forward is to curve your thinking slightly and approach your efforts to establish a TGT with the thought that it is never the what that the teacher did or did not do, but rather why they did what they did. This culls out of the equation the mistake atmosphere and transforms it into an almost Socratic exchange, requiring deeper thought, deeper and purposeful reflection, and deeper reasoning processes.

Sinek describes his "Golden Circle" as being made up of three superimposed circles starting with the WHY at the center, then moving outward to the HOW, and then to the outermost circle, the WHAT of the organization. "The *why* is the purpose of our actions; it communicates our causes and our beliefs. The *how* is about the process, the actions we must undertake in order to make our *why* a reality. Finally, the outermost circle is the *what*, the result that we wish to achieve, because of our *why*, and through our *how*" (Sinek, 2009, p. 37).

Follow Me

Sinek also writes of the "Law of Diffusion." In business, "…a company has to attract a basic 15% to 18% of the market and they are on the way to success" (Sinek, 2009, p. 120). Success does not mean gaining everyone's allegiance right away. Gaining a 15% initial following is strong, because when people buy into the fundamental values of the company or product, the company has a foothold in the industry, and then it is only a matter of time before it diffuses into the larger market.

The same lesson applies to a leader who is trying to propel a faculty forward. It is a fact that there will always be people who oppose any kind of change, who will not cooperate, no matter what. This should not stop you! You should focus on attracting those members of the faculty who share your same values, who are excited about the prospect of their growth potential, and who feel empowered to fulfill the mission of their profession. Once there is a *core followership* (that 15% to 18%), the Law of Diffusion will come into effect, and innovations like a TGT will spread to more and more people. You will, however, always have those with a red magic marker.

Going back to Greenleaf for a moment, he stressed that there must be a balance of power for an organization to have lasting success. A partnership will not be active when only one individual holds all the power, or when a selected few individuals have power and others do not. If one person dominates, there is the possibility of that leader developing *coercive control*, at which point all the efforts put forth by followers will cease (Greenleaf, 2009).

Every individual should be encouraged to articulate their ideas/power, and use them to create victorious scenarios and reach a shared objective (Moxley, 2002). In other words, employees work together to orchestrate a shared vision as they individually and collectively understand the *why*, establish direction, resolve obstacles, and value the significance of their work (Moxley, 2002).

Collaboration

You are creating a school ethos built on collaboration for teacher growth via a TGT. Collaboration is reflected in time spent together to discuss and come to consensus on educational goals, progress toward goals, and areas in immediate need of growth - - all based upon student outcomes. Collaboration within an educational setting is essential, because you and the teacher need to determine his or her growth trajectory. *Where are we starting, and where are we heading* (please notice I did not write the word *ending*)?

It is important to start small by selecting something you both feel is *actionable* and *growable*, and will create and sustain student success. You want to start off on a strong, productive, mutually agreeable initial step. This is a decision that needs to be a shared one.

And, you do not capitulate and walk away from the table if the teacher essentially says, "Everything's fine, and I don't see a need to grow." Now who would ever say something that stupid!?! Well, unfortunately, you will be surprised! (I submit to you that it has been my experience that the weaker the teacher, the more resistance you will encounter.)

It certainly helps if the teacher feels that they belong to a strong and caring organization with a strong and caring principal who is seen by the faculty as always having the best interests of the kids in view. This fosters an atmosphere of understanding of organizational goals, and the motivation to be part of the solution and progress toward established goals.

Pass the Quill and Ink Bottle

One of the true tests of the collaborative tone and practice that you are forming with your colleagues is when pen is applied to paper (or a keyboard pounded) and subsequently the information is archived. It can make people nervous and kind of moves the needle from a simple collaboration among colleagues to *someone is taking notes* of what was said around the table - - and can it be used against me going forward?

The stark reality is that it is necessary to put pen to paper and use the Teacher Growth Trajectory charts (see Appendices C, D and E). Pragmatically, it is one piece of your **evidence** to provide to a superintendent and/or board of education should you need to demonstrate and have archived your attempts to encourage support a teacher's growth. There is also the unpleasant concept of demonstrating that the teacher has *not grown* to the level you require in order to maintain him/her in the district. Do not be so naïve as to believe that someone in central office is not *evaluating you* as you meander through your workday. So you also need to compile and archive **evidence** of your own actions.

Of course, during an evaluation of *you* as a principal by the district superintendent or assistant superintendent, Teacher Growth Trajectory charts are golden as an indicator of your work with the faculty. You cannot be Pollyanna and imagine your work with teachers will also not be a point of evaluation by those in central office assigned to evaluate you (and monitor *your growth*).

Frankly, self-preservation requires that you maintain a "paper trail" of what you have attempted and accomplished in order to improve instruction school wide. It tends to be an ugly subset when you notify central office that you do not want to continue probation or grant tenure to someone. You a need an excellent reason; hell, you need reason<u>s</u>! You need to demonstrate - - with **evidence** - - why. You need to delineate clearly what you have done to support the teacher prior to this determination.

Remember, this can easily become a legal matter if the teacher being let go feels discriminated against or has other accusations that he or she was not treated properly. You will feel, if it comes to this, that you are on trial - - and, by the way, *you will be!* Your ducks (associated paperwork) need to be in order.

You cannot be leading the movement to create wonderful and outstanding learning opportunities for kids if you are not the principal! You are *not* sacrificing others for your own professional gain, you are simply making sure every brick on the road toward student achievement is the best brick it can be - - and yes, you have my encouragement to paint the bricks yellow!

Growth Trajectory Charts are simply a collection of notes, plans, next steps, resources used, and other aspects of the TGT. You and your administrative staff will never be able to remember everything that was done by each administrator for each teacher under the TGT initiative, so maintaining copious notes is prudent.

Frankly, it also serves you well that the teacher knows you're keeping notes! When I headed off to the Army, my father told me: 1) keep your head down, 2) never volunteer, and 3) watch out for anyone with a clipboard (they are taking names and notes, and you do not want to be a note)!

Prepare Your Comments

You don't want to read a script, but you do need to be clear about what you are going to discuss with teachers during TGT meetings. This helps you stay on track and stick to the issues. You also need to maintain some kind of longitudinal record of the teacher's growth plan. What was discussed, and what actions were taken on your part and the part of the teacher, need to be archived and regularly updated. Document everything with a date. The teacher needs to see you recording all this information for three reasons.

1) It maintains a track record of what was said, done, and why.
2) It highlights the importance of what you are doing.
3) It will most certainly gain their attention!

Be Specific

Discuss with the teacher their TGT plan and seek their continued input regarding how well they think they are developing. Initially, make their input 85% of the process, so they gain confidence in you and your willingness to *listen deeply*, and in the TGT process itself.

Your more instructional opinions can be added later on down the road, especially if the teacher has skirted the issue(s) you want to place on their growth trajectory agenda. This ensures that you stick to facts, and leaves less room for ambiguity. Remember to stick to what you have viewed firsthand - - the **evidence,** not conjecture. You'll quickly find the ice beneath your feet is thin if you start giving feedback based on anything other than **evidence.**

Limit Your Focus

A TGT feedback session should be a discussion of no more than two items on the teacher's growth trajectory. Any more than that and you risk the person feeling attacked and demoralized.

You should also stick to behaviors the person can actually do something about. Negative personality traits cannot be changed (although you can make a teacher aware of them). I once had a teacher who was very sarcastic. And while I appreciated and actually enjoyed her sarcasm in a non-professional conversation (light, everyday comments about life in general, spouses, ex-spouses, kids, friends, in-laws and outlaws and other relatives, that kind of thing), she also unfortunately brought that sarcasm into her classroom. I would get complaints about how she spoke to kids. I brought up the sarcastic exchanges that she had with her students - - with **evidence** - - because it was having a significant negative impact on student learning. Once she was able to read her own words, she understood the line crossed and amended her ongoing discussions with her students.

A good rule is start off with something positive. This helps put the teacher at ease. It also lets them *visualize what success looks like*, and this helps them take the right steps next time. It also indicates that you see and recognize their success.

Provide Specific Suggestions

It is important for you to realize that complex learning, as feeding-back, feeding-forward, and feeding-up, will *initially* appear to teachers as a spiraling-up process. Repeated attempts are often necessary for the teacher to develop proficiency, and you understanding and effectively communicating this to them will support their process.

Make sure you and the teacher know what steps need to be taken to stimulate growth. The main message should be that you care and want to help the teacher grow and develop. Set goals and make plans to monitor and evaluate progress. You may not agree on everything, so it's a good idea to ask the teacher to provide their perspective of what their growth trajectory might look like. Use phrases like:

"What is your reaction to this (after you have shown them **evidence**)?"
"What do you feel would be a good start for this year's TGT plan?"
"Will you allow me to add a comment or two?"
"Do you support this growth trajectory focus?"
"As you purposefully self-reflect, what are your thoughts?"

"What do you see as your first step?"

"What would you be most comfortable doing as the next (or first) step?"

Listen attentively to what he or she has to say, and try to get them to offer suggestions. You want them to be a huge and growing part of the TGT plan.

Initially, they might not realize or even believe that they have the ability to control the direction and/or steps in this process. When you make a conscious effort to give feedback on a regular basis, you demonstrate that feeding-back, feeding-forward, and feeding-up represent a powerful means of professional growth. Performed properly, feedback is not agonizing, demoralizing, or daunting, and by couching the feedback in the form of a growth trajectory assists in limiting the downside.

It is often less what is said than how it was said!

You Just Slammed the Book Shut and Said, "Wait! I Have a Faculty of 105. I Can't Do All This!!!!"

OK, prior to you bailing on me because you have a school with 900 kids and a staff of 105 spread across many, many curriculum areas, please allow me to inject a modicum of reality.

A TGT is a long, long, looooong plan of action. Nothing will be accomplished in the first year, nor will it be completed in five years! Certainly, within a three- to five-year window, fruits of your labor (and that of the teachers) should be visible - - think buds on a tree in May.

Yes, I know what you're thinking. You're thinking, "Wait! I have to make a decision about tenure within a short window, *and* you previously said to let questionable and/or less than effective teachers go in two years!"

Well, that, my friend, is why you get paid the big bucks!

The Process

The reality is that because tenure is decided in within four years, you are forced, in my opinion, into making a decision about new teachers in two years.

Watch, listen, ask questions, and then let your gut take over. If you are attentive and have a clear understanding of what *great* teaching is and is not, you will be able to know whether or not this teacher will eventually work out. He or she doesn't have to be *great* by the end of the second year, but you need to see that the potential is present! If you have fulfilled your moral obligation to invest time and energy in these neophyte educators, your decision will be clear. (Why just two years, you might be asking. Well, my response it simple. You have *my kids* in those classes each year and the longer you protract your decision the longer you are expos-ing/subjecting *my kids* to inferior teaching.)

Create a process that is introduced and initiated by you in a general discussion with the faculty, noting your altruistic goals and that a trajec-tory for teacher growth will be created for every member of the faculty (*every* being the operative word here). This is first accomplished at a gen-eral faculty meeting, and then with various grade levels, special area teachers, and/or at department meetings that you attend with the depart-ment chairperson.

The reality is that this is *not* something you will be starting in Septem-ber of your first year as principal. You will be spending that first year get-ting to know and understand the existing culture of the school, getting to know the kids, parents, fellow administrators (building-level and central office) and - - oh yes, the teachers. You will be marking your territory from week one, and will visit every class every other day.

Assessing the culture of an organization usually takes an administrator about one year. Only by sharing a few cycles of communication, listening to feedback, and observing reactions to real situations can you truly know the stakeholders of the school.

There will be cliques to discover, interpersonal relationships to under-stand, a history to learn based upon politics, dependencies, strengths, and areas in need of growth. Only after a year will you know who the early adopters are, who will be recalcitrant, who will initially resist change, and who will support change, and why.

After this first year you can begin to anticipate reactions, rally support groups, establish trust with like-minded teacher-leaders (people of your ilk), and really start the process of rolling out the TGT concept. Carrying the above process to its predictable outcome, you will be ready in April to commence the introduction of the TGT process. If you are reading this book as an established principal, April is still the best time to roll out the concept of a TGT that will start in September.

You are highlighting your sincere belief that *professional growth is the key to mastery of pedagogy by your constituency of quality educators who are in the school.* The longest of journeys is always begun with one initial step!

However, prior to April, you need to have a series of meetings with your building-level administrative support staff: assistant principal(s), curriculum directors, department heads, and any administrative personnel whose responsibility it is to monitor and support student learning. If you are rolling out this concept to the faculty in September, then precursor-planning meetings must commence in early spring of the prior school year.

"Here is my plan to increase the educational success of our students," is your opening remark, *"...and I need your support to make it happen..."* is your follow-up statement. You are not going to present reasons such as "...to raise our assessment scores" or "...to terminate less effective personnel."

What you do say is, *"We are embarking on a trajectory to establish growth patterns for all our teachers and, in so doing, enhance the academic capabilities of our students based upon the growing pedagogical expertise of our cadre of educators."*

Please open the floor for discussion, and certainly after presenting your TGT plan, ask your cadre of administrators for their opinions about how to institutionalize and establish the process. Do not ask, *"...are you all with me on this?"* or *"...can I count on your support?"* but rather, *"I would like your opinion on how best to accomplish this task."*

At that point, provide the cadre of administrators with some handouts (copies of the Appendices), and <u>please feel free to buy each of them a copy of this book.</u>

You Know What Happens When You Assume

Please do not assume that every one of your administrative team members will run to jump on this TGT bandwagon. I have seen just as many dysfunctional, recalcitrant assistant principal(s), curriculum directors, department heads, and other administrative personnel as I have teachers operating in a less-than-appropriate fashion.

This is not a "do you want to...." It is "here is what I stand for in the process of improving opportunities for kids, and are you coming along on the bandwagon, or am I dragging you along from behind? For fear not, one way or the other, we are heading down this road."

Too strong? Too intimidating?

I am all for shared decision-making, because I am not the brightest light in the sky, nor am I the sharpest crayon in the box. However, there will be times when you must make clear that it is "my way down the highway." After all, you are the principal.

In reality, what are you really asking your administrative cadre to do? Simply buy into the concept of improving academic opportunities for kids, by asking teachers to purposefully reflect on their classroom pedagogy as an outgrowth of the observation process and the development of professional growth trajectories.

And, OK, a little more paperwork! OK, a few more conversations with teachers! And, just between you and me, never forget that there are also administrators with red magic markers!

Beg and Plead

I have always been a better-to-beg-for-forgiveness-than-plead-for-permission kind of person. However, it would not be a bad idea to call your superintendent, request an appointment, and ask him or her to come over to the school. The reason you want him or her in the building is because in her or his office the phone is always ringing, or the secretary breaks into your conversation to say the president of the board of education has popped in and is waiting to see you.

At the school, his or her attention will be more focused. Present your TGT concept and plans - - detailed plans - - for implementation. What you want, of course, is her or his blessing to move forward.

It also will not hurt, when you are discussing this with your cadre of administrators, that you can then throw in, "...when _____ (add the first name of the superintendent) and I discussed this, he/she immediately came on board with the plan."

Are We There Yet?

There will be people who will take on the role of Pope Sixtus IV, who for years asked Michelangelo when the Sistine Chapel ceiling would be finished. Teachers will want to know when their TGT will be done, accomplished, completed, and finished! I always had one response to that question: *when has one breathed enough to stop?*

Now, here is your hill to climb. It can be a hill, or it can be Mount Everest. It will all depend on how this is presented to the faculty.

What you want to avoid is having them believe you think they are substandard. You have been there a short time, and your face has been seen everywhere, all the time, and therefore the faculty will take 2 + 2 and come up with 5!

They will believe you think they're terrible at their jobs, which will be followed by the indignant; "Who the _ _ _ _ does he/she think she/he is, coming in and telling us we need this!?!"

You never said that, but it's likely to be what they think, and tongues will be wagging in the Faculty Room.

Most dentists I know don't work on Wednesdays - - look, a four-day workweek for you! However, if you are like me, the cadaver part of dental school would be a deal-breaker.

My advice, should you decide to finish this book and continue as an administrator, is to realize that the majority of teachers who say and think this are scared. Scared of you, and scared of the process.

This is where the one-on-one TGT voyage will work in your favor. Many teachers will embrace this opportunity to discuss their work, their results, and their profession - - as long as the first thing they see you doing is *listening!*

Assessment of the Paradigm Shift

The proof that the shift toward TGTs has produced the desired results will come from many sources, not least of which will be enhanced student academic achievement. When teachers grow professionally, students improve, and certainly it is possible to measure that quantitatively via longitudinal data analysis from both state and local assessments.

A less formal way you can measure growth is through *anecdotal **evidence** of teacher satisfaction*. When it is evident that people enjoy coming to work, either because they tell you they enjoy it, or they smile all day, or they line up for extracurricular projects/activities, or they are first to volunteer for what they see as another opportunity to grow, the overall success of everyone in the school will inevitably grow too.

You must never fear asking teachers what they think will make them better educators, and subsequently encouraging them to take a leadership role in making it happen! I have always had one simple goal, and I felt if that goal was achieved, it would be indicative that everything else was working.

My goal was <u>for teachers and students to look forward to Monday mornings</u>!

A Little Chapter Closing

It is important for you to approach the concept of observing teachers and the subsequent development of a TGT as teaching teachers through feeding-back, feeding-forward, and feeding-up. You are giving feedback, not grading a teacher's performance. Grading has a negative connotation, and gives the teacher no information whatsoever about how they're doing and/or what they are accomplishing.

- What is the teacher's level of performance, and how far are they from a high performance level (greatness)?
- Where are they now, and how do you get them to where they need to be?
- How are they viewing their own growth potential?
- How are both of you specifically addressing the above through a growth trajectory?
- Is the teacher aware of and prepared to be purposefully self-reflective?
- What does the teacher require in terms of support that you can provide?

Engage in diagnostic, analytical, investigative, pinpointing assessment. Where is the teacher right now, and what do _the two of you_ need to do next, and then next, and next, and all the subsequent next steps to maintain a sufficient and sustained growth trajectory?

The combination of: 1) collaboration, 2) building consensus, and 3) shared decision-making is an ideal model for schools and, in theory, it is as positive an experience as waving the American flag, Mom, hot dogs and apple pie (I wish tiramisu was part of that package. Don't you love a _great_ tiramisu?)

These three elements combined create motivation and much-needed ownership in the establishing of goals, mission, and vision that in return will reflect positively on student achievement. Having written that, and wishing that it might be so, the truth is you might need to grab the hand of some people and accompany them on this journey.

Truly, when administrators and teachers are motivated, they have ownership of their own leadership and teaching. Subsequently, they are more willing to go above and beyond to relate goals and sub-goals to their own experience, ultimately motivating students to achieve at a higher level.

You, as an effective leader, are a role model who creates consensus through collaborative decision-making strategies that in turn are built on a two-way trust between administrators and teachers.

Building such an essential climate for success can only be achieved through eliciting *commitment* from the staff, and yet there will be times when you need to put the hammer down and declare that *this is what we are doing.* Please do not be afraid to do this, because gaining consensus from a large and highly opinionated group (be it the faculty and/or the cadre of your building-level administrators) is almost impossible. Be gracious if it happens, but be demanding of the outliers if it does not!

You are either going to be hired as someone outside the district who is brought in to be the principal, or you will ascend from inside the ranks of your current district. Making the changes as an already-known commodity in the district will be the hardest. Coming from outside, you will be the Young Turk riding into town, unknown to all.

Everyone will assume you were hired based in large part on what you said in the interviews and what the superintendent and board of education want, and they wanted you and your ideas, concepts, theories, goals, vision, and so on. So you have your honeymoon period and natural fear of the unknown on your side (actually, this sounds like my first marriage).

But whether you're homegrown or an outsider, you need to allow the time for people to get to know you and your collaborative style. Changes like this require time and effort. However, you can't be like the football coach who was hired on a three-year contract but had a four-year plan!

This process of Teacher Growth Trajectory is slow, and individualizes processes that obviously can never be accomplished simply by announcing it. It requires a huge buy-in from the entire administrative team, and it will also never be fully accomplished, and certainly never to the degree you want, if teachers are not involved as part of the growth trajectory plan.

The question becomes, how can you overcome long established and adhered to practices that prevent teachers from making themselves, their ideas, and their quality pedagogy visible to other teachers? You are trying to create an ethos of voluntary teacher growth paths that spreads around the school as fast as a case of pinkeye or head lice does in a classroom, except with a more pleasant outcome for everyone (I predict that within the next 15 seconds you will either rub your eye or scratch your head)!

Chapter 5
Teacher Attitudes Toward the Observation Process and How to Ameliorate Them

People are hardwired to be self-protective.
~ Author Unknown

According to Malcolm Knowles's theory, there are basic assumptions of adult learning, and two of them always stand out to me:
1) Adults have a psychological need to be self-directing.
2) Adult learning is primarily intrinsically motivated.

The fact that adults are focused on self-direction means that it takes effort to get them to work collaboratively, which may explain why so many people are reluctant.

Secondly, if adults are intrinsically motivated by the desire to better themselves, how can administrators expect them to support one another in an era where numerical scores serve as teacher ratings (and rankings in their minds), and build a competitive atmosphere rather than a collaborative one?

What needs to occur is the refining of the process, the ethos associated with the process, and the eventual expected outcomes. It must move from a pure rating system to one that *supports the growth process* of a teacher. This refinement must be a physical one *and* a mental one for all parties concerned, with a mutually-agreed-on road map of purpose, intent, and roles within the process.

Stick a Needle in My Eye

Theoretically, observations are intended to be the means for you to help educators grow professionally. However, many teachers have a negative association with the observation process and would prefer to have the title of this section occur rather than be subjected to the process.

Your job will be to:

1) Never bring a needle to school, and
2) Create a collaborative system that defeats this phenomenon.

How difficult will this be in the era of numerical rating of teachers? Darn near impossible! I wrote "darn near," *not* impossible! Teachers simply do not feel autonomous if they are being observed, judged, and evaluated by a supervisor (there is that S-word)! As long as both parties perceive teacher observations as noxious or cumbersome, it will not serve its purpose. As long as numbers or ratings are associated with the observation practice, there will never be a comfort zone.

While you could be mandated to provide this kind of reprehensible information in order to comply and, frankly, keep your own job, *it doesn't mean it has to serve as the underpinning of your teacher growth plan.* You need to make sure everyone understands that this TGT process is *not* a static one, where the parameters are statistical, but rather an evolving project that is embedded in teacher growth.

Mark Twain said it best: "There are three kinds of lies: lies, damned lies and statistics." Let the faculty know this is your mantra. You believe nothing the numbers show, but rather what you have seen in the classroom, and what you and the teacher have shared and included in their TGT.

The educational system in America always fluctuates in dramatic fashion as both state and federal governments try to rescue what they see as a failing system. It is political fodder, pandering to those who want their politicians to do something about education in America.

There will always be new educational initiatives. Ones within recent memory are/were Regents Action Plan, No Child Left Behind, Race to the Top, and the more recent addition of Common Core, which is now Every Student Succeeds Act (ESSA) - - and hold the phone a little longer and ESSA will eventually fail and be changed as well. Stay tuned, because next year the newest, latest, greatest, never-fail rescue of our embattled educational system will be debuted. And, it too will fail, because it will be politically and corporately generated and not a product of educators!

Educational funding is always connected to new initiatives, and while they may be well intended, nevertheless they are hog-tied by people initiating these programs who have no idea what takes place on a daily basis in classrooms.

Most of the initiatives eventually become unmitigated disasters. More important, these changes have most times negatively impacted the way we view and implement teacher evaluation. A cast-iron mold with one remedy prescribed for all education's maladies does not work, or embrace academic diversity.

Simply put, all these attempts look to cure both cancer and a broken leg with the same prescriptive remedies.

A Different Lens

How do principals influence others and initiate action in an environment where teacher observation is not viewed as being productive or even viewed positively?

The initial step must be to express and demonstrate that you view the observation process *through a different lens*. Rather than expressing this in detail at a large gathering of staff via a faculty meeting, my suggestion is that you initiate the concept through individual, grade-level or departmental forums.

Your philosophy and subsequent actions will be focused on establishing well-planned and thorough teacher growth trajectories (TGTs) that are individualized, attainable, and built on **evidence** from observable classroom practices. You will be managing TGTs based upon teacher need, desire, and self-reflection.

I think it's important to insist that teachers continually ask themselves whether their students learned from and can effectively apply the material they just presented.

Does the teacher subsequently have the **evidence** to substantiate the concept of success? A teacher cannot know what to work toward if they don't know where their students currently are, and the level of each student's performance. If you create a culture that constantly asks these types of questions, it will be commonplace to reflect on what is being accomplished in the classroom.

It is important to be relevant, and when teachers can see the impact (or lack thereof) that a lesson has had on a student, they can become more motivated to change their methods of instruction to better assist and support their students. Being able to chart student growth and proficiency through some form of running record will support and empower teachers to continue to reflect and revise their TGT when necessary.

Your Purpose in the Observation Process

The purpose of classroom observation is to determine the current level of performance regarding a teacher's ability to foster their students' capacity to analyze, write, verbalize, and problem-solve. Teacher observation is necessary to assist him/her in their growth and development into a *great* teacher for *all* students.

The feedback you provide (feeding-back, feeding-forward, and feeding-up) is key to how teachers grow as a result of a TGT and, subsequently, apply their teaching skills.

Someone has to be watching, and it is your j-o-b to do so. Many times, teachers are unable to see the structure of how their lessons are implemented and internalized by students. It is not that they don't have the desire, but they are literally too close to the process to view their actions - - or even, at times, the results - - analytically.

It takes a fresh set of eyes to see what the teacher is unable (or possibly unwilling) to discern. You possess a depth of knowledge of effective pedagogy, and this is paramount to the teacher's success. This is due in large part to your effectiveness in pointing out *specific and clear* **evidence**. This **evidence** must be based on examples of what are the teacher's *direct and purposeful actions*, and (and this is critically important) the subsequent result of those actions (or lack thereof) in the classroom.

A Drop in Relationship to an Ocean

It is extremely important that educators in today's schools have enough pride in what they do, and genuinely care about their students enough, to strive for professional growth.

Kouzes and Posner (2012) wrote that leaders "...mobilize *others* to want to struggle for shared aspirations" (p. 30). This is why *leadership is a relationship* and, as a time-strapped leader, you will need to cultivate those relationships toward serving teacher growth. It is the courageous principal who allows and encourages this type of teacher investment by stepping to the side and recognizing and allowing *great* teachers to step forward.

Nothing sums up the *give a little and get a lot* concept better than when Japanese writer and philosopher Ryunosuke Satoro was quoted as saying, "Individually, we are one drop. Together, we are an ocean."

Just Get Over It!

One of the first things you will hear from teachers is their concern about the *subjectivity* of your response to their work, your write-up of their observation.

They need to get over it! Yes, it is subjective, because you are the one in the classroom making decisions about what you are seeing and hearing, and about the subsequent results, which are - - most important - - based upon some form of end-of-class assessment, and not indiscriminately about how you *feel* about the lesson.

I have sat through countless attempts, both on school district and statewide levels, to calibrate inter-rater reliability between principals observing the same teacher as he or she is giving the same lesson. All of these attempts, in my opinion, failed miserably. In fact, the New York State Department of Education has abandoned its initial efforts to do so. No two people can or will see the same thing, although they are observing the same event, at the same time, from the same angle, and with all the same players.

The factor that negates inter-rater reliability is that each administrator has biases that enter into the observation process.

There! I wrote it, and I stand by it!

But what creates the leveling influence is the inclusion of **evidence** from the lesson. A predisposition is automatically erased if it can (or cannot) be substantiated by **evidence**.

You should not be concerned at all about "...your pedagogical bias..." which will be thrown like a gauntlet by some teachers. It is why someone drives a lime-green BMW and someone else an arctic white. It is why someone puts ketchup on his or her eggs and others wear black socks with sandals. One cannot legislate good taste or, for that matter, what looks or tastes good. Therefore, how can one possibly get administrators to all agree on what is effective within the classroom? The leveling agent is and can only be the **evidence** provided by the teacher as he or she is delivering the lesson, and subsequently supported by rates of student growth.

To counterbalance the inevitable, three (3) components are a must for *every* observation to help level the playing field for the teacher being observed by the administrator sitting in the back of the room.

- Did the teacher reach out to *all* members of the class successfully, based upon each child's learning style/need?
- Did the students learn the main point/focus of the lesson, and can they subsequently apply what they learned?
- Did the teacher conduct some degree of assessment prior to the end of the class?

Regardless of an observer's desire to see pedagogy a certain way, was the desired end result accomplished via the pedagogy utilized and the manner in which the teacher engaged the students with the information?

Without becoming too Machiavellian again, did the ends justify the means? These are the only foundational elements that really matter.

Poppycock

In the spirit of fairness, and to remove as much as possible the stigma of subjectivity, you gather **evidence** from the lesson, which has been *provided by the teacher*, to substantiate your points about the effectiveness of the pedagogical path in terms of student understanding and potential application.

Period! End of story!

This is the only thing you need to prove, and you will remove all (OK, almost all) the negative bias built up around less effective observational practices.

The chant that you were biased - - for whatever reasons the teacher dreams up - - is negated to a large degree. And you don't refute the teacher's statement that you are subjective and biased, you merely keep turning back to the **evidence** *the teacher supplied*. You make sure your point is not, *"...look, I am correct,"* but rather that, *"...this is merely the starting point for our growth trajectory discussion, and the **evidence** points out where to begin."*

Regardless of how the teacher argues that the kids love him or her: *"...look, they are all really happy in class..."*, *"...the parents love me..."*, *"...I come to school early and stay late..."*, *"...I am the faculty advisor for the student government..."* and, of course, the inevitable, *"...I am the winningest football coach in the history of the school..."* - - it's all poppycock!

Bottom line, and the *only* line, is *what are you doing in the classroom, and what is the subsequent end result, and here is the **evidence** I gathered directly from you.*

Your New BFF

Evidence is what you will use to establish your credibility with the teacher. While there will be times when you and the teacher disagree about your interpretation of the **evidence**, there remains the factual **evidence** of what was said and done (and potentially accomplished).

While interpretations may vary, the facts cannot be reasonably disputed. It is this **evidence** that you will constantly be referring back to, time and again, to make points about what pedagogical practices are present or not present - - and, by extension, based upon **evidence** - - which ones were *effective!*

Frankly, **evidence** is your friend, *your very best friend!* Think of going to a party, and you aren't sure who will be there, but you do know at least one person will absolutely be present. Naturally you will seek that person out as soon as you get to the party. That person is *evidence.*

Establishing yourself as a proficient gatherer of **evidence** will earn you respect as a person who is not inclined to make subjective judgments! The biggest gripes most teachers have about the observation process are:

"It is unfair because of the subjectivity that is being employed by the administrator."

"Oh, he doesn't like me because I speak out at faculty meetings."

"I am active in the teachers' union, and administrators are out to get me."

"I didn't support the principal during the last initiative, and he/she is now angry with me."

"He/she has never liked me."

You know quite well that I can go on for pages and pages, but I will stop here. The teacher dreams it up and then adds whatever degree of paranoia they feel is needed to make their point.

However, it's all blown away by your new BFF! Outstanding use of **evidence**, drawn directly from the observation and the set of activities taking place in the classroom, blows all the comments above, and those like them, out of the water. Ah, life is good with your BFF!

Sans **evidence,** all you are doing is passing on an extremely *subjective opinion* based upon what? Well, only your opinion. And you don't want to be caught standing around with that sticking out! Providing the teacher with **evidence** to support what you witnessed - - yes, it can be seen as proof, but you should try not to go that route. Avoiding the use of the word *proof* solidifies perceptions your work in gathering **evidence**, initially for the benefit of the teacher, and ultimately that of the students.

Hot Chocolate

Later in this book I will write about how and when to lay this trump card on the table, but suffice to say at this point that the culling out and effective use of **evidence** is 84.4% of the observation process. Knowing which piece is the stronger **evidence** to substantiate your point(s) will come with time and practice.

Evidence serves to dispute a huge degree of the subjectivity associated with the observation process, and creates the perception that you are an effective, straight arrow, and call-it-as-you-see-it kind of person. You are using what was done in the classroom to make and prove (if necessary) *supportive* comments about the lesson.

The **evidence** serves as the springboard for the TGT. Don't use it as a "gotcha," but rather as a supportive awakening for teacher growth.

One of my former colleagues stated it this way when he approached a teacher during a sensitive component of a post-observation conference: *"If I were you I'd want to know that I..."* and *"Here is what was said, done, and the subsequent degree of accomplishment* (**evidence**, boys and girls), *so let's look at what we can do to build upon and further support this significant foundation that you have commenced to improve student success."*

My goodness, put that way, I'd buy hot chocolate from him while I'm sitting on the beach on July 4th!

Florence

The key word here is *support!* I cannot impress upon you more strongly the concept that must be repeated and maintained in your mind - - your mantra, so to speak - - that everything, with an emphasis on the word EVERYTHING, you do must be *in support of teacher growth* and its subsequent *impact on student learning.*

Eat, sleep, drink, breathe and put into your everyday practice this concept. Your ability to work with teachers in a more collaborative manner will hinge on their knowledge, understanding and TRUST that you are gathering information in *support* of their growth, their Teacher Growth Trajectory.

I must add one important point that I am sure many of you have come to at this juncture. As previously noted, the word *proof* is a combative word, and is read as a way to prove your point to the teacher. The word establishes, in and of itself, a less than collaborative environment.

I never, ever used the word *proof,* other than between the front and back covers of this book (our secret). Even when the process did not go well, and I was embroiled in a situation with the teacher, the union building representative, the union president, and the assistant superintendent for instruction. I never pointed to something and said, *"Here is the proof!"* The word **evidence**, because of its legal association, also is a somewhat inflammatory word when used to make a point.

"Here is what I saw..." "Here is what I heard..." "Here is what the students said (or did)..." and *"Here are the results of..."* are four alternate routes that get you to the same place, but the route is more scenic, more acceptable, and has less negative legalese. You want to head as far away as possible from any legally-inspired jargon and more toward a Florence Nightingale, *I am here to help you* approach.

I will continue to use the word **evidence** (and possibly even throw in the word *proof* every now and then). However, keep this between us! Create your own verbiage, your own approach, and your own *persona.* Just make sure you do not turn into *persona non grata.*

So, What Is Evidence?

Evidence can be what the teacher said and/or what the teacher did. It can be what the students said and/or did. It can be handouts or information presented during any part of the lesson. It can be results of assessments. It is extremely important that what is utilized as **evidence** is tangible, something seen or heard or hardcore tangible, such as projects, handouts, seatwork, and test or quiz results.

Now this gives rise to the next logical question dealing with what is tangible. Because the lesson will probably not be recorded, neither the oral part nor the physical part, **evidence** needs to be the *reasonable and logical notations by you of what transpired during the lesson.* It should not be and cannot be expected that every word and action of the teacher or students can be written down.

However, you need to learn to maintain a high degree of concentration that allows you to view and hear what is taking place and, at the same time, make notes, either written out or using an electronic device to record what has happened *and* what did not happen (and probably should have).

Evidence Gathering

I am about to scare the stuffing out of you, because I'm about to list everything you should be looking for while you observe a teacher.

My tongue was firmly in my cheek while I finished amassing the list, because I do realize it's impossibly long, and certainly beyond any human's ability to fulfill as the observee, and beyond the ability of the observer to notice, record, and comment on every single one.

What will inevitably happen, as you gain experience and get to know the ability level of each of the teachers, is an almost instinctive ability to know where to look and what to look at, and, further, to understand what are the most important points to bring to the attention of the teacher.

It is a puzzle made of many parts that requires time to put together, and, if done well, you and your colleague (as well as *your* kids) will benefit greatly.

OK, Fasten the Chinstrap on Your Helmet

- You look for a formal introduction, possibly linking previous lessons to the one about to commence, with a clearly stated lesson aim or goal.
- Are supplies, materials, and other teaching tools ready, with no time wasted pulling them together?
- Is the presentation clear, as succinct as necessary, and not totally dominated by teacher-talk?
- Are links established to make the lesson and set of activities relevant and connected to past classroom experiences?
- Are processes modeled by the teacher, and does he or she pause to see if students have any additional input and/or questions prior to them being set to task on independent work associated with the lesson?
- Does the teacher monitor students while they are working independently and/or in small groups?
- Is the teacher cognizant of when some re-teaching needs to occur based upon ongoing assessment, and how it is best accomplished?
- Is there a synopsis of the lesson near the conclusion, along with an appropriate assessment, using either a review of task cards, exit tickets, or some other form of assessment?

- Is homework discussed and linked to class activities, and is there a succinct precursor to the next lesson for the subsequent meeting of the class?
- Are students being appropriately challenged, via differentiation based upon their learning styles and/or needs, to support how they learn best?
- Does the teacher finalize the lesson with an invitation to anyone in class requiring further support, and does he or she indicate when it will take place?
- Does the teacher establish a warm and inviting environment where questions are encouraged and met with respect?
- Are there a generous number of students being called upon (both hand-raisers and non-hand-raisers)?
- Is there a degree of interaction between students on the topic?
- Are the students appropriately challenged and engaged, and do they seem interested in the work and what the teacher has to offer?
- Is there a mutual respect demonstrated at all times?

I know this may sound silly or superfluous - - but lastly, are the students and teacher having fun? Learning can be fun, and I am always warmed by the sight of students and teacher engaging in learning and at the same time having fun.

The Curse

All the above should keep you busy during the time you are in the class - - *any time you are in the classroom!* Not only are these the things to look for/sense while in the classroom for formal observations, but they also are absolutely the things I absorb as I am doing my walk-arounds and establishing my presence every day!

Trust me, it does become automatic in time, and at times it is a curse. I can unequivocally tell you that there will come a point in time when every one of the above criteria will be so ingrained in you that you will automatically run them through your mind the second you walk into a classroom - - *every* classroom, *every* time, *every* day - - ergo, the curse!

Evidence of Student Learning

In addition to the above, providing **evidence** of *student learning and acquisition of skills* is the most important indicator of teacher effectiveness.

Evidence of student learning can come in many forms, such as state and district standardized tests (I cannot believe I just wrote that), classroom assessments (pre- and post-test), homework, quizzes, questions and answers, verbal presentations, debate, group projects, and/or portfolios. You can begin assessing teacher effectiveness through the use of these various forms of student assessment.

However, relying solely on the above **evidence** would not determine teacher effectiveness, but would provide knowledge that would help you to increase teacher effectiveness via a planned growth trajectory formulated from all the **evidence** provided from the above endeavors.

The Elbow Mac Lesson

During a formal observation of a second-grade teacher, I was shown an introductory lesson on the correct use of commas and quotation marks. After a brief lesson introduction, each student was provided with a long strip of paper, and each student was to write one of the sentences the teacher provided to them, each student having gotten a different sentence. Once the sentence was written, the students were given some elbow macaroni and a small amount of Elmer's glue to place commas and quotation marks at the appropriate locations on their sentence strip.

Best lesson I ever saw? No. Cute? Sure. Was it fun for the kids? Yes. A couple of days later, the teacher was able to show me early writing samples, and then the newer ones that reflected the use of commas and quotation marks subsequent to the elbow mac lesson. I was satisfied that the lesson met its goal and students were able to apply what they learned going forward. I wrote up the lesson based upon a highly satisfactory outcome -- end of story? Not so fast!

There were seven teachers on the second-grade level, and the next year I saw the exact same lesson presented by another second-grade teacher, and a year after that, two other teachers dragged the lesson out for me for one of our prearranged formal observations. *I was being duped!* They shared among themselves that it was a lesson I liked, and therefore it would guarantee a good observation report for whatever teacher used it.

114

On one level I was pleased that they had shared an effective lesson, and that they were talking with one another about pedagogy (or were they talking about what pleased me during a formal observation?).

At the first faculty meeting the next school year, when the agenda rolled around to observations, I took out of the large paper bag I had placed upon the table a large box of Ronzoni Elbow Macaroni, whacked it down on the table with a great flourish, and said, "I have had more elbow macaroni than I will ever need!"

The entire faculty broke out laughing! I had eventually caught on to them, and apparently the entire faculty (not just the second-grade teachers) was aware of my apparent passion for elbow macaroni. Certainly I was happy they were sharing a good lesson that worked well for young students, which was more important to me than anything else. We all had a great laugh, on me, and we moved on.

Question: how would you have handled that situation? I was a new principal, in my fourth year, and this was before I started to use a pre-observation conference!

Thank You, Sylvia

Giving every student a gold star (or its equivalent) at the end of the day, regardless of performance, will only perpetuate teachers who are only there to collect their paycheck every two weeks, and/or ones who haven't a clue.

I once had a veteran teacher who parceled out easy lessons so all her students could appear to achieve. This was by all accounts a simplistic and ill-conceived mind-set. Her heart was seemingly in the right place, everyone got an A, and everyone (kids and parents) felt really good at the end of the day (and school year).

At a post-observation conference after one of her lessons I formally observed, I took her to task, and not the first time, for providing work that was too easy for the grade level, and sans any form of significant and grade-level-appropriate challenge.

Her innocence was almost Forrest Gump-ish. She insisted that all her students were doing extremely well in her class and always had, for years. I reiterated my position about how her students (*my kids!*) were not being significantly challenged, and therefore not learning and progressing, especially when compared to the work being performed by students of other teachers on her grade level.

With that, she told to me wait a minute, and she dashed to the front of the classroom and retrieved her grade book. She proudly opened it and pointed out how <u>everyone</u> in her class got an "A," and therefore, she was "...a *great* teacher, and my students are learning everything they needed to know."

And thank you, Sylvia, for proving my point!

Bad Recycling

No one wants to be reminded of past mistakes, errors, or efforts that did not come to successful fruition.

Successful educators do not reuse the same lesson(s) year after year. After all, the class is not made up of the same students, and they certainly do not have the same academic needs. "If it is October 21st, then it must be time for the October 21st lesson," is not the academic progression you should condone, expect, or see!

However, *great* teachers do continue to build on the successes of the previous year, and strive to not repeat past mistakes. This cannot be done if experiences of the past year are forgotten or not thought about from the last day of the school year to Labor Day. It *can* be achieved, however, if they become a serious part of any purposeful self-reflection.

You need to stay engaged and continue to provide the necessary upwardly spiraling growth path for each teacher from year to year. Creating an opportunity at the beginning of the school year to discuss with teachers their self-imposed goals inaugurates a new year of growth. It establishes an appropriate mind-set, and/or at the very least it serves notice that you *have not forgotten the TGT mind-set*, and that you are persevering forward, onward, and upward! And using your TGT Charts (Appendices C, D, and E) while discussing goals at the start of the school year will surely impress to the teacher sitting with you.

One issue born out of human nature is that good teachers often plateau professionally. It happens because they aren't given the ongoing support and quality professional growth incentives that are critically necessary to help them develop into *great* teachers, or even to sustain their performance as *great* teachers. One must look at and practice the art of supporting teacher growth through a TGT in a multi-faceted manner, as opposed to the one-and-done observation process of pre-observation conference, observation, and post-conference, and then "see you in a few months when we must do this dance again."

Merely applying one component of the process (the three-pronged observation plus pre- and post-conferences) will never be sufficient. While the three-pronged approach may satisfy a contractual obligation, in contrast, the TGT process targets teacher effectiveness through a layered and spiraling approach that is dependent on the observed growth needs of teacher.

While you observe to fulfill a contractual obligation, the layers of a TGT fulfill a moral obligation to create the best educational environment for students by way of enhancing teacher effectiveness through their professional growth. When this is complimented with unbiased, constructive feeding-back, feeding-forward, and feeding-up techniques, and when post-observation work includes collaboration and motivation, you will see movement toward collegial support and ultimately teacher growth.

This looks good on paper, of course, but unfortunately, for too long the notion of the observation process has been tainted by teachers' actual experiences of the process, most of which has been negative because it wasn't properly framed and/or presented as a teacher growth model.

The objective of classroom observations is to *serve as a platform to take off from* for teacher growth. At best you will use the observations to help guide teachers to enhance their planning, instruction, classroom environment, and possibly even their professionalism. Theoretically, both formal and informal observations are meant for you to help teachers grow professionally.

We've discussed the fact that many teachers have a negative association with the process. People simply do not feel autonomous if they are being judged, evaluated, and observed by someone in a powerful position over them. So in theory one might argue that allowing teachers to observe and support colleagues might be the best way to go. Of course, in theory Communism works. However, even Pollyanna wouldn't believe that a system like that is doable, given state department of education requirements, and teacher contract obligations, and strict adherence to the delineation of the process.

The bottom line is that teachers do not want that type of responsibility. However, *great* teachers, as observable role models on a carefully, specifically prescribed basis, can serve as a means toward an end in supporting other teachers, and will be a critical asset to your teacher professional growth endeavor.

In your role of principal, I would suggest that you use a combination of collaborative and directive informational behaviors as keys to your feedback pattern. As you establish your pattern of proactive intervention strategies, a more directive approach needs to be held in abeyance, and only used if a collaborative environment isn't working, or is not working fast enough for the good of your students.

When a principal approaches teacher growth in a collaborative fashion, she or he shares the decision-making process with the teacher in a joint effort. When utilizing a more directive informational approach, the principal gives suggestions for professional growth, and hopes (and an occasional prayer isn't out of the question) the teacher will integrate these changes.

Damn, the Principal is Taking Notes

A mid-September meeting with each teacher, to ask about their students and the individual plans they have for them, will certainly also get them thinking and hopefully planning, especially if they see you referring to notes from your previous meetings with them. I think it is important for you to know about the academic (and social) needs of as many students as you can.

Nothing, NOTHING, n-o-t-h-i-n-g made me feel more a part of the academic team then knowing about the long-term growth pattern of specific kids. To be able to articulate their year-to-year progress to the current year's teacher is fantastic, and boy, does that impress parents when you can speak knowledgeably about their child off the cuff, when you see them in the hallway or at an event!

Don't Give Me Any Static

As long as both teacher and administrator perceive teacher evaluations as noxious or cumbersome, they will not serve their purpose. Embrace the mind-set that what you are doing in terms of teacher growth through the observation process is *a pedagogical evolution* more than a static process. You are adding a twist to the grind of observation by turning it into an upward growth model mind-set, and not a punitive or negative process. The end result is simple and recognizable, and there are two things you need to readily admit to as part of the observation process:

1) The sustained pedagogical growth of a teacher, and
2) The removal of a less-than-the-highest performing teacher.

If you aren't admitting to both, you're kidding yourself and those around you, and you won't gain the fullest cooperation.

Spend a preponderance of time up front working with your newer staff members, building their skill sets, and feeding them a growth trajectory mind-set for their continued professional growth. You are seeking to weed out (yes, I wrote it) those who do not have, at the very least, the *potential* to be *great*.

By dedicating yourself to that endeavor at this early stage in your relationship with these teachers, you'll not find yourself married to an incompetent while pursuing futile efforts (tenure laws are simply too strong) to remove the teachers later on in their careers.

A Video Camera, A Video Camera, My Kingdom for a Video Camera! The Best Method Is One We Apparently Cannot Use

Research from Harvard's Center for Education Policy suggests that many teachers believe classroom-based observations are inherently subjective and biased. As a result, teachers may dismiss the feedback they do receive and fail to grow from the process.

Still, a report from the Brown Center on Education Policy at Brookings in May 2014 shows that if these challenges can be overcome, observations can, in fact, improve the efficacy and accelerate educator growth.

But how can they be overcome?

Without question, a classroom video would help building administrators provide teachers with better feedback and support. However, in this day and age, that simple and highly effective growth tool is almost never utilized. Frankly, videotaping the lesson and set of activities is THE key to undisputable **evidence**-gathering, and would serve as the definitive method to implement teacher growth patterns. It's amazing and frustrating that something so easy to do is so off the planet in terms of do-ability.

Classroom videos present an accurate depiction of the teacher teaching. With the ability to pause and rewind, video technology provides explicit **evidence**, and a reference point for both teachers and you. Therefore, feedback can be thoughtful, specific, holistic, empirical, impartial, and objective, thus enabling teachers to more readily accept feedback and grow from it. With video, it's possible for subject-matter experts to review instruction for more relevant and actionable support. Video provides the common **evidence** that initiates the meaningful and common reference points teachers need to accept feedback and grow.

Video can allow teachers to:
- Receive more frequent, meaningful, and actionable feedback on their instruction.

- Evaluate their own practices and identify opportunities for growth through purposeful and specific self-reflection.
- Get personalized and specific support for their content area.
- Ensure written observations and written evaluations are accurately and fairly based *solely* upon **evidence**.
- Share best practices and effective techniques, and collaborate more effectively with other teachers.

Classroom video captures actual practices in real time, making the observer's feedback more relevant, unbiased and valuable. Using videos of instruction opens the door for a new way to use informal and formal observations to provide teachers the support they need to feel confident in their classrooms.

To improve pedagogy, teachers must understand what their current teaching methods are, and this is impossible to do based only on their own perceptions, or even feedback from observers. A classroom is a dynamic environment, and there is always a lot going on that can be missed in the moment.

Here are some important guidelines for helping teachers feel comfortable and successfully capture video of their own classrooms:

1) Make sure to communicate that the use of the video is to interpret what is going on in the classroom, not judge it.
2) Allow teachers the ability to control who is going to be watching the video of their classroom instruction.
3) Work with teachers to set purposes for viewing the video before the actual filming, and stick to them during the reflection and feedback process.
4) Commit to the idea that the overall goal is to always be growing their practice.

Paging Dr. Merlot

After more than three decades of observing teachers, dialoging about the observation in pre- and post-observation conferences, and subsequently writing up the results, it is my opinion that there is only one way that observations will be productive.

The process is clear, it is simple, and it brings me back to my college days as a Fine Arts major. In painting class, for example, the professor would assign a theme, such as the use of hue to bring out mood and/or emotion in the observer. We were all told to return to class in three weeks with no less than four paintings demonstrating the parameters of the assignment. The professor noted that she would be in the studio during class time each week if anyone wanted to run anything by her in terms of the assignment.

Now here is the best part, and one I believe would be most useful for teacher growth trajectories. On the fourth week we all returned with our paintings. One by one, we each placed our work on the numerous easels around the room, and then our peers commented on our ability to reach the desired outcome as established by the assignment parameter.

Did we reach the target goal of the activity? Interestingly, "yes" or "no" were never acceptable responses. I learned a great deal from my peers about what worked and what did not during those sharing meetings. The critiques were never given with malice or disdain, and every bit of input was delivered in a professional manner.

Now here is the most interesting part, at least to me. *I listened more attentively and deeply when the person discussing my work was someone whose work I admired and whose opinion I, therefore, respected!!!!!!!!!!!!!!!*

What are the implications for you as an administrator? I want to keep this book under two hundred and seventy-five pages, so I will let you reflect on your own.

Imagine, if you will, teachers supporting other teachers with my Fine Arts model, using videos of their teaching during their growth trajectories! The results, I believe, would be phenomenal! If I could just convince everyone of this, patent the process as my intellectual property, and collect royalties. Hawaiian beachfront condo, here I come!

King of America

Boy, if I were on each state's Board of Regents, or Commissioner of the State Education Department, or King of America, guess what I would mandate! Give every single teacher a visual recording device and a tripod, and let them record as many videos as they want. Then have them select three or four colleagues to share videos with.

Why? Because in so doing, the teacher has already gone through the process of viewing the various videos he or she made, and established a self-selection using purposeful self-reflection!

I call it the Dr. Merlot Teacher Growth Trajectory Model, because I would serve some red, grape-based, adult beverage at the teacher-sharing sessions. OK, I know what you're thinking: a) red wine gives me a headache and I, therefore, only drink white, and b) where is the administrator's portion of this process, other than serving as a sommelier?

I'm so glad you asked!

Let's say you're involved in the beginning of year two of this process. The teacher and her or his colleagues have spent a year working together, beyond earshot and the view of the principal (although you are still having a significant presence in every classroom).

In September/October, you commence your formal classroom observations and conduct the process of pre- and post-conferences as well. However, at the pre- and post-conferences, the teacher can use the videos he or she selects to share with you which demonstrate growth in areas they have selected. The selection needs to be meaningful - - having a direct and significant impact on students learning - - not simplistic, managerial tasks.

And here is an interesting twist; they supply the **evidence** of growth! Oh my, I think I just felt the earth tilt slightly off its axis. All hail, the new King of America!

No Man or Woman Is an Island

Sans videos, we now move back to the reality of the day. The process we know as teaching continues to remain dominated by extreme isolation from one's peers. Nowhere in corporate America is the underlying tenet of staff dominated by as much isolation of individual employees. These days wall-free collaborative environments dominate corporate America where ideas, theories, best practices, and individual growth are fueled and supported in a collaborative fashion. This can be seen everywhere except the educational system of the United States.

My *wall-free* vision is not one that will take us back to the open classroom era of the 1960's, where multiple groups of youngsters were educated in a vast space, with no walls separating groups of various ages and academic focus. My *wall-free* metaphor means that teachers communicate with each other regularly about pedagogical practices, and visit each other's rooms regularly while their colleague is teaching. It is performed because Teacher A knows that Teacher B has something to offer him or her that can help build their growth trajectory.

You, as principal, can support that endeavor by creating the structures - - time and your commitment - - needed to allow this to occur, *regularly*.

Privacy of Practice: Isolation Is an Enemy

As long as teaching and processes for teacher growth remain marked by extreme teacher isolation, it works to the detriment of teachers and their students. Autonomy of practice for teachers only guarantees that some teachers will have the freedom to fail.

Privacy of practice is an ugly term, and one that some teachers feel emboldened by and, at some point, even protected by, or even entitled to.

Hogwash! And having spent time in rural Indiana, I know exactly what hogwash looks and smells like. There is no privacy of practice!

If you want to work as a teacher -- at least in a school where I am principal -- there is *no* privacy of practice! You may enter your classroom with four walls, a floor and a ceiling, and you may shut the door behind you, but you are not an atoll unto yourself.

Isolation, the antithesis of collaboration, is a harmful practice that creates nothing and can, in fact, be harmful to professional growth. In an isolated environment, people (teacher and principal) can become delusional and think things are progressing smoothly and effectively.

Isolation inhibits vision, growth, varied experiences, creativity, problem-solving, and dialogue, as well as one's view of reality (remember Sylvia?). A teacher who works in isolation and consistently creates initiatives or changes based on their own personal viewpoint will not achieve a high degree of success. This is because they are the only one they are bouncing things off of.

Additionally, a principal who cannot create a buy-in by faculty or other stakeholders is in equal peril. This type of leader rules by coercion and intimidation, does not motivate staff, and refuses to involve them in the growth process. *Isolation is the thief of growth.* It creates potentially false impressions and *allows a mirror to serve as feedback*.

A way to thwart the concept of privacy of practice from teacher to teacher is to implement the previously mentioned *Community of Inquiry* (CoI). Establishing individual TGTs for each teacher in no way diminishes the need, use, and importance of learning communities.

Using *Community of Inquiry* results in improved teaching practices, which in turn result in improved learning for students. When teachers collaborate, it produces greater success than when teachers work alone. In order for an organization to benefit from the CoI concept, the school must have a strong leader who believes in collaboration (that is *you*, by the way). Rather than be the type of leader who simply tells people what to do, it is up to you to set an example of teamwork.

Wildfire

When a change needs to be made within the building, for whatever reason, use committees who work together to create plans. This assists in creating a culture within a building that two or more minds are better than one.

It is also imperative for you to understand that if one wants to have a CoI in action, where teachers can share ideas, you must allocate time for teachers to do so. You must create opportunities for these meetings to occur. Perhaps teachers are given coverage for their classes in order to meet, or time is assigned before or after school for CoI meetings.

Think of the impact if *you* were to cover a class, thereby freeing up a teacher for one period every two weeks! Think if you and an assistant principal or department chair each covered a class while those two teachers met!

Now you are not only verbalizing the word collaboration, but you are lending your physical support as well. Word of this kind of support spreads like a wildfire in California, and not only will it be greatly appreciated by the staff, but you will be heralded as someone who talks the talk and walks - - well you know. Plus, this collaborative culture thwarts a teacher's demand for privacy of practice, since it is alien to the practices already in place supporting collaboration.

Rosetta Stone

Working with the human species is complex. People are always caught up in their own insecurities and concerns about how other people view them. I think we are the only species on earth who feels that way - - although when Gracie, my cat, does something silly or awkward, she immediately looks around to see who's watching her, and I get the impression that she's embarrassed.

I think you need to look upon certain basics as the Rosetta Stone of how to approach everyone (not as the foreign language program, but as something that provides crucial clues to understanding).

Traditionally, teachers have been observed by administrators and *told* what they did wrong and how they should improve. The TGT process is one of colleagues (teacher and principal) working together to improve student performance through enhanced pedagogy.

You must work to remove the *telling* part from as many situations as possible. A process that has the capacity to open communication between you and teachers is indispensable based on the diversity of teachers' abilities and subject expertise. Observations should serve to help teachers build and subsequently sustain pedagogical growth, not to demand compliance.

They Talk to Each Other

Yes, teachers talk to each other! Colleagues who are of the same ilk are in classrooms before school, after school, or during lunch when they elect not to eat in the Teachers' Cafeteria/Faculty Room. Some/many also socialize with each other outside of school, and Dr. Merlot, when available in even moderate amounts on a Friday after school at local adult beverage dispensary, can get tongues wagging.

How you treat one teacher will be shared with others. My hernia repair was not half as bad as I had heard it would be, and yet passing a kidney stone was so much worse than I had heard. Fear or calm is developed via the passing of tales around an open campfire, or its 21st century equivalent, after school on Friday night at a watering hole serving adult beverages at a prodigious rate.

People look for fairness and consistency. They want to hear that a person's pre-conference, observation, post-conference, and write-up weren't as bad as they thought it would be, and that it was more challenging but had a bigger reward than most had expected. You want that same word-of-mouth spreading about their TGT! They want to hear that their fellow teacher's hand was held (not literally), and that there was no judgment, no consternation, no intimidation, and they got to speak and *you listened*. The unknown is always scarier than reality, and the next teacher in line for the process is all ears.

That does not mean you should portray everything as a rose garden. There will be thorns (sorry, this was too easy, and I couldn't pass up the metaphor). People to whom you had to be very matter-of-fact because they are not willing to collaborate will cry foul, and those with an axe to grind will claim there was more vehemence than in actuality.

The experience for most will be favorable. They will see the degree of importance you place on the reflection process, and on your support of their growth through a TGT, and will cautiously and yet optimistically (because they are happy with your approach) believe you are teaming up with them for the benefit of their pedagogical growth. They will remain cautiously silent and somewhat under the radar, afraid to stand up to or appear against the more dark-side voices, until the tide turns and they see there are more Jedi than Sith!

Baseball players don't practice by listening to speeches about their swing; they improve by hitting thousands of baseballs. In fact, many players have access to a video of themselves at bat; literally from the moment they sheepishly walk off the field into the dugout during a game, and can see what they did wrong (or the pitcher did right) to strike them out. Standing next to them is the batting coach and/or a teammate who happens to hit that pitcher well, and each is supporting the player who struck out with advice that the player can apply during their *very next time at bat*. If a baseball player gets only four (4) hits for every ten (10) times they are at bat, they would be in the Hall of Famer on the first ballot and be the best hitter in baseball history - - with only four (4) out of ten (10)! Now think of the dire straits if only four (4) out of ten (10) students in a teacher's class were successful. Not acceptable!

I truly believe you will never, n-e-v-e-r really change those who do not want to grow, or who view themselves as requiring no growth despite significant **evidence** to the contrary. They prefer to sit on the bench and ignore what might assist them. However, it will be the people who are listening quietly, not joining in with colleagues getting the tar, feathers, rope, and pole. They are your candidates. They understand! They appreciate the work you are doing with them. Will they speak out to support your efforts with them? They will not - - especially after seeing that the red X people have an abundance of extra tar, feathers, poles and ropes.

Let's Not Be Naïve

The observation process is steeped in layers of mistrust and ineptitude. There are as many facets to the process as a well-cut diamond. The problem is the perspective that each participant brings to the process.

When teachers view the observation process as a measurement of their ability, and you view it as an opportunity for them to grow, the polarization creates a situation that is less than conducive. I would consider anyone who believes that decisions about the employment status of a teacher aren't made during the observation process to be extremely naïve. They can and should be made as a result of your awareness of what is happening in the classroom. It is an awareness that teachers carry with them from their non-tenure days.

As previously written, I know eleven teachers who at one time worked in our school and no longer do, and that was due in huge part to the observation process connecting me to their inability to teach effectively. I also am aware of a few teachers who retired in their first year of eligibility due to my observations of their work and my subsequent write-ups and conversations with them.

Therein lies another effective dynamic of the observation process. However, the process of removing an ineffective teacher from the system is built around the due process of observing the teacher teaching, and the constructive support you offer. With that as a mainstay of the removal process, denying that it exists places you in a position of not being ethical, trustworthy, or, quite frankly, honest.

During the course of 35 years, there were eleven (11) people who parked their car in our parking lot and eventually vacated their spot by the end of their second year. To deny it happened is ludicrous, and to pretend that the observation process did not *significantly* contribute to the outcome is equally ludicrous.

Frankly admit to it while you also make that situation work for you. Forgive me, but fear can be a very strong incentive! The fear experienced by teachers during the observation process is because it is a reality. In states where tenured is the carrot at the end of a very short stick (only a brief few years) decisions must be made very quickly. I have had first dates with women that seemed to last longer than it takes to give a teacher tenure, and the result of tenure is a marriage for life.

Dream on, Don

A system that would allow for a five-year apprentice (team-teaching) period, where the neophyte teacher is paid and a principal-selected mentor teacher compensated as well, would allow for the growth of a neophyte teacher and support a realistic timeline of expectations for the development of their potential prowess.

I have had teachers walk into school after going through the hiring and induction process with Styrofoam packing peanuts statically clinging to them because they were so new. The bell rang on the first day of school, they entered their classroom, and they closed the door behind them. Other than me walking into and around their classroom, conversations from time to time based upon pointed questions I would present to them (not merely, "Hey, how is it going?"), and the observation process, I knew little about how effectively they were doing their job.

Yes, data from testing would provide me a clue, but not immediately. Comments from students, phone calls from parents (probably mostly negative in nature at that early time of the year) would help to adjust my understanding. I also had colleagues, trusted colleagues, who I could subtly go to and ask, *"How do you think things are going in Room 231?"*

Nothing about the present induction system was developed to build skills, and very little about the process centers on professional growth. Yes, many times the new teacher was formally supplied a mentor by district administration, for one year, and that, I am sure, was better than nothing.

However, the qualifying factor, as I noted previously, would be the competency of the mentor. We need a better and more complete induction to our profession for neophyte teachers. However, nothing I say or write will change the process, and all we can do is work within the current, albeit inept, system of where teachers have a short period of time to prove themselves or they are out!

Never let the systems in your school allow an inept teacher make it into tenure status. That is why I give new teachers only two (2) years, and never let a questionable teacher reach their third year. Too many things can happen in that third year that might allow a teacher to eventually slide into tenure.

Attitude

John Maxwell often writes about attitude and how it can be a person's most important asset. He reports on a study completed by the Carnegie Institute concluding that only fifteen percent of success is due to an individual's initial training. The study goes on to conclude that eighty-five percent of success in any endeavor is due to personality, with the number one trait being *attitude*.

Think of the attitude of a teacher, alone in his or her classroom on their first day, week, and month of their teaching career! Now, when you walk in and around the classroom:

- Is that teacher seeing you as a helper, a supporter, a colleague, or someone who is judging them?
- What kind of induction did this teacher experience when they entered the school?
- How did you approach him or her, and what did you say?

How much time did you spend with them, and what did you offer them in terms of creating and sustaining their professional growth - - especially at this early stage?

This certainly invites the question of how one can cultivate the proper *attitude* in the teachers you are working with. How can you develop and create a viable attitude among teachers so there is the *best chance* of success, not only for them, but for their students as well, because you can't judge the success of either one without taking the other into consideration.

What Is *Your* Attitude? Try This on for Size

First and foremost, I have the attitude that the students in the school are my children, and I am loaning them to a teacher on a specific grade level, or in a course, for a period of a school year. You might have noticed how many times on previous pages I have referred to students as **my kids**.

At the end of the school year, the teacher is essentially finished with them, and they will be returned *to me* for distribution for the following school year. So *my attitude* is that these children are *mine*, and what are you (the teacher) going to do *with* and *to* them? I'm not sure if this is a rational mind-set in your eyes; however, who in the school is the most constant and consistent person in the lives of children in school *year after year*? Possibly two people: you, serving *in loco parentis*, and the person working in the cafeteria for the past twenty years, dishing out mac & cheese on Fridays (however, I do not look good in a hairnet)!

The advantage this *attitude* confers is one of *ownership*. One is more likely to care and cautiously oversee something they consider theirs, more than they would for something that they do not consider themselves responsible for. This then leads one to the quandary of creating an *attitude* of caring on the part of the teacher for those students under her or his guidance for the school year.

In my mind, and as simplistically as it can be presented, the fact that I take such care and concern for *my students* automatically places a teacher on notice that I care, my *attitude* being, take really good care of *my kids* this year (or else)!

Kemosabe

A principal is responsible for establishing or setting the tone of the school culture and environment (I know you know this). An authoritative-style leader engenders apprehensive compliance in their staff. "The use of coercive power tends to result in alienation" (Chance 2009, p.35).

Either through structural constraints (scheduling, confinement to classroom and from proximity to others) and/or with other isolating conditions that permeate the school environment, teachers may become lone rangers, feeling they must stand for themselves against an ongoing tide of demands from students, administrators, parents and the curriculum. They pull up the drawbridge and stock the moat with alligators and piranhas.

This is hardly an environment where a teacher can flourish, grow, and positively impact the culture of the school and their students. You subliminally support all these concepts by a lack of presence and a *lack of dialogue with each teacher*. You are creating paranoia among your staff, absent your visibility and conversations about pedagogy and what you stand for in terms of betterment for your kids, and a lack of candid and purposeful conversations leads to this paranoia.

Amid the backdrop of the pressures of teaching, and there are many, a strong and visible leader can be a "...dealer in hope" (Napoleon Bonaparte), and thwart the previously-mentioned concept of privacy of practice that could be prevalent, by fighting against and not accepting the "...conventional school model characterized by dependency, hierarchy, and professional isolation" (Glickman et al, 2010, p.40).

By turning to the "...collegial school model characterized by purposeful adult interactions about improving school-wide teaching and learning" (Glickman et al, 2010, p.45), you create the most fulfillment in a faculty. A cadre of educators engenders mutual respect through their ability to work together, creating a strong collective vision and shared decision-making through open communication and feedback in a CoI learning community you created and seek to sustain.

You calmly instill urgency about meeting or exceeding student needs through teacher growth, and subsequently achieve a high level of student learning.

Impact of External Factors

The bottom line is always this: what did the students learn?

Paul Bambrick-Santoyo (2010) stresses in <u>Driven by Data</u> that we should not be focusing on *how much teachers are teaching*, but rather on *how much the students are learning*. It nonetheless still rests with your opinion and analytical proof of student performance. The question is easily answered when results are excellent. No one is suspect when the results are good.

The issue becomes more muddied when the results are poor, although they can be, in part, based upon extenuating circumstances. For with poor results comes the issue of *student innate ability* added into the process, and how effectively the students can use information exposed to them versus the teacher's ability to teach. What is the definitive correlation between the two?

- Can the teacher be held fully responsible for a student not being able to demonstrate proficiency based upon the student's learning disability?
- Can a teacher be held fully responsible when there is a lack of academic support at home?
- Can a teacher be held fully responsible when the student's native language is not English?
- Can a teacher be held fully responsible when there is a lack of adult supervision after school hours?
- Can a teacher be held fully responsible when English is not spoken in the home?
- Can a teacher be held fully responsible when the best (and maybe only) meal a child has all day is lunch (and possibly breakfast) in school?

This is where the trust factor starts to really come into play. No standardized or in-house assessment takes any of the above into consideration. The assessment spits out a number, and you will be in dire straits if that is all you use to develop your judgment of a teacher's ability.

However, the questions begging to be asked are:

- *How can teacher growth support some of the students struggling under the conditions noted above?*
- *How can teacher growth enable the teacher to counteract or at best diminish, the impact of some of these conditions?*

According to Colin Marsh and George Willis (2003) "many neophyte teachers begin their careers with beliefs that date back to early contact with their own teachers" (p.200), and some of these new teachers will use methods that were presented to them when they were students. To be effective, areas of learning should:

- Apply to all students, regardless of their place on the developmental continuum.
- Define a wide range of performance, therefore, accommodating learning goals for every student in the classroom.

Look at the subtle differences in the discussions that could ensue. Instead of asking the teacher *why* did these students perform poorly and *mitigating* some of the causative factors as not relevant, you are asking the teacher what can *we do* to support these students?

There is a huge difference, which quite possibly can create *a huge difference in the way the teacher subsequently views you!* The above questions cannot be offered as an excuse for poor performance. However, it can be accepted as a highly significant contributing factor for poor student performance. This leaves open the door to these questions: how do we help these kids, and how do you (the collaborative administrator) help teachers to help them.

Moo

You must replace the conventional mind-set of teachers, and the associated negative connotation of the observation process, with a more congenial approach associated with a teacher growth mind-set.

Again, it's possible I am being too kumbaya-ish. However, I do not think I am being too pie-in-the-sky and naïve in this approach, because what we have left absent the teacher growth mind-set is what we currently have, and have always done, and that puppy isn't working so well.

My strong suggestion is that your mantra becomes *teacher growth through collaborative TGT development.* It would be impossible to make desired teacher growth and the observation process separate, because where would your basis for planning a Teacher Growth Trajectory (TGT) come from if not from the observable practices of the teacher? Which in reality draws the administrator into the observation process when teachers ask, "Why are you asking me to grow in this area? What have you seen me do (or not do)?" You need to link the two as you inevitably would peanut butter and jelly. Since jelly by itself is too sweet, and peanut butter by itself sticks to the roof of your mouth, they need and require each other, and so do teacher observation and the foundational components of a TGT. And please don't forget the ice-cold glass of cow juice!

A Little Chapter Closure

From Homo erectus up through the early 21st century, teacher observation by administrators has been the bane of many professional educators. The process is necessary, if for no other reason than to draw focus and attention to pedagogical practices being used in the classroom by a teacher, and their impact on his or her students. In most cases, administration saw it as a major function of their responsibility to *pass judgment* on the efficacy of the teacher and the pedagogical practice employed by the teacher. On the other hand, the teacher saw it as something he or she must endure and hope for the best.

What needs to occur is a refining of the process, the ethos associated with the process, and the eventual expected outcomes. It must move from a pure rating process to one that supports the professional growth of a teacher. This refinement must be a physical one *and* a mental one for all parties concerned, with a mutually agreed-upon roadmap of purpose, intent, and roles within the process.

Chapter 6
The Advantage of Conflict

Conflict is not the enemy; it is simply the path to peace by taking the long way around.
~ Author Unknown

Conflict is unavoidable and largely unpleasant. However, while not inevitably essential, it can serve as a genesis for germinating ideas and resolutions to problems and/or plaguing issues. In order to make conflict as productive as it can be (and this will not be easy because of the emotionality embroiled in the process of conflict), it will be necessary to map out your approach to the person with whom you are in conflict. It is not impossible, and is certainly worth the effort.

Understand Conflict Because It Is Going to Happen

Your ability to handle conflict is essential to the overall effectiveness of the professional Teacher Growth Trajectory concept. (I threw in the word *professional* because you will be using the word as extensively as Captain America uses his shield. As you know, I love the term *professional maturity*, because it is something I expect from every adult in the school.)

To succeed at handling conflict, you will need to learn and understand how to motivate people, and to deal with their variety of emotions. Although dealing with the emotions of staff members is not on the priority list of many researchers, it does provide leaders who are capable of addressing these issues as an opportunity to motivate maximum productivity and create a more productive work environment.

You must be able to create an environment that is conducive to positive interactions with teachers. For the most part, teachers want to feel *important* and *valuable* to the overall goals and objectives associated with the school. There will always be some who are more fixed on their VACA (either at Turks & Caicos or Aruba), and you will from time to time run into a teacher (or two) who only want to be told what to do and when to do it. While you will never allow them to abandon adherence to the teacher growth trajectory concept, they can have a pass if they don't want to get involved in the decision-making process.

However, they need to understand that if they self-select to not buy into the collaborative system, then they have no voice, and must capitulate to whatever decisions are rendered to them in their TGT. If the teacher selects to acquiesce out of the process of having direct input into their TGT, they are then into a system they cannot criticize later, and they need to just follow along like a sheep. That doesn't mean, however, that they can neglect their responsibilities to *my kids*. If they do not want to give me their opinion, fine. But refusing to give 110% to *my kids* will never be tolerated.

Do not be so drawn into a fight that you *forget what you really want* in the first place! You do not want to *win* as much as you want progress toward teacher growth. The progress can be only an inch at a time, but an inch forward is better than a yard backward.

Render down the issue to make it clear to all involved (although in most instances it will only be you and one other person). In order to do this, it might be necessary to take a step back.

The immediacy is not important; however, the thought process is. This can mean stopping at a certain point and indicating *let's think about what was said and what we are looking for, and let's meet again early next week.*

Please remember you are looking to develop a colleague, not create an enemy. You will be amazed what a weekend can do to internalize and perpetuate resolutions. This is not an avoidance of the issue. It is a recalculation: a reflection period, during which the issue is not ignored.

The brief postponement allows everyone to consider a possible repurposing of desire, progress toward an acceptable outcome, and a reexamination of the path that will get people on the track toward a successful outcome.

Reflection-_in_-Action and Reflection-_on_-Action

Reflection as a method of learning falls into two categories, according to Daniel Sullivan and Christopher Wiessner (2010). These categories are "reflection-_in_-action" and "reflection-_on_-action" (Sullivan & Wiessner, 2010, p. 42).

Reflection-in-action refers to thinking about what is happening in the moment it is happening, and _reflection-on-action_ is reflecting on the action after it has taken place. Experiential learning is how most of us learn. We experience, and we learn from the experience (I reflect, for instance, on my first marriage, since I never want to repeat that catastrophe). However, Sullivan and Wiessner believe that _learning without reflection may not be learning at all_. Reflection has an important role in experiential learning.

From Attila the Hun to Mother Theresa

One of the most effective things you can do is climb into the penny loafers of the person you are engaged in a conflict with. Because chances are the person will not be doing the same thing, and will not be enlightened enough to see your perspective, or even want to. They will be firmly entrenched in their desired outcome, which might be as simple as you going away and leaving them alone in terms of their classroom pedagogy - - which, of course, you will not do!

Begin looking at the issue from their perspective. Doing this allows you to see some possible compromise avenues that can bring you closer. Remember the inch you will settle for is initially the first step down the road to teacher growth.

Process these questions in your mind:

- What do they want?
- What are they facing if they acquiesce to your desire?
- What pressure(s) are they under by their own doing, and what do they perceive you are doing to them?
- What is important to them?
- What is their experience, and do you think they are capable of bringing to fruition your desired outcome?
- What support should you offer?

Money on the table, *they are not* thinking about any of these questions. However, after you think through the questions above, you will be shifting your persona from Attila the Hun to Mother Theresa. You have now basically positioned yourself on their side of the table, and the result will be to your advantage.

No One Has Ever Been Turned Off by Someone Willing to Listen to Them

There are some people who simply prefer to be sheep, and that's OK, as long as it is their conscious decision and not them taking a step back from the process because they have not been invited into the canoe. Everyone is invited, and frankly, you need everyone to be there. So put out the welcome mat (repeatedly, if necessary).

It will be your responsibility to relay this understanding to every member of the staff, one at a time. I have found it to be extremely beneficial to explain to those teachers who sheepishly confess they have nothing to add to the goals and vision of the school just how much they potentially can contribute.

This is where your expertise as a *deep, purposeful, and intentional listener is significantly important*. Ask what they want to occur in their classroom, or what they would like to see their kids able to do - - and then sit back and *just listen*. No one has ever been turned off by having someone listen to them! You might be (and hopefully will be) very surprised at what some people have to offer *once they are asked!* Some people wallow in the mind-set that, "Oh, he/she doesn't want to hear from me." You cannot allow those people be isolated in their self-imposed quicksand.

Emotions and Conflict

Emotions are many times the precursors to conflict. Regrettably, emotion is the unstable part of human beings.

Joyce Hocker and William Wilmot (2014) wrote, "Constructive conflict resolution depends upon our ability to work with and transform, not close off or repress, normal human emotion" (p. 190). They also discussed how conflict is equivalent of a light switch when it comes to emotion. Emotions change when conflicting situations arise. As humans, we equate our emotions with facts, and that is the biggest error and cause of conflict. The following is a set of principles of emotions in conflict Hocker and Wilmot (2014) developed:

- Conflict depends upon sufficient emotional arousal.
- Emotional events trigger responses.
- Intensity of emotion varies through the conflict process.
- We experience emotion as good or bad, positive or negative, pleasant or unpleasant, and helpful or destructive.

We become emotional because something is at stake for us - - possibly our identity.
- Relationships are defined by the kind of emotion expressed (p. 193).

Frank De Witt, Lindred Greer, and Karen Jehn (2011) expounded on conflict, which they defined as, "The process emerging from perceived incompatibilities or differences among group members" (p. 360). They postulated that there are three types of conflict within any organization: relationship, task, and process.
- Relationship conflicts occur when disagreements emerge from personality, values, and belief differences that emerge within any process, such as establishing a mutually agreed-upon growth trajectory (TGT).
- Task conflict occurs with disagreements over the content and outcome of tasks. Here is where you and the teacher disagree on what was observed and/or what the teacher did or did not do.
- Process conflict is tied to task conflict, because it accompanies the logistics and responsibilities of accomplishing the growth as established in the TGT.

Overall, these three conflict types noted by DeWitt, Greer and Jehn are based on power imbalances. You will inevitably experience a tangled web of these types of conflicts as different teachers react differently to your attempt at constructive collaboration and a planned TGT.

Friction

Your values influence the decision-making process and its consequences by filtering information and defining the possible alternatives for resolving the dilemmas. You serve as a conduit, and if the conduit is not smooth, it causes friction, and friction (remember your science class) produces heat, and heat produces negative conflict - - the last thing you want in your school. While I waxed poetic about conflict not being bad within a school, since it can lead to a heightened awareness and the kind of dialogue that produces the best results, *friction is not conflict*. It is what is left over if your handling of conflict is not performed well.

Conflict in close relationships such as a school faculty environment are inevitable, so the chance of ending your school day having experienced some type of conflict is probably even-Stephen.

The reason conflict is constantly occurring is because people see situations differently and may not always agree on the desired outcomes. Conflict, according to research, is based on perception, opinion, or beliefs among people (Prieto-Remón, Cobo-Benita, Ortiz-Marcos, & Uruburu, 2015).

When an opinion is accepted without belief, conflict still exists, but is avoided by choice; however, it can fester. This avoidance is actually detrimental to the entire situation, because it essentially increases an isolation behavior and increases stress in the situation (Hackett, Renschler, & Kramer, 2014). Effective communication is essential in the avoidance, prevention, and resolution of conflict (Nwogbaga, Nwankwo, & Onwa, 2015). David Nwogbaga et al. further state that the role of communication cannot be underestimated (2015).

Joyce Hocker and William Wilmot (2013) discussed how patterns in our behavior and responses to conflict could be categorized into five conflict styles. The five conflict styles are avoiding, obliging, dominating, integrating, and compromising. The category in which your style belongs depends upon your degree of concern for others and concern for yourself, and your attitude toward TGTs. **Pop Quiz!** Which of the five would be best for integrating the TGT ethos within a school?

Detractors

There will, of course, be detractors of the TGT movement. Surprise! What you will not hear will be from those complaining to their union behind your back. The union will need to come up with a reason to be on your case, and after your dismissal of Privacy of Practice, you will next hear from them about "…too much standardization, where is our freedom to teach within our classroom the way we know best…" or something along those lines. All on behalf of teachers who do not want you in their classrooms because they are terrible at what they do, and are afraid you and everyone else will find out and support those kinds of statements!

You will be accused of trying to standardize teaching in the school, and taking away academic freedom of choice from educators - - which, oddly enough, is the very outcome tenure was originally attempting to discourage.

Here is what I always did. I found someone doing the right thing, at the right time, for all the right reasons to meet the needs of *my kids*, and I said to others, "I want you to do what they're doing, and I will help get you get there!" If anyone wants to call that *standardization* or *lack of academic freedom*, then by all means be my guest!

Frankly, I adore the concept of standardization. (Yes, I am a standardizer!) Find me a *great* teacher, and then get everyone else to do what he or she is doing. Where do I sign up!?! I would respond with what might appear to be hairsplitting, but standardization is not quite I am really looking for, which is instead *a commonality of quality practices*.

Someone's teaching gets better with time, patience, adjustment, practice, adjustment, practice, adjustment, and more practice. With a solid observational process in place, you can assess and suggest adjustments regarding the teacher's lessons, delivery, classroom management, assessment, differentiation, data-driven instruction, preparation, and more. You can offer the struggling teacher time to observe a stronger teacher and practice with that teacher.

Next you need to be patient. The last thing you want to have is the new or struggling teacher becoming frustrated.

However - - here we go again - - for a non-tenured teacher, your patience needs to be *no longer* than two years. You have two years to decide whether or not to bring the teacher back for their tenure year (year three). If a teacher cannot prove to you within two years that they are within the realm and/or at least potentially within arm's reach of *greatness*, I would strongly suggest not bringing them back for that third year.

In my opinion you are looking for a natural-born teacher, not a manufactured one. It is a buyer's market. There are plenty of people looking for teaching positions. Perform your due diligence, and hunt for and find potentially *great* educators!

By the way, I have consistently had positive results from people who put their career on hold while they raise their own children, and once the children are school age are looking to come back into the profession!

Oh, Charlotte

We have all been exposed to and intimately involved with teachers who have been observed by administrators and then told what they did wrong and how they should improve. Most of the state education departments across our country have mandated that administrators follow a strict hierarchical observation system based on the work of people like Charlotte Danielson.

I am sure Charlotte is a nice person, means well, and has been well compensated for her work that in most places has taken on an almost biblical magnitude. Rather than having colleagues work together to improve instruction that will inevitably lead to better student performance, the hierarchical observation system has resulted in an intensification of an environment of inspection, control, and reporting on highly specific parameters. While these processes have allowed for a common gauge of expectations between teacher and administrator, with the help of a standardized rubric that serves as the basis of the observation process, it really is the same process we have always used, but with tighter, more stringent adherence to guidelines.

Unfortunately, *the process is more to rate rather than to propel growth.* And equally as unfortunate, that is how many educators (teachers and administrators) want it!

I Am Not Anti-Union, I Am Just Anti- Some of the Things They Do

Working with a teachers' union can be very frustrating, and can be a regular source of conflict. One of the tenets of the Ten Commandments of Teaching, as delivered from Mount Sinai by all teacher unions, is that their teachers are all created equal.

As I have previously written, according to many presidents of teachers' unions, there are no differences among teachers in terms of quality of their pedagogy! There are no teachers better than others! One teacher cannot be compared to another in terms of ability, proficiency, or skill! Any attempts to classify teachers in a hierarchical fashion is blasphemy, and building-level administrators who attempt to do so will be forever banished in the minds of the union into a sort of anti-union purgatory, and let me hear an *Amen, Brother!* as you place your hand upon the teacher's contract!

The issue for you will be that once you have witnessed *great* teaching, how can that effectiveness be optimized school wide?

I have been extremely careful to explain that all this effort to create TGTs cannot be performed by you and you alone, even with your cohort of fellow building administrators firmly on board the growth train. It would be extremely taxing, time-consuming, and pretty much darn near impossible - - if you are the only ones stoking the fire of growth! This is why building an ethos of self-reflection, collaboration, and self-growth is so critically important, and why you will tolerate, and even at times support conflicts, because of the potential end result that the conflicted dialogue brings to fruition.

Many times what brings the teachers' union into the mix (conflict) is when a teacher says, "Look at what he/she is trying to do to me! I am already a *great* teacher." This teacher doesn't want to deeply internalize and take charge of their growth beyond what currently exists, because they feel they do not require it.

Just as we inspire students to take charge of their own education, we must instill the commitment that teachers will ultimately be in charge of their own TGT - - with you as their support system! Sans that eventuality, the growth train may leave the station, but it isn't getting very far down the track.

Russ Marion (2005) writes, "Effective leaders are able to correctly diagnose worker readiness, and to adapt their leadership styles (task behavior and relationship behavior) accordingly" (p. 141). Situational leadership theory affords the flexibility to acknowledge differences, whether strengths or weaknesses, and subsequently build on the strengths and/or ameliorate weaknesses.

What You Need to Establish in Your Mind to Avoid Conflict

As a teacher of teachers, how comfortable will you be with that role, and how will you develop a comfort zone that allows you to lead in that capacity?

It will be essential to capitalize on conflicts as open and candid discussions taking place about teacher growth and the ability of the teacher to see him or herself as a learner in this endeavor. This role reversal is many times not an easy one for a teacher to fully accept, and can be the causative factor in the conflict.

What you need to establish in your mind to avoid conflict.

What makes a good lesson, and what distinguishes it from a *great* lesson? Understanding this subtlety and being able to express it so a teacher fully "gets it" are critically important on a number of levels.

First, you must be able to express to that effective teacher what he or she needs to do to become a *great* teacher. Broad-brush strokes will not work. Specificity will be important.

Second, once you understand what effective and *great* teaching look like, it will be easy - - and easy it will be - - to recognize a poor lesson and an ineffective teacher.

What you need to establish in your mind to avoid conflict.

Which is it: insufficient teacher knowledge, or her or his ineffective use of pedagogy? Don't get caught up in the minutiae. He or she is ineffective if they cannot see why their teaching is not working, and how building a growth trajectory will correct the issue(s). Salisbury steak and hamburger are the same thing - - chopped meat!

What you need to establish in your mind to avoid conflict.

What is your approach after observing a poor lesson?

Part of the process is making it just that: a process. Not simply a reaction to one observation, but rather by linking the acts and student progress to the observation**s**, and to see their upwardly spiraling growth, or lack thereof.

Think of your feeding-back, feeding-forward, and feeding-up as central to a teacher's growth process, not peripheral. The event or events within the context of an observed lesson should not be considered outliers, nor should they be view as an isolated event, but rather viewed and evaluated within the context of their TGT.

With that process in mind, what isn't working, and what are the essential elements that might be missing or poorly utilized? My suggestion is to use the time you have spent in the company of *great* teachers, and contrast how and what they do compared to someone who is not achieving the same student-based results.

You need to be intuitive, insomuch as your determination that it is not working for *my kids* with that teacher, and prescribe alternative efforts based upon what you have seen in other venues (classrooms). Your vantage point and your eyewitness experiences are what you wish every teacher had the opportunity to see and share. However, absent that possibility, your job is to serve as the conduit by which best practices are shared and repeated in other classrooms. You are a catalyst for change.

What you need to establish in your mind to avoid conflict.

What are the characteristics of the learning task that students find meaningful and authentic?

What you need to establish in your mind to avoid conflict.

What does it mean to teach for meaning?

What you need to establish in your mind to avoid conflict.

How can you leverage feeding-back, feeding-forward, and feeding-up for teacher growth?

Providing isolated feedback doesn't equate to feeding a continuum of teacher growth strategies as part of a series of conversations, ideas, strategies and concepts that you and the teacher are working on for growth. This is where copious note-taking and a specifically written-out TGT are critically important. Your feedback must be *targeted to the current need.*

What you need to establish in your mind to avoid conflict.

Feedback should not be editorial in nature, but rather supportive.

It is not the amount of feedback (and too much can be oppressive), but rather the quality of the *specific* feedback, which is then seen by the teacher as part of your support of their growth. Feedback that serves to teach - - not judge - - defines, illuminates, and guides teacher growth. You are not being critical. You are being informative!

What you need to establish in your mind to avoid conflict.

As you approach the observation process, both you and the teacher must come to realize that you are not grading what you see, because grading implies you are taking points away based upon a listing of what was wrong, and that is not helpful.

What you need to establish in your mind to avoid conflict.

What can you say/do that is going to make a difference?

What you need to establish in your mind to avoid conflict.

You are not teaching through feedback if the teacher is not listening. How do you create a communication roadway, a two-way street that will allow teachers to listen and also realize you are listening to them? What you need is a two-way roadway of shared understanding.

What you need to establish in your mind to avoid conflict.

What will you be looking for that signals differentiation is taking place?

One of the fundamental areas to observe is the degree of differentiated instruction in the classroom. When this type of instructional practice is used, the curriculum can be better implemented for academic growth and personalized student success. Since teachers are implementing the curriculum in their classrooms, your involvement in looking for and commenting on a differentiated approach will be critical, especially since this is probably one of the main deficits you will regularly encounter.

You will need a toolbox of practices to recommend to teachers, and encouraging differentiation for those who are not doing it to the degree necessary is one of the more important tools.

My initial question would never be *"...why aren't you..."* but rather along the lines of *"...how are you addressing the individual needs of each student in the class?"* Then I would listen! I would never assume it wasn't occurring just because I didn't see it at that point in time, but rather that at that particular point in time I didn't see it.

Remember, differentiation can take place in many different forms. You can have groupings based on ability that may be in the form of leveled reading groups. You may have groups based on interest, such as students researching different animals of choice. You can also differentiate by project, when a topic is taught and a project is assigned, but the final project is different for each student.

A differentiation by-product may also be that one student may take a written assessment, but another student writes a poem as an assessment (how anti-state assessment is that?!?). Others may present orally to the class, while another can conference with the teacher.

One final way to differentiate is via cooperative groups. Students are assigned to a group, and a peer leader is assigned as an amanuensis or reader to help facilitate the work being done. The leader is the peer tutor.

As an observer, I look for **evidence** of some sort of differentiation in any of these forms. I ask for the data (reasons and outcomes) to support the teacher's differentiation decisions. The process of discussing differentiation alone can lead to an awareness of each student's academic need on the part of the teacher.

If a teacher is not differentiating, I look at the lesson I observed with the teacher; see how she/he could have differentiated the lesson, and which method would be the most appropriate for *that* lesson and *those* students. I also arrange for the teacher to visit classrooms where I know differentiation is taking place, so the teacher can see it happening in real time.

One last key differentiation point; please don't expect to see it, or instruct the teacher to do it all the time. If you do, you will appear unrealistic, unsympathetic, and highly unreasonable. I would much prefer to have it done during the most important times and areas of the curriculum, rather than a cursory attempt on a more regular basis.

What you need to establish in your mind to avoid conflict.

You should not assume that teachers will be responsible for their own growth if you do not state that you expect it, or if they don't realize you will be a resource for them. Therefore, what can you do as part of a teacher growth trajectory to stimulate a purposeful, reflective practice and subsequent pedagogical growth?

What you need to establish in your mind to avoid conflict.

What questions should you be asking?

One way to foster teachers who are not engaging all their students is to discuss the strategies they are using to reach the outlier student in every classroom. I am not only talking about the students who are not doing well, but also those who are high performers but also simply getting by without extending themselves.

This opens a conversation with the teacher about what strategies they are employing, and if there are none, then provide a forum for discussion and/or suggestions. Being direct and simply going at the non-differentiated instructors might cause defensiveness and damage the give-and-take you hope to maintain with the teacher. Sometimes going in the back door brings the teacher around more quickly when they see you are concerned about every child in their classroom and the discussion is, at this point in time, more general because it is simply a discussion.

What you need to establish in your mind to avoid conflict.
Your response to a teacher who charges you with trying to standardize what is taking place in classroom.

What you need to establish in your mind to avoid conflict.
How to infuse positive attitudes and encourage growth.

What you need to establish in your mind to avoid conflict.
How to cement in the mind of every faculty member that, "A leader is a dealer in hope" (Napoleon Bonaparte).

Dealing in hope means you encourage instead of cut down, compliment instead of criticize, and provide constructive feedback instead of offering only negative statements. By fostering hope in your colleagues, you help support the overall educational environment for everyone involved. This *hope* is necessary for teachers, students, and parents, and directly impacts what is learned and how.

What you need to establish in your mind to avoid conflict.
Helping the teacher see the importance of the degree of academic relevancy for all students in the class.

What you need to establish in your mind to avoid conflict.
The importance and significance of the TGT process.

A Closing Thought About Conflict

Argument, disagreement, quarrel, discord, controversy, opposition, and dispute are descriptive words used to explain the exchange between people who are engaged in conflict. Conflict can be expressed through active engagement or passive avoidance (what I call Ostrich Administration, i.e. sticking your head in the sand and hoping that the conflict goes away by itself). When conflict is prolonged and unresolved it can impede academic success, diminish professional growth, and damage relationships (Bradley, Anderson, Baur, & Klotz, 2015).

The experience of conflict has the potential to produce negative *but also* positive outcomes because of the dialogue(s) it can produce. Positive outcomes offer the opportunity to create meaningful changes when the conflict is recognized, and you take the initiative to: a) identify the conflict, and b) take progressive, proactive, and well-orchestrated steps to ameliorate the conflict by creating an environment of deep, purposeful listening with intent to find a solution (*not win*, but find a working solution, reaching consensus at least, if not outright agreement).

Negative outcomes can include the disintegration of relationships, reduced productivity, and increased stress (Bradley, Anderson, Baur, & Klotz, 2015).

Also, please do not be Pollyanna about this. The disruptive faculty member wants to win! However, you are taking the higher road, thereby establishing *your* professional maturity!

The conflicts will not go away on their own - - and the TGT process can and often does bring conflict to the surface - - and left unfettered it can become disastrous. This is not the time you want to practice Ostrich Administration.

A Little Chapter Closure

With a well-delineated TGT and a standardized common language fostering growth, the expectation is huge. However, results will be significant when compared to the older observation processes that used whatever parameters and criteria the administrator wanted, often not known to the teacher until after the observation was completed.

You need to influence how teachers perceive you, and how you perceive and place them in the observation process, adding and making it clear that *this is a growth process, not a rating process!* You don't need to be the leader of a supervisory (yuck!) process as much as you need to be the leader of a collaborative process for teacher growth through a TGT.

This entire process will cause some conflict, so *be prepared by giving a great deal of thought to how you will handle it.*

If you view your responsibility to observe teachers, and note the support, practices, and resources needed to sustain self-reflected and collegially-developed professional growth, you have then broken the process down to its bare bones. However, the idea should be one that the process is collegial in nature and not unidirectional (emanating from only one source). You dissuade conflict with this mind-set and practice.

Chapter 7
Building Trust

At the end of the day, people follow those who know where
they're going. ~ Jack Trout

Historically, if school leaders fail to build a culture of trust, teachers refuse to participate in activities to promote change (Bridgeland, Bruse, & Hariharan, 2013).

In short, teacher expectation of positive outcomes must exist before they engage in any process that requires trust (Tschannen-Moran & Hoy, 2000). Expectations decrease proportionally based on teacher perception of amount of trust, which they equate to distance between themselves and a leader (Thomsen, Karsten, & Oort, 2016).

In some ways trust is like a living organism, because it also has a life cycle (Kutsyuruba & Walker, 2015). You must understand and learn how to build and sustain trust through the conveyance of confidence. You can do this by actively engaging in purposeful listening and honest communication that expresses genuine respect for each faculty member's professionalism, contribution, and expertise (Weiner, 2009).

First Blush

At first blush it might appear that it would be easy to observe a teacher and render an opinion based upon **evidence** regarding the effectiveness of their efforts.

After all, you are the boss, and what you say matters, and obviously you're always correct (believing this means you have never been married). It is a common misconception that the person with the most authority has an easy time simply because it appears that they get to tell people what to do, when to do it, and how to do it. Many times teachers comment that those in leadership positions don't remember what it is like being a teacher, and that a leader's job isn't nearly as difficult as teaching.

New principals are often disillusioned once they step into the role and realize holding the title doesn't immediately give one the authority or respect necessary to get the job done. On the contrary, one quickly learns that leading a group of people is extremely challenging, and providing critical information to assist in the growth of teachers is oftentimes more of a method to assuage rather than a demand for conformity based on your title. None of these techniques - - assuage, demand, or conform - - are applicable to a TGT and the successful growth spiral you are seeking. In fact, they are the antithesis of what you are seeking!

It is a Matter of Trust

It will be your job to be both a guide and an inspiration. According to Anthony Bryk and Barbara Schneider (2003), trust "...makes it more likely that initiatives will diffuse broadly across the school, because trust reduces the sense of risk associated with change. When school professionals trust one another, they feel safe to experiment with new practices" (p.104).

In Practicing the Art of Leadership: A Problem-Based Approach to Implementing the Professional Standards for Education Leaders (2017), Reginald Green wrote, "To obtain commitment, trust must exist between leaders and followers, and that trust has to be developed in a reciprocal manner" (p.122).

There are many ways in which you can earn the trust of the staff. They all stem from one source: *maintaining your professional integrity*. Integrity means that your actions are in direct alignment with your words. Your words and deeds are directly, unambiguously, and steadfastly focused on educating children, and thus the best interests of the students are the foundation of *every* initiative communicated to your colleagues. In this way, *your integrity is cemented in your role and purpose!*

Devin Vodicka (2006) cites four key elements needed in the facilitation of trust:

1) Consistency

Leaders who are consistent are trustworthy, because they create in others a sense of safety since expectations remain the same for everyone within a given context. In our situation, that context is what is best for students. The consistency is important as you work with colleagues, because people will judge you on how you interacted with them as compared to how you interacted with others.

2) <u>Compassion</u>

A compassionate leader respects the professionalism (my concept of the professional maturity I expect from everyone) of every staff member who is rowing in the canoe with you. It will be your job to enumerate what professionalism stands for in the building, and the first step in that process is modeling your professionalism every single day! Compassionate leaders create a feeling of safety, because teachers believe it is not your intention to harm them. They also know through your words and subsequent deeds that students come first, always!

3) <u>Communication</u>

When you communicate effectively with staff, you are taking into account their professional opinions and showing that they are valued as professionals. People feel most comfortable communicating with a leader who is seen as compassionate and consistent, because they feel a sense of respect from you, and they believe their opinions will be valued and not chastised - - as long as they are student-centric!

4) <u>Competency</u>

A component that, if not present, will be like kissing your sister (Again! I think I need a different metaphor or you will think I require some serious therapy) is competence. This is most important because it is your role to create an environment conducive to productivity in both teaching and learning. If you are not seen as pedagogically competent, no one will listen to you, and the other three keys just make you a nice person - - great to have a beer with, or sit down with Dr. Merlot on a Friday after school - - but you won't be seen as an academic leader; you will not be viewed as competent.

"Highly successful principals have the exceptional ability to build relationships. To build trust they have interpersonal skills that allows [sic] them to communicate openly with stakeholders and give them the opportunity to help and to have a voice in the decision-making" (Gray and Streshly, 2008, p.3). Susan Gray and William Streshly go on to write, "Leaders build relationships with diverse people and groups especially people who think differently. Focusing on relationships is not a gimmick but a means of laying the foundation for sustaining improvements over the long run" (2008, p.15).

This process provides the needed ownership on the part of the teacher, with you serving as a sounding board, a wall to bounce things off of, a guide and sage, as well as someone holding onto the seat and running alongside as they are learning to ride their bike.

This will be very difficult to establish, because no matter how much you appear as a warm and fuzzy father or mother figure who's only there to help, you are still the boss, and viewed as someone who will ultimately be making a judgment about their ability within the classroom. All I can offer you is the suggestion that this is going to take time, it is going to be done with baby-sized steps, and will at times make your neophyte teachers uncomfortable - - until *what is developed?* Oh yes, TRUST!

As an effective leader, you create collaborative decision-making built on a two-way trust between you and ***individual*** staff members. Wow, a word written with **bold**, and underline, and *italics!* This must be really important! The key word here is ***individual***, obviously!

What may not be so obvious is that you need to approach your trust development process *one teacher at a time.* You will never win over an entire faculty by standing up at a faculty meeting and saying, *"Trust me!"* This certainly will not work if you are the new principal and this is your first faculty meeting, because no one knows you - - yet! You will be developing relationships - - *cautious ones* - - one faculty member at a time. You will be sharing decision-making on pedagogy one teacher at a time. You need to apply a *calculated consistency* in every endeavor in terms of your approach and expectations.

However, how a teacher arrives at that destination is more in their hands than yours. Respect their knowledge, respect their skill sets, respect their philosophy, and respect their pedagogical approach until they prove to you it is not working and that they do not deserve your respect.

Mistrust is an Aliment That Can Be Cured

Fred Hoyle, Fenwick English, & Betty Steffy (2005) contend that in order for teacher observations to work, teachers have to view them as a positive process for achieving the innate rewards of professional growth. They argue that, "True professionals need open, threat-free workplaces that nurture self-expression and respect" (p.106).

This kind of environment does not occur naturally or organically; you, as a gardener (an administrator), must cultivate it.

Mistrust is an ailment that can be cured. *It is not so much a single-dose remedy as it is a long-term treatment plan.* As with any effective treatment plan, the mind-set of the patient or, in this case, the teachers within the school, needs to be emotionally tied to and involved in the plan. Teacher growth is not a map handed to a teacher, but rather a guide showing various roads, which can be traveled to reach a destination, with you by the teacher's side, serving as a guide. As per Robert Frost, it can still be the road less traveled - - as long it gets everyone to where they need to be - - and it can make all the difference.

Empowerment

Empowerment allows a learner to achieve ownership of learning. When a learner is empowered, the potential is endless (Arias, 1996).

Given this premise, it is up to you to empower teachers (the learners in this case) to grow through your feeding-back, feeding-forward, and feeding-up, and the delineation and subsequent application of that feedback via a TGT. You are providing advice (feeding-back, the *What*), hoping to reach a level of understanding and practice to move forward (feeding-forward, the *How*), and providing the reason(s) for future application (feeding-up, the *Why*).

The truly effective, long-lasting, and most positively powerful motivation is for you to reach within those who follow and flip the switch that turns on empowerment. Coercion is short-term motivation achieved through the use of power and fear. Not the best road to head down. Long-lasting trust is built with time, effort, communication, and determination on the part of the leader, all of which your build through empowerment.

The four building blocks of trust are: time, effort, enthusiasm (passion), and effective communication.

- Time is for working with those who would follow, to share visions and goals while explaining and showing the value of the TGT. Take the time to explain, and to deeply, purposefully, and intentionally listen to colleagues.
- Effort is the leader believing in what they are doing, as well as modeling and sharing this vision of what the results will look like. A building block of effort is commitment.

Enthusiastic communication is taking every opportunity to share, with passion and conviction, the value of teacher growth - - what it means, and how will it make us better for the good of our kids.

Communication is also deep, purposeful, and intentional listening to those following this TGT path. They must have input that may/will alter what the growth trajectory looks like via their empowerment, but not where it will end up, for that is your call, and your call alone - - and it is set in stone.

If you have no passion, then you will never be able to ignite passion in others. You will need to work hard and passionately about teacher growth in order to hold the image of the empowered TGT and its positive fruition in front of those who you are asking to follow.

I think several interpersonal constructs are necessary to encourage teachers to be purposefully reflective and autonomous about conceiving their growth trajectory.

First of all, the culture of the school needs to be supportive of these efforts by providing opportunity for purposeful reflection, and you must model and place significant value on self-reflection.

Pom-Poms are Optional

Teaching teachers is similar in many ways to coaching. A coach's job is to show an athlete how to do something, and then to get them to do it.

For instance, tennis players don't practice by listening to speeches about groundstrokes; they improve by hitting thousands of practice shots. Pilots don't watch Prezi presentations about flying; they spend hours in simulators and then flying with a more experienced pilot by their side.

Teaching is no different. Unless participants can truly practice peda-gogical techniques, their skills will not improve. When you think about it, nearly all a coach's teaching is done through feedback. Maybe five percent of a coach's time is spend telling a player how to do something, while the remaining ninety-five percent of the time is spent watching the person perform, and then providing feedback.

As previously noted, realize that communication is what is *heard,* not what is said. So getting the teacher to accept your feedback requires that it be delivered within a context that makes the teacher receptive to it.

This is especially important when the feedback concerns issues with the teacher's performance. Accepting sometimes difficult feedback re-quires a certain type of relationship with the person providing the feed-back. We tend not to accept feedback from someone we do not *respect* or *trust.* This is why much of your job will be spent *cultivating a relationship* with teachers, which will help make the teacher receptive to the feedback, and motivates them to grow professionally.

However, one of the biggest mistakes a principal can make is to provide nothing but *cheerleading* in their feedback. Teachers need an *honest* ap-praisal of their work, backed up with informative data and specific references, or he or she will soon decide the cheerleading is basically meaningless.

You will have some teachers who will prefer to live in the Land of Oz and accept your cheerleading as the gospel, and will consequently merely maintain the status quo.

The Path

What I am really talking about here is showing teachers *a path* toward sustained growth.

Learned helplessness is the tendency to give up when one believes that nothing they do can alter their circumstances. A teacher can fall into this trap, and a principal who simply points out problems can help exacerbate this belief.

The way out is for a principal to include not just feedback based on a teacher's pedagogical issue(s) and the gathered **evidence**, but also on how to ameliorate them by providing feedback that propels the teacher forward. Visualizing a path can have a direct effect on a teacher's emotional state, and thus their willingness to accept a TGT.

We all covet praise, and I don't want to say that praise never has a place in teacher growth plans. That would be ludicrous. But principals often think praise alone is a path to motivation, and *this isn't true*.

Constant praise sans constructive suggestions with **evidence** can appear empty, shallow, or even an attempt to placate a teacher.

It can demonstrate a lack of critical examination of a teacher's work, which is not only a poor reflection on you, but points to you shirking your responsibilities. It also plays down the teacher's efforts to improve and can cause a teacher to feel you don't care. And that you don't hold him or her and their applied effort toward pedagogical *greatness*, as well as the improved performance of the students, in high regard. Eventually empty cheerleading recedes into the background and becomes white noise.

Make sure to embed any praise within examples of what a teacher is doing well, and how they are making progress toward their goals. This way, the teacher knows you are observing their work, and can get a sense of what they are doing well. In other words, be specific, *very specific*, about what they are doing well, and what you are praising them about. This will go much further than empty cheerleading, and will enhance the motivation for the teacher to continue with their TGT.

People are motivated when they recognize they have been empowered to be in charge of their own growth trajectory. They will feel valued and respected, and *it will build trust*. It is your role to provide the resources and parameters for pedagogical development.

Again, when people feel their input has value, they are more likely to take on more responsibility. You must also provide encouragement and time for this growth model. You need to be a resource, communicator, role model, observer, motivator, ombudsperson, collaborator, and facilitator. Additionally, you personally providing daily valet parking would be nice, but probably will not crack into the top 10.

Mr. Watson

While this is not a game, it is in many ways game-like. You have ascertained via observations and pivotal **evidence** that a teacher needs to grow in a certain pedagogical area (or areas). Based upon a high level of trust you have earned, teachers view your input as worthy of consideration, and views the gathered **evidence** as compelling, based upon that established trust. And at that point, like Sherlock Holmes would say, *the game is now afoot!*

The game is over (*I think it's Mr. Plum in the library with the candelabra*) if the teacher reflects on your previous dialogues and has come up with a self-developed growth trajectory plan. All you need to do after that is support his or her effort with needed resources, be they time or something tangible, so they can apply their growth trajectory to ameliorate any issue(s). *Good gravy, Marie, I love being a principal!*

Anything less than consistent application of their TGT requires your intervention, through a continuum of dialogues and actions, to build trust which will then assist in moving the teacher along and onto the desired growth trajectory. It is hoped that after a year or so of this kind of assistance, the teacher will be able to reflect and take command of their own TGT, with you serving as a resource person. That process is spelled E – M – P – O – W – E – R – M – E – N – T!

Sometimes there is resistance to change (err, most times). Most often this resistance to change isn't not wanting to grow, but a fear of the unknown and giving up the warm, fuzzy blanket of a known process. And, as odd and ever-so-ridiculous as this sounds, the consistent old school process of you coming into the classroom - - infrequently - - doing your perfunctory observation, writing it up, and delivering it to the teacher once or twice a year, and that's it (regardless of the conclusions) is comfortable because that's how it's always been done.

Think Intravenous Drip Bag Approach

Probably one of your first less-than-positive encounters will be with that teacher who will give you that inevitable line, "I've always done it this way, and it has worked well, and that is why I don't see a need for a growth trajectory, whatever that means, for me."

The immediate issue then becomes, what interpersonal skills do you have that will be essential for developing a positive and sustainable relationship with this teacher? How do you go about building a bridge toward trust? What is and where is the **evidence** that you will use to provide the person with an alternate opinion (prove them wrong, in so many words), and in what manner will you meter out everything you want to tell this teacher.

We are not talking avalanche here, for you will surely lose them if you hit them with too much at one time! Think intravenous drip bag in terms of how fast (and steadily) you will need to move ...drip ...drip ...drip ...drip, with that teacher and, quite probably, the majority of the teachers within the school.

Trust Essentials as Related to a TGT

There are three essential questions that will enable you to initiate the teachers into the TGT concept. You first ask them to purposefully reflect on these questions:
- What do you want your students to learn?
- How will you know the students are learning?
- What will you do if you discover that students are not learning?

These are, in fact, trust-inducing questions. They don't diminish trust, but rather cut to the core of a teacher's purpose in a school. The next step employs the same set of questions, but now you have asked him or her for the **evidence** to substantiate their answers.

The first time these questions should be presented is at a faculty meeting where discussions about the overall establishment of individualized teacher growth trajectories can be discussed. These questions are harmless and nonthreatening, but do cut to the essence of teaching. You are asking them to think about their teaching and where they see themselves and/or would like to see themselves growing from a pedagogical standpoint. These are also foundational questions at the outset of a pre-observation conference.

When and Where?

It is only fair to present this in the spring of the year prior to when you begin instilling the concept and practice of Teacher Growth Trajectories in the teachers.

You have never mentioned this as a by-product of the observation process. You are not being disingenuous by not linking the two, but why do it? You are not thinking observation for numerical ratings or ranking purposes, you are thinking *I am in your class watching you teach, and let's then talk about your pedagogy and its direct impact on all your students.*

The word you need to never forget is the word *all*. Why?

The reason the word is important is because there will be teachers who disregard students they consider outliers, students the teacher considers outside the norm. For example, special needs students, students with language differences, gifted students. Some teachers even consider all students new to the school as the responsibility of others. For example, the Resource Room teacher, the ENL teacher, the AIS teacher, and others like them are staff members to whom some teachers will mentally shift academic responsibilities to lessen their responsibility. You cannot let that happen! The entire faculty needs to buy in, and not be selectively culled out.

I do not, in my mind and heart, see TGTs as an attempt to be a snake oil salesperson to the faculty. If you believe in this concept of teacher growth trajectories in your heart and mind, and it is evident through your conversations and deeds, then they too will *eventually* buy into it. The key word here is *eventually!*

It cannot become part of the ethos and lexicon of the staff if you don't use this as your mantra. It is directly related to the observation process - - of course it is! You will obviously be in the room observing what is going on, but there is no need to verbally associate one with the other. Though it is implied and obvious, you will not acknowledge the hippo in the room, because it is superfluous and potentially explosive. And, as previously mentioned, you are taking the higher road, potentially one less traveled upon (thank you, Mr. Frost), and that *will* make all the difference!

What you will need to discern is what type of engagement and encouragement will move the teacher off Square One, and *that will be different for each teacher!* Which is why that type of engagement and encouragement is not a faculty meeting discussion, but rather an individualized one.

A Trusted Litmus Test

And are you willing to extend trust to others? As a leader, you need to emanate trustworthiness or others will not follow you. Trusting yourself first and then extending trust to others will give you *the right* to have others trust you. Remember, you cannot talk your way out of a situation that your behavior got you into. Building trust is crucial to your long-term influence as a leader.

The staff has to trust that you are not there to *catch them messing up*. They need to understand you are on the side of students, and therefore, by extension, on their side. Collaboratively, you have the same macro goal in mind. As principals, we are, in a sense, partners in the educational process, and working toward the betterment of our students. At the same time, you are situated higher on the district organizational chart, and sometimes that leads to paranoia or a naturally adversarial relationship. So it is important for you to establish (and hopefully maintain) an atmosphere that is affable and based on mutual trust and respect.

As previously noted, the predominant way you can accomplish this is by being visible. The best principals do not take up residency in their office, but rather in the halls, the classrooms, the cafeteria, the music rooms, gymnasium (word of caution: stay out of the Faculty Room), and, of course, classrooms. *A huge part of helping teachers feel comfortable is familiarity.* If you frequently pop into the room for four minutes, it will just seem like a normal day, a normal occurrence. Absent this normalcy, an inauthentic ethos permeates and can led to mistrust.

A Little Chapter Closure

Always demonstrate respect, even if the person doesn't deserve it! It is illogical to expect respect prior to extending it to others. Personally, I think teaching well is one of the hardest jobs to do correctly, and I hold the position of teacher and those that do it well in highest regard. I demonstrate that honor to each teacher until someone shows me that they don't deserve to be in that company. I recognize that teachers are the experts, and I ask questions so I can become smarter about the profession. I do this until someone demonstrates that they aren't that smart and/or proficient.

Finally, I honor teachers who are long in the tooth. I cherish their extended experience and the knowledge that comes with it.

Remember, as the new kid on the block, that these are the people who built the block! Honor their experience until proven otherwise. Take on a learner's manner and mentality, and trust will follow you home like a lost puppy.

I would like to share the Chinese poem I had on the wall in my office for the day when you can post it on *your* office wall.

> Go to the people.
> Learn from them.
> Love them.
> Start with what they know and
> build on what they have.
> But of the best leaders,
> when the task is accomplished and
> the work is done
> the people will remark,
> we have done it ourselves.
> ~ Lao Tsu

Chapter 8
How Do You Recognize Great Teaching When You See It?

> If you have respect for people as they are, you can be more
> effective in helping them to become better than they are.
> ~ John Gardner

In every successful school, developing *great* teaching is at the forefront of a leader's educational agenda, since it provides the best chance for student success.

This agenda requires you to understand "...what good teaching is, what it looks like in action, and how students should interact, respond, and shine" (Glickman, 2002, p.3). Within this, "...certainty can become arrogance and dogmatism, but uncertainty can become permissiveness and the acceptance of all teaching [as] having equal merit" (Glickman, 2002, p.3). This is a runaway train heading downhill that you do not want to board for any reason (whatsoever).

In order to steer clear of this pitfall, you must understand where each teacher stands professionally. To be successful in supporting teacher growth, you must first recognize what *great* teaching looks like and sounds like while you observe the classroom's occupants in action.

The art of teaching includes finding exciting ways to present the material. You must be cognizant that today's students are accustomed to having a new stimulus approximately every seven (7) seconds. Just look at today's movies, television shows, and especially commercials. While I do not advocate the every-seven-second stimuli teaching methodology, a knowledge and understanding of *how* today's children are being feed information commercially would be an important insight and consideration. Some topics are more exciting than others, and *great* teachers must be very creative in order to keep their students engaged. Chalk-and-talk is no longer cutting edge, nor is it very effective.

What must be clear to you initially, and eventually made crystal clear to the faculty, are the concrete performance indicators for identifying *great* teaching. The development of *great* teaching needs to be at the forefront of your drive and passion, and those attributes must *not* be kept a secret!

I respectfully refer you back to the barriers to generating *great* teaching throughout the school:

1) The pedagogical isolation that a classroom teacher can experience as he or she works within their solitary classroom.
2) The self-disillusionment that their isolation can cause when they're never able to watch other teachers teaching.
3) The damage caused by repetitive presentations of the same pedagogy, year after year, regardless of the yearly change in target population in their classroom.
4) The lack of purposeful self-reflection absent focused conversations about what he or she is doing and the subsequent results for students.

The inability, based upon prehistoric mores, to identify *great* teaching and making it available - - in-house - - for others to see.

As previously noted, if you are not passionate about something, then others will not be passionate. If you accept nothing but the best from yourself, then others will not have a laissez-faire attitude.

And when someone is not pulling their load verbally, or demonstrating less than a team spirit, it is your responsibility to stay on their case. They are accepting a salary (plus a pension, health and dental insurance, 403B, and more) to instruct students toward success. If you ascertain, based upon **evidence**, that their practices are not having the desired outcome, then your job is to assist in modifying those pedagogical practices.

I have been amazed at the fact that some teachers seem to *forget what they are being paid to do* or that there is a higher expectation of them beyond merely coming to school and lecturing! Many think showing up at school is sufficient to justify a salary! Many think they don't need a growth trajectory because they have been doing the job for so long that they are experts. However, never accept seniority as a signal of, or evidence of, *greatness*.

There really isn't a single definitive exemplar to help you recognize *great* teaching. You have to see this and that every time when you are observing a teacher. As I go through all the components of *great* teaching, I see that some happen continuously, others infrequently, and others randomly. This doesn't mean a lesson is poorly delivered unless it has *all* those parts. It simply means that certain concepts and/or practices were not needed, not required at that time, or would have been superfluous within the context of the lesson.

Therefore, it leads one to the obvious conclusion that a teacher <u>knowing what to put in and what to leave out is also a sign of *greatness*</u>.

However, I am not letting you off the hook, so don't think reading the following pages isn't important. The narrative is important for you to know, and for your teachers to grasp, both conceptually and practically. These are things *great* teachers have in their arsenal, and things you need to be aware of while you cultivate growing teachers successfully. And you want a bumper crop every year!

Chickens

A southern tobacco grower of over 30 years sees the handwriting on the wall and knows growing tobacco will never be the same again. His farm and his livelihood are slowly but steadily decreasing as more and more people stop smoking. He seeks the counsel of a trusted and intelligent friend, who suggests something else for him to raise - - chickens!

Eventually, after some soul-searching, the farmer buys 10,000 chicks. A week later he purchases 10,000 more chicks, and a week after that he purchases an additional 10,000! The following week, the friend who convinced him to switch from tobacco to chickens calls and asks the farmer how everything is going. "Terrible," said the farmer. "Things are not going well; everything is terrible!" His friend asks why, and the farmer replies, "I don't know. I can't figure it out! Either I am planting them too deep or too close together."

The chicken lesson is an obvious one in terms of my thought that people will need and subsequently function better with hands-on guidance. Notwithstanding the collaboration and empowerment that I hope I wrote eloquently about, none of that can come to positive fruition sans guidance. Guidance can be a resource or set of resources; guidance can be building a relationship among teachers who can pedagogically benefit from the relationship; and guidance can even be you pushing a little (without bursting the balloon between the two of you).

Label and Define *Great* Teaching

The closest I can come to putting a definition on *great* teaching is, "The teacher's ability to use various ways of teaching according to a variety of learning goals and student learning styles" (Glickstein, 2002 p. 203).

If *great* teaching is so difficult to define, how would a principal be able to tell what *great* teaching is? Thankfully, there are many noticeable attributes to look for when observing a teacher to determine their effectiveness. In the classroom, academic performance of students is only one slice of the pie - - albeit a huge one - - amid all the components needed to determine the effectiveness or ineffectiveness of a teacher.

Students should be actively engaged in the lesson and be able to personalize the material as it relates to them. The delivery of instruction should be appropriate to the cognitive level of the teacher's audience.

Teachers must establish expectations and routines for their students to cultivate a climate conducive to learning. These routines and expectations must be visible to you, and it is your responsibility to look for them and ask about them if you do not see them.

In essence, *for the duration of the instructional period, all students should have an equal opportunity to be successful*. In principle, and to bottom-line it: isn't that what *great* and engaging teaching is at the end of the day?

It is certainly the bottom line for me. What has the teacher done or not done to create those equal opportunities, and, if they haven't, what can *you do* to assist him or her? In order to promote this type of environment, a mutual respect must be established based upon your relationship with the teacher.

Having Skills and Applying Appropriate Techniques

Previously, I touched upon the concept of effective teaching versus *great* teaching. There is a difference between *great* teaching and effective teaching.

Great teaching requires a purpose *beyond* effective teaching. It is possible to have effective teaching without having *great* teaching.

Things like student engagement and improved academic performance can be helpful in measuring effective teaching. *Great* teaching can be quantified as students achieving mastery and an understanding of the relevance and application of what they are learning. It is also somewhat measured by the degree that the student takes responsibility for her or his own advanced learning beyond the teacher's initial input. Ideally, the convergence of both will yield not only the highest academic performance, but also more important, meaningful learning that can be applied to future situations, both in and out of the classroom.

Teaching is a practice that requires skills and actions, not merely knowledge of certain content areas. *Great* teaching includes the use of learning goals and objectives to keep discussions focused by maintaining student engagement, asking purposeful, objective-oriented Socratic questions, listening and responding to students, connecting student ideas and contributions to learning objectives, and tying up or summarizing the discussion and relating it back to the learning objectives (Ball & Forzani, 2011).

Teachers must motivate and engage students in active and deep learning. Teachers who are considered *great* make the purpose and process of learning relevant and explicit for students through modeling, demonstration of content, and active and engaging lessons (Wray, Medwell, Fox & Poulson, 2000). *Great* teachers build on prior knowledge, connecting learning to a student's real-life experiences, frequently checking for understanding, and ensuring that they are addressing the needs of all learners through the use of differentiated instruction (Sandholt, 2011).

Paint by Numbers or Born to Be?

According to Deborah Ball & Francesca Forzani (2011), "The practice of teaching effectively is learnable..." (p.42), and those who teach must have the opportunity to develop the necessary skills and knowledge. Administrators should then identify specific practices that are fundamental to supporting *great* teaching and student learning, as this is at the heart of building an effective system for professional development (Ball & Forzani, 2011).

I could not *disagree* more with Ball and Forzani!

I do not believe you can teach greatness.

In Chapter 5, I noted John Maxwell's point that a person's attitude is his or her most important asset. A person's attitude certainly cannot replace basic skill sets, and is not a replacement for a deep understanding of how children learn best.

I always lean toward teachers being born and not made. It is not the broad brushstroke of *can they* or *can't they* teach, it is the subtle and firm enhancement of existing intrinsic qualities and abilities, and not a Pygmalion metamorphosis. Under these conditions, a person's attitude is crucial, and goes a long way to substantiation of Maxwell's thesis. However, a positive attitude does not a *great* teacher make - - Ooops! Now I sound like Yoda.

Kissing Frogs

I believe it is possible to standardize pedagogical practices and teach people to do them in a logical, predictable and reasonable manner.

However, I do not want a paint-by-numbers teacher in the school. Again, I firmly believe teachers, *great* teachers, are born and not made. As an administrator, I have hundreds of potential educators to select from whenever a job opening is advertised. I am of the firm belief that my time and energy - - a huge amount of time and energy - - must be dedicated to this process. I will subsequently kiss as many frogs as necessary in order to find a prince or princess - - a natural, born-to-be educator.

Characteristics of *Greatness*

There are a number of key characteristics that should exist within a *great* teacher. *Great* teachers should be committed to:
1) Learning
2) Balancing content delivery with developing learning skills
3) Possessing strong instructional skills
4) Being fair and unbiased
5) Being able and willing to collaborate with other staff members, and, most important,
6) Being willing and able to purposefully reflect and adapt based upon student needs

Additionally, Linda Darling-Hammond (2009) found that *great* teachers possess such important qualities as:
- A strong general intelligence and verbal ability
- Strong content knowledge
- An ability to promote higher-order thinking skills
- An understanding of learners

Let's Get Physical

To attain success when collaborating teacher growth, you must first recognize what *great* teaching actually looks like, sounds like; what it feels, smells, and tastes like, and what the results *should be* as a result of the lesson taking place.

If you are thinking locally and microscopically, then your focus should be on what's happening today, this hour, this minute, and this second in the classroom you are observing. Do not try to embrace the huge and expansive overall picture of your school. Look at it one brick at a time.

It will be the parts and the events within the classroom every day and every hour and every minute that will allow for positive outcomes on a school wide basis. It is the *purposeful* compounding of *purposeful* events that creates a highly significant and *purposeful* whole. It is a long, long journey that is accomplished one small but significant step at a time. And as the Grateful Dead sang, *...just keep truckin' on!*

Build-A-*Great*-Teacher Workshop

Developing a basic framework to use and a set of guidelines to identify *great* teaching must be done in order for you to identify *great* teaching. How interesting would it be if, while you are designing your roadmap toward *great* teaching, that you *engage the expertise of the teachers for input!* Talk about collaboration and inclusive building of the underpinning of the school. Not only are you seeking input from highly qualified people, you are also subliminally getting every one of them to think about their own pedagogy as the criterion for excellence.

There are these Build-A-Bear Workshops (stores) where you can obviously build your own stuffed bear. Imagine if you will, a faculty meeting under this premise, except that instead of building a bear it was called Build-A-*Great*-Teacher Workshop!

No finger-pointing, just an open dialogue, with teachers brainstorming in small groups with felt-tip pens and large sheets of paper taped to the wall where each group can write down their thoughts about what constitutes *great* teaching. Subsequently, the groups get together and create one final chart that outlines (builds) the attributes of a *great* teacher.

What would you do with the list of attributes? Make copies and give one to each teacher? Laminate it and post one in the Faculty Room? Would you point to it and refer to it often during pre- and post-observation conferences?

Bar Raising

There has been a huge cloak pulled over parents' eyes today in terms of what is being considered *great* teaching. Parents have been led to believe that assessment results are the sole indicator of teaching ability. Simply put, students scoring high on standardized assessments have been taught well, and those who don't perform well on assessments indicate a lack of effective teaching.

There exists a national demand for testing, and that has created this disastrous slogan and mantra: please repeat after me, *"We need to raise the bar* to improve student achievement!"*

The concept of *raising the bar* is a cute little catchphrase that has caught the fancy of the media and the public. However, why are we raising the bar for students who cannot even reach the preexisting bar? What have we done to support those who could not reach the original bar? Now we have said to these kids, you couldn't reach expectations (the bar) in the first place so, in order to spur you on, we will now set the bar even higher from you!

And the compounding implication is that teachers who cannot get their kids to the newly heightened bar are seen as ineffective. This is what you get when educational initiatives are placed in the hands of lay people, corporations, and politicians!

It is also why the definition of *great* teaching has been confused with the ability to cover all the standards required by the state.

Ideally, the *great* principal realizes that <u>great teaching is the way knowledge is developed</u>, not merely covered. For this reason, *great* teaching across all curriculums seeks to absorb the attention of all students.

Which leads to this question: How does a teacher make the students feel individually connected to the lesson? How do they build relevancy into the lesson? This engagement is even further intensified by the enthusiasm and passion of the teacher. This type of engagement promotes individual student perspective and subsequent student ownership. If the student doesn't feel ownership, or at least potential ownership down the road, under the guidance and support of her or his teacher, then all hope is lost.

Great teaching enables students to build and apply critical thinking skills. Students will eventually leave the supportive confines of school and will need those critical thinking skills, as well as the ability to find accurate information, in order to be successful in life.

The foundational principle of any educator must be the development of each student's ability to think and reason. These skills support the formulation of viable responses. Hence, critical thinking must be evident in student interaction; whether in collaboration with other students, or while the teacher facilitates the lesson in progress.

Think of the wealth and/or surplus of information available on the Internet. Students need to think critically and reason through the process to determine accurate from inaccurate information when they don't have a teacher sitting beside them. It many times is more important to understand how an answer was derived rather than the correct answer at the time. The process - - how the student is thinking, and *what steps did the teacher take to elicit the critical thinking process* - - is what is most important.

Additionally, as you make observations (both formal and informal), it is crucial that you evaluate the cognitive demand of the questions and activities being presented - - the Socratic questioning strategies - - since they should be developed with the cognitive process in mind. Your ability to identify *great* teaching that includes personal passion, engagement, and tiered Socratic questioning and activities, is ultimately the fuel for effective learning, and is the major component in the development of a successful school.

All the above needs to be part of the teacher reflection process, the process where the preamble is almost as important as the correct conclusion. Regardless of whether the answer was correct or not, within this particular venue, and at this time and place, the teacher needs to be confident that the *correct process* was utilized, and the theory behind the concept was understood by the students.

Poor computation skills (for example) can be addressed later. It is not the answer that is important at this point; *it is how the student arrived at the answer, the reasoning and logistical path the student took, that is crucial.*

Sit back and think for a moment about the deliriously wonderful discussions you can have with teachers about this! Now this is a dialogue that can move the pedagogical needle via a Teacher Growth Trajectory! This is a professional discussion that marginalizes the *what did they get on the test* concept.

The concept of *great* teaching, therefore, transcends statistical outcomes alone. Putting a label on *great* teaching would be remiss if isolating one specific style or model as paramount. It would be as unfair to the students as it would be the teacher. One size does not fit all. *Great* teachers are the ones who are constantly engaged in ongoing dialogues of *purposeful* self-reflection concerning their pedagogy, and who continuously seek steps toward pedagogical growth.

Great Teaching Subsets

Teacher-to-Student, Student-to-Teacher, and Student-to-Student Interactions

A component of *great* teaching that I look for would be through the lens of observing teacher-to-student and student-to-teacher interactions. Teacher-to-student interactions come in two forms, verbal and non-verbal, with both being extremely important to the overall success of the learning process.

Verbal teacher-to-student interactions can be used to motivate, encourage, question, and even discipline students as needed to maintain academic focus within the classroom. These interactions are vitally important to the success of every student and their level of comfort in the classroom.

I look for teachers who present energy in front of the class and when they speak to students, they speak in a dynamic way that avoids a monotone voice (Bueller..., Bueller......, Bueller.........) and shows respect for students while still maintaining a strong classroom command and class leadership role. The verbal communication that is used can also be shared among students so the classroom isn't completely teacher-centric.

The nonverbal communication cues that I look for in a *great* teacher include:

- Eye contact with students
- Positive gestures to reinforce good behavior, such as head nods and open-hand movements
- An attentiveness that signals the teacher is interested in student responses
- A willingness to reteach as needed
- The distribution of Socratic questioning that allows for layered and in-depth responses
- Proper professional attire, because I believe it shows respect for the students, the institution, and the profession
- Posture that includes enthusiasm

Students take note of these subtle yet important clues whether they know it or not, and therefore they have an impact on students when they're in the classroom. Likewise, these interactions can create a welcoming classroom environment that allows all students to feel comfortable and positioned for learning.

As previously noted, professional maturity is important, because students want to respect their teacher. Verbal sarcasm and acerbity have no place in the classroom, and a teacher who models those behaviors will surely get them thrown back at him or her. These are not your fraternity brothers or sorority sisters, they are your students.

Any teacher who has put his or her students into small groups knows that orchestrating effective student-to-student interactions takes deliberate planning and preparation. You might be familiar with some common strategies like 'turn-and-talk' or 'pair-and-share,' which can give every student the chance to speak and begin processing her or his ideas and the ideas of others. It also provides them with outstanding opportunities to listen to peers and to provide productive feedback to them.

On the upper levels, suggesting (and even insisting) that students address the class with their concepts in semiformal situations allows for students to feel their voice is being heard. People do not write or speak solely for themselves. Addressing the class serves as a platform and provides students with opportunities where others will read and/or hear their opinions, and can open doors of creative expression and/or provide opportunities for students to drill down deeper into concepts, theories, and positions on issues.

Facilitator

Building productive communications into classroom routines will not only address academic standards, but also help prepare students to transfer those skills to increasingly complex tasks.

Great teaching is about listening, questioning, being responsive, and remembering that each student in the class is different. The question for you becomes, has the teacher reached/attempted to reach every student?

Please do not fall into the belief that the most important part of a lesson is the information the teacher delivers to the students (think lecture). I believe the opposite can be true. A *great* teacher should be an expert in playing the role of *facilitator*. This means they are listening and questioning so the students can delve into and drill down deeper into the topic at hand.

Too often teachers feel they must be doing something significant when being observed. It may sound funny, or like the antithesis of what should be happening; however, constant talking by the teacher doesn't translate to *great* teaching. Is the teacher talking and going on and on to impress you, the observer? This can lead to too much teacher talk and throw the lesson off from what a *normal lesson* would look like if you weren't in the classroom.

Again, this is where collaboration, communication, and trust come into the picture. In my opinion, <u>it is less about what the teacher is doing/saying in the front of the classroom and more about</u> *what the teacher is causing or facilitating to happen in the class*.

It is also important that you view teaching in both the short and long term. Having only a snapshot of a teacher's performance is not nearly enough to make an informed decision about what their TGT should look like. This is why many times a teacher may feel they have had a limited opportunity to demonstrate effectiveness (translation: *you are not present in the classroom enough*), and that can lead to too much teacher talk, and this becomes where the teacher is trying to impress you in the short time they have with you (think Speed Dating).

This is easily remedied by your *regular* presence in the classroom, and through regular and effective communications with the teacher. Your presence in neophyte as well as veteran teachers' classrooms is imperative. Simply because they have a good track record doesn't mean you should avoid walking into their classroom.

Content Delivery

Great teaching is also synonymous with *great* delivery. Enthusiasm is rarely faked well (or is it well faked?). You know outstanding teaching stems from genuine enthusiasm and knowledge of the content area. *Great* teachers lead students to understanding by the best means possible, based upon the students' readiness for the skill, and by offering various routes to meeting the objective. This exemplary teaching method features natural differentiation of a lesson based on multiple areas and modalities of understanding, with each sub-section recognized as the teacher caring enough to make the lesson concept understandable to them.

Student Engagement

Great teaching begins with the ability to engage students. When a teacher is using best practices and maximizes their instructional time, it does not invite the opportunistic poor behaviors that result in behavioral disruptions in the classroom - - or at the very least it significantly reduces them.

Students who are engaged are more active participants in their own learning. Students feel this is *their* teacher, because the students know this teacher really cares about them and their social and academic growth. In fact, they can assume ownership of their own learning as they progress through the grade levels.

Without this engagement, teaching becomes the dumping of knowledge into vessels, known in our profession as students, sans true meaning, understanding, or the ability to apply the knowledge dumped into these cranial containment units, aka their brain. Grasping and holding the attention of students, engaging them in dialogue, and then sending them on their way still wanting more are hallmarks of *great* teaching and the teacher's ability to engage and mentally hold onto students.

This is a hard concept to teach teachers who don't understand the significance of that ability; ergo, *look for the natural-born teacher.*

Providing Useful, Relevant Context

Tied very closely to the idea of student engagement is the idea of context. Providing context is an important step in engaging students, but it also helps them focus on the important points of the lesson by assuring that it is being viewed through the appropriate lens.

Some lessons and subjects lend themselves to an easy access to context. However, other lessons require more work, but without context a lesson can quickly lose its effectiveness. An ability to offer more than one point of contextual reference is important to ensure the teacher has met the needs of all students. Students subliminally read that effort as a teacher who cares about them and how they learn most effectively.

A Safe and Respectful Environment

I am not talking about a physically safe environment here. That's non-negotiable. I am talking about an educator who works to create an environment where a student feels comfortable taking measured academic risks.

In order to maximize educational opportunities, students need to be willing to ask questions, volunteer answers, share thoughts, and take part in discussions in a nonjudgmental atmosphere that encourages their active participation.

A teacher must take great care to model appropriate listening and interaction behaviors for all students in the class in order to assure that they develop within the classroom. The seemingly innocent sarcastic remark or good-natured ribbing can tear away the comfort zone a student feels in the classroom if the right relationship and classroom atmosphere have not been developed. This only comes down to one finite point that you will be looking for within the classroom: *respect.*

Has the teacher created an atmosphere of respect within the classroom? That critically important tenet can only emerge from one source - - the teacher. If the teacher isn't demonstrating respect for her or his students, then the concept is going nowhere. There will be no respect back to the teacher from the students and, unfortunately and devastatingly, there will be no respect among the students - - not an atmosphere where students feel comfortable expressing themselves.

Have you seen the movie *Freedom Writers*? There is a scene where Hilary Swank (Ms. Gruwell) says to a student, *"...you don't feel respected, well maybe you're not, but to get respect you have to give it."* The student replies *"Bull_ _ _ _! Why should I give my respect to you? Because you're a teacher? I don't know you. How do I know you're not a liar standing up there? How do I know you're not a bad person standing up there? I am not just gonna give you my respect because you're CALLED a teacher."*

I often think about this scene, and it's really true, especially when you hear of teachers who have been caught doing unethical and illegal acts and behaviors, from cheating to having sexual relationships with students.

Unfortunately, students don't naturally have the same sense of respect for their teachers that some of us did growing up. So dialogue with your teachers from day one is about boundaries and communications, interactions, and respect in the classroom - - and their use of social media! Tell your teachers not to assume that they will automatically get respect. It is earned (and I'm not so sure that's a bad thing).

I am always concerned when I hear teachers trying to be hip, on point, or in the mainstream with comments, verbiage, or kids-speak to try and establish their creds (credibility) with their students.

The first point to realize is that the teacher will never, ever be able to keep up with the street lingo that goes down and changes faster than a New York minute - - which, by the way, is 59 seconds. A teacher's attempt to win students over in this manner will be disastrous.

Students want their teacher to be an adult professional, professionally dressed, knowledgeable, and sincerely caring about them. Their sister-or-brother-from-a-different-mother is their peer-friend, and the teacher will never be that person. Do not allow your teachers to *disappoint* their students by trying to be someone they are not, or trying to reach students by being something they are not. Students need teachers for inspiration, not friendship.

Higher Order Thinking

Another component of *great* teaching is the use of questioning and discussion techniques. This is typically an area of weakness for many new teachers, and it is even an area of weakness for some veteran teachers.

I place a very high value on a teacher's ability to push - - yes, I wrote *push*, but I only mean it metaphorically - - students to ask and answer critical questions about the topic at hand. *Great* teachers know using a Socratic questioning strategy works best, and sets the stage for students to realize that there are no one-word answers, and follow-up questions are developed to solidify a student's understanding and/or reestablish the way an answer was presented. These are the higher-level questions in Bloom's taxonomy.

It also provides a window into deeper learning, logic, reasoning, and applying critical judgments to a concept. Kids like to be asked what they are thinking and why, and this is where a teacher's effectiveness in setting up a *respectful classroom* ethos is critically important to a successful learning process.

A teacher who can tap into his or her students' intellect and have them analyze and evaluate novel situations or problems has done far more than simply *depositing knowledge into a student's cranial containment vessel.* He or she has gotten to the heart of teaching by asking students to think in a critical and responsive manner. Many students are content to receive knowledge from the teacher whom they perceive to be the all-knowing authority. Socratic teaching happens when a teacher challenges students to uncover knowledge through dialogue and penetrating questionings based upon their initial response.

- How did you come to this idea/concept/thought?
- Why are you standing behind it?
- What would be an alternate way of looking at this issue?

Wouldn't you love to hear a response from a student to the following:

- What were some of the ideas/concepts that you didn't use, and why?

Differentiated Instruction

Great teaching uses a variety of modalities in order to reach numerous learning styles in the classroom and reinforce concepts in different contexts. Differentiated instruction benefits all students across all ability levels, and *great* teachers will plan a variety of instructional strategies within a lesson in order to accommodate all students.

Let's Not Get Physical

There is huge physical side to the art of teaching. It never, however, involves the physicality of touch, because I would strongly argue against *any* physical contact between student and teacher. This prohibited physicality includes the seemingly innocent, poignant, and gentle touching of an arm, back, shoulder or hand during a conversation as an effort to comfort and/or reassure. You may mean it that way, but the issue is *how will it be receed?*

There is really no safe place to touch a student, because it is so dependent on how the student will respond to the touch - - and it is, in all instances, *indefensible.* If you witness a touchy teacher, buy him or her a sensory-based hand toy, and they can use that instead of touching. However, can a student be as comforted by the use of other attributes rather than a physical touch? Well, of course. For example:

- Eye contact. The great teacher tries to make eye contact with each student throughout the presentation.
- Voice fluctuation. The great teacher varies her or his vocal pattern throughout the presentation.
- Facial expressions. The great teacher uses a variety of enthusiastic facial expressions.
- Hand gestures. The great teacher continually shows the palms of his or her hands during gestures.
- Use of space. The great teacher has their room set up to allow students to see and be focused on where the teacher wants that focus. The great teacher moves, points, shows, and varies their position in the classroom.
- Excitement. For the great teacher, this might be the twelfth time in twelve years that he or she is teaching the same pivotal concept. However, the teacher displays the same excitement and wonder as they did the first time they ever taught it.

Demonstration of what was learned. The *great* teacher culminates the lesson with an informal assessment of what the students learned. While paper and pencil quizzes have their place, there are some other ways to create an effective ending, ones that excite the students. For example: Exit tickets on Post-Its slapped to the door on the way out, highlighting two things each student learned. The teacher takes an empty basket and places it on top of her or his desk and then has the kids crumple up their exit ticket and shoot it into the basket on their way out the door - - they love that!

Do Not Create Islands

It is important to provide students with feedback, so they can see relationships between assignments and areas of study and start to develop their own understanding of the relationships between everything they're doing in the school. Students have a natural instinct to compartmentalize their work, and this has been educators' fault, because we have math during math period, science during science class, history in history, and English during reading and writing time. A *great* teacher builds and allows students to see and use all the disciplines as tangential to each other and, at times, overlapping entities, and not islands unto themselves. This is learning through understanding. As students become more efficient at critical thinking about the totality of their work, they buy into the process of learning as a continued motivation, not merely grade attainment.

Not the Same Old

The art of teaching includes finding new and exciting ways to present the same material. Some topics are more exciting than others, and *great* teachers are creative about how they keep the students engaged. The choice of materials or grouping of students could also significantly impact student engagement.

Flexibility and Responsiveness

Great teachers demonstrate flexibility and responsiveness in their instruction. Sometimes the students just are not getting it. In that case, the teacher needs to be flexible enough to slow down or alter the instructional plan accordingly.

This is difficult for some teachers, because they equate not finishing a lesson with failure. They also see you sitting in the rear of the classroom and are afraid that if they don't stick to the script you discussed in the pre-observation conference, it will have a negative impact.

This is definitely not the case! The failure is actually continuing at a pace/or process that loses students and yet the teacher never recognizes it, and thus failed to alter/adjust the pedagogy. It shows that the teacher doesn't understand his or her students, and is not flexible enough to alter plans in order to address the students' immediate needs.

Recognizing and understanding the needs of the target population allows for the slowing down or stepping up of the pace, as well as the elimination of or light touch upon other areas. This ebb and flow allows students to reach the desired end result, and clearly demonstrates a teacher's proclivity for putting the needs of their students above all else.

If someone were to observe a well-taught lesson, they would see teaching by someone who is flexible throughout their lesson. They have a plan in mind, but are able to determine the direction to take a lesson in the moment (the most appropriate teachable moment), as well as the change-ups in questioning and the need to review or reteach when the students are not able to move forward.

Furthermore, *great* teaching allows for students to be engaged and involved in their learning. At the culmination of the lesson, students are asked to apply their knowledge to complete a demanding task. Their success with the task can be used as a measurement to see if learning took place, and to what the degree the lesson and set of activities were effective. If the teacher fails to do this, then they need to accept responsibility for their ineffectiveness. One of the reasons teachers remain ineffective or stagnant is the lack of adequate support by their principal.

You have a responsibility to ensure the success of your students by creating an ethos of teacher growth, and, as a consequence, increased student acquisition of knowledge.

When teachers have confidence in themselves - - and the *confidence in you* that will allow for him or her to alter the original lesson plan based on their read of the students during the lesson - - it is evidence of a fantastic relationship between you and the teacher! It speaks volumes of the growth culture you have created within the school. It is at a time like this that you come to realize just how well you have helped your teachers understand and believe that you are there as a collaborator, not a judge!

Content Knowledge

In order for a teacher to effectively impart concepts to students, her or his content knowledge needs to be solid. It is not enough for a teacher to merely be one lesson or chapter ahead of the students.

A thorough knowledge of concepts is necessary to allow for natural curiosity and *organic (natural) progression* by the students. By having a rich understanding of the content, the teacher can troubleshoot when students do not understand a particular concept, and they can also plan ahead so the concepts are presented in an organized, meaningful and engaging manner.

Additionally, by being an expert in the subject area, teachers are able to offer both remedial information as well as enrichment for students who are working at a faster pace. Having a solid knowledge of the content allows for increased ability to diversify and differentiate lessons. However, the teacher must never forget that what comes easy for them based upon their knowledge may not come easily for their students.

But is content knowledge enough to make up for poor pedagogy? My daughter had a high school physics teacher who certainly knew his way around a physics lab (no, not Einstein); however, he was a sucky teacher! He knew his stuff but could not teach it. So content alone is no guarantee of pedagogical success. He could explain why which would hit the ground first, a feather or a bowling ball, if both were dropped at the exact same moment from a height of 100 feet, but his teaching ability put three-quarters of the class on the ground and right in the path of the bowling ball.

Classroom Control

Having control of the classroom is also a sign of *great* teaching. Control does not mean silence and desks in straight rows, although it can mean that if the circumstances warrant. Having *great* classroom control includes keeping students on task and engaged, making them curious but not to a point of distraction, with a noise level of wonder and controlled excitement. Classroom control could easily be a subset of respect.

Great teaching is about knowing where to start, and where you want to end up, and how to begin and end in an enthusiastic yet controlled fashion. And a *great* teacher also knows what to do in between, in a controlled fashion, to help the students learn.

Having good classroom control includes keeping students on task and engaged. We had over 850 boys and girls in school, and an assembly program was always somewhat unnerving, since I knew if the presenter could not maintain interest, the assembly would become a somewhat noisy and disconnected place 30 to 40 minutes into the presentation.

I was always impressed when the Animal Man came to school with his menagerie. When he said, "OK, we need to be quiet before I can bring out the next animal..." you could hear a pin drop! The first few years, I would always ask myself why this was happening, and then it dawned on me. *He had something the kids wanted*, and they were willing to behave because they really, really wanted to see what was next! They wanted to see the six-foot python, the baby monkey, the tarantula, the baby lion cub, and others. They listened and were unbelievably attentive because they were fascinated, and that is the concept you look for - - sans the tarantula - - in the classroom.

Can your teacher do that day in and day out, or at least come really, *really* close?

Continuous Assessment

There needs to be teacher desire to continuously develop systems that assess students and potentially modify their instruction to meet each child's needs. A comprehensive assessment plan is essential to *great* teaching. Educators should continuously question their efforts in terms of lesson development and the strengths and weaknesses of their students, and use data gathered from assessments to guide their practice. A teacher should use a wide array of assessment vehicles to determine the strengths/weaknesses of students, and to gage the effectiveness of their own teaching. The teacher must be open and receptive to modifications of their pedagogical practice based upon assessment results.

Student Engagement

Student engagement in the lesson and rapport with the teacher are critically important. Students must feel there is a purpose for what they are learning, a degree of relevance that can be immediately applied, or one that they can see being used in the future. This requires that teachers find purposeful and realistic ways to introduce material, ways that have direct relevance to the lives of the students.

This is where the anticipatory set can come into play within the construct of a lesson. This is more than a *play catch* environment, where the teacher throws out the questions and the students toss responses back to the teacher.

Is the pedagogy a matter of merely dispensing and directing student responses to known facts that will appear on future tests and, therefore, it must be known - - or is it content the students view as relevant and useful to them?

Planning

One of the first cornerstones of *great* teaching is the planning/preparation aspect of the instructional process. *Great* teachers spend a significant amount of time planning for their classes, and developing comprehensive units of study that align with state- and district-level curriculum, as well as assessments that are varied in terms of design and how they measure what students were intended to learn. Remember the Lincoln quote when asked how long does it take him to chop down a tree? Factored into a *great* teacher's planning are the learning styles of the students and preparation of lessons and activities to encourage academic growth in areas of weakness while also promoting their strengths.

What to Look for During Observations

Now you have completed most of this treatise, you might reflect on this additional list with a sharper resolve and a more in-depth understanding of why each component is important, and why working with a teacher to grow toward addressing each of these areas is critically important for your students. The critical elements I would look for when observing a teacher are:

- Were the objective of the lesson and set of activities clear to students, with materials and equipment ready? For example, was time wasted during transitions within the lesson?
- Were the students motivated? For example, is the stage set to engage the students, and what is their demonstrated attitude?
- Did the teacher facilitate student participation, or was it strictly 'chalk-and-talk?' For example, are the students encouraged to ask questions, to think and to challenge?
- Were there accommodations for the special needs of students and/or an understanding of the various learning levels of students in the class addressed, to enhance their participation and increase the potential for their success?
- What were the various modalities of responses available to students to demonstrate ownership of the concept(s) being presented?
- How did the teacher manage instruction? For example, did the teacher manage time effectively, was there a smooth flow of information, were directions clear, and did the teacher have a summary/closure/review?
- Did the teacher check for understanding at various times during the lesson? How was this accomplished? What was the result of this action?
- Did the teacher demonstrate respect for all students and use effective communication skills? For example, did they have a rapport with their students? Were their voice, intonation and body language effective? Did the teacher model appropriate communication skills, such as correct grammar and spelling?
- What were the various forms of end-of-lesson assessments, and did they afford each student the opportunity to present what they learned in a manner that indicated to the teacher their level of understanding?
- Did the teacher assign meaningful independent work, and how did they monitor it?
- Was the assigned homework related to the work during class?
- Was there a conclusion to the lesson with an appropriate mini-review and setup for the subsequent lesson in the subject area?

Yes, this list is extensive and might, at first blush, seem daunting, in that you need to remember to look for all of the above. But with time and practice, this list will become second nature, and will put you on autopilot while you observe a teacher at any time and at all times.

Think of it this way: trying to explain to someone how to tie their shoe - - where to place each hand and each lace, and the order of the process required to successfully tie a shoe - - is daunting. At first. However, each of you knows how to tie your shoes based upon what? The same thing that gets one to Carnegie Hall.

I walk into a classroom, and I scroll through in my mind each and every one of these attributes and requirements as easily as falling off a log. You, too, will develop the skill set necessary to fall off a log!

Sharp, An Additional Take on Lincoln

One of my hobbies is cooking, and I find creating meals for friends and family a joyful experience. As part of the mise-en-place process, in addition to getting ingredients ready, I always sharpen knives I know I will need.

A sharp knife doesn't stay sharp, so it must be honed and sharpened time after time throughout its life. When the knife is sharp it is easy to keep it performing optimally. When the knife is left to get dull over a long period of time, it becomes extremely difficult to use and does not perform at its best.

I apply the same concept and principle to the art of teaching, as well as to *the art and skill of being an effective leader*. There needs to be a regimen for sharpening oneself on a regular basis - - and note I did not write "every once in a while" - - as it relates to pedagogy and leadership. Very little in this world self-perpetuates, and most certainly people do not self-perpetuate over the long haul, or even from year to year. This is where you, as the building leader, must:

- Create an environment where people purposefully self-reflect on their efforts and the subsequent results (and this includes you and your efforts).
- Appreciate that the use of the observation practice and subsequent collaborative prescriptions for growth must be ongoing.

It will also be interesting to see what you *purposefully* develop for yourself as you self-reflect on your efforts and, most important, the *results* of your efforts! The lingering question will be <u>what will you do if your efforts do not come to fruition and achieve the ongoing evolution you are seeking</u>?

- How about reviewing everyone's ongoing TGT during a rainy, dreary weekend, to see where each teacher is, and the gains made (or lack thereof)?

- Taking a realistic look at your red X-ers to see if you have converted, or even partially converted, any.
- Gauging your patience. Has it decreased or increased, and why?
- Visualizing to see if the TGT process is really not working, or if you're expecting too much too soon?

Taking your assistant principals out for a couple of adult beverages one afternoon and having a candid conversation about where everyone thinks the teachers are in this process. (I do believe there will be a direct correlation between their increase in candor and veracity proportional to the amount of adult beverages consumed - - so be patient).

A Little Chapter Closure

Great teaching enables students to build and demonstrate critical thinking skills. These skills support the formulation of viable responses with relevant meaning, and when followed by praise for the effort (think growth mind-set), they encourage what psychologist Albert Bandura labeled as self-efficacy, as well as a sense of accomplishment. Hence, critical thinking must be evident in student interaction, whether in collaboration with other students or while the teacher facilitates the lesson in progress.

Additionally, as you conduct observations, it is crucial that you evaluate the cognitive demand of the questions and activities being presented, since they should coincide with the ability level of your target population and desired student growth.

Your ability to identify *great* teaching that exudes personal passion, engagement, and tiered questioning and activities is ultimately the fuel of operative learning, and is the major component of the growth pattern of a teaching cohort of a successful school.

Your job will be to take all the pieces that constitute a meaningful, focused, productive, and highly effective lesson and consider what is missing within the context of the above, both while you observe a teacher, and when you place everything into a *logical, reasonable and obtainable (doable)* TGT plan.

It must support teacher growth to reach new heights of pedagogy resulting in student growth, but not shock the stuffing out of the teacher when you present it. Now that is leadership!

Chapter 9
Your Role in Establishing *Greatness*

Few leaders achieve greatness for any considerable length of
time by stumbling upon solutions to problems; for most leaders,
leadership is a deliberate and purposeful practice in which self-
awareness is critical.
~ Bill George

Effective Instruction

The bottom line to each and every conversation I have with a teacher regarding the effectiveness of her or his instruction never dwells on the concept of what they taught or, for that matter, how they taught it initially.
The sole barometer is all about *whether or not the students learned and
can apply what was taught*! *Great* instruction is not about whether or not
or how a subject was taught, but rather the results. And frankly, from that
point you then move back to *how* and then *why*.

You will, I promise, have teachers say during your post-observation
conference, "*...but I taught that...*" in response to your discussion of his or
her pedagogy outcome.

What you need to expunge from the mind-set of teachers is that *teaching something* doesn't mean it's time to move on to the next topic. Teaching
something alone does not satisfy the importance of the act of teaching,
because the teacher is not looking at the *result* of the action, but simply
the action.

You are looking for the result, and so should the teacher. Your only
concern with the action is if the result is not good!

You need to enforce and reinforce in the mind-set of the teacher - - simply and simplistically - - that it is not about whether they *taught* the lesson because it was in the planbook or in the chapter of the textbook, and it does not mean that after it's been taught, the students *are automatically ready* to move onto the next concept or lesson. The act of teaching something is not the passport to move on to the next concept.

As previously noted, early on in my career as a principal I was observing an extremely veteran teacher (how about that for being politically correct?) whose lesson I felt left a lot to be desired. It was way too easy (remember first grade teacher Sylvia, and also the second-grade macaroni lesson?).

You may find this happening quite often, because teachers want to provide you with a lesson and set of activities they know will be a home run. These are lessons that have worked well in the past, or at least curried favor with past principals. These are easy lessons, with no one daring to step outside the box, but rather staying home with the fireplace on and the cat on their lap on top of the afghan in the Lazy-Boy with a cup of hot chocolate.

You are being set up if this becomes the norm! It can never be the exact same lesson, because the kids (the target population) will be different from year to year. It doesn't mean the teacher is ineffective, it just means *they planned for you being in the room* and applied the subsequent "boxed lesson" *as opposed to planning specifically for the kids in the room*.

This is the ancient and typical dog and pony show people trot out when the principal comes in for an observation. It is, in my mind, most egregious, because the teacher is planning for me and not for *my kids*. However, bring something like this up to the teacher, and the teacher turns into a defensive linebacker! It will not be the first time, nor will it be the last, when a well-intentioned discussion about teacher growth got caught up in the emotional personalization of, "Oh, so you think I am not a good teacher!"

Just Get It Right - - It is Your Future as Well

As the person conducting observations, you need to be purposeful and intentional about how you use the process. Feeding-back, feeding-forward, and feeding-up means nothing if it isn't the *right* feedback, for the *right* person, at the *right* time, and focusing on the *right* stuff.

At its most basic level, observation is nothing more than noting and *judging* - - there, I wrote it! I am making a judgment call regarding what I am witnessing! Next it will be my job to remove the *stench of subjectivity* from the judgment call, to the best of my ability. I don't want the teacher to get a whiff of it!

If I am to be fair to those being observed, subjectivity will need to be removed and replaced with (our BFF) **evidence**. This is the only way to accomplish objectivity in terms of you being seen as fair. However, I am less concerned about the person I am observing seeing me as fair - - and I do not perseverate on the concept, because it is an uphill boulder-push, since the observation process is an emotional experience for the one being observed.

With that thought in mind, should a third or fourth party see the written observation, I want that person or those people to view it as fair. I, of course (once emotion is removed and clarity has replaced it), want the teacher to view my input as unbiased. Most of the time the observation write-up is between you and the teacher, but there will be times, as I previously noted, when your superintendent and/or assistant superintendent (and possibly the union president) will read what you have written.

Write an observation that a teacher doesn't like or deems unfair to them, and all manner of people can become engaged in the process of analyzing what you have written.

This is why writing an effective observation is so important. It will be a piece of history that can and mostly likely will be viewed by others, from superintendents and board of education members to the president of the teachers' union and the attorney representing the union. This will certainly occur if the teacher deems your write-up to be wrong, unfair, discriminatory, or disciplinary in nature.

Given the potential audience, an accurate, well-written, grammatically correct and logical document is a baseline priority that *must* be met. It is an important document that has a dual reflection: it reflects on the teacher you have observed, and it also *reflects on you* and your observational, writing, and communication skill sets, as well as on your ability to work with people. As you are judging and making a decision about the teacher, people are also making a judgment about you. Of course, no pressure there for the non-tenured principal!

The people who are making decisions about you and your future as an administrator will view your written efforts as an indicator of your effectiveness and ability. Union representatives will eye you as a formidable adversary if your writing has ample **evidence** to support the points you are trying to make about the teacher's pedagogy during the lesson that you observed. You will be amazed at how the observation process and the ancillary components are seen as such a major indicator of your proficiency.

The process should never be taken lightly. If you do, you will be the only one who does!

Teaching Channel

As has been previously written, some will argue that *great* teaching is a subjective concept.

You stand a pretty good chance of hearing that argument from teachers, especially those who are not recognized as being *great*. However, I submit to you that you should, in a fairly non-subjective manner, present concepts of *greatness* to the faculty prior to applying them to individuals in the school.

Do the Build–A-Great-Teacher Workshop (although I may not label it that way). Also, bring into faculty meetings Teacher Channel videos of teachers teaching and have a discussion at the conclusion of each video as to *what was powerful* and *what was less powerful* in the pedagogy that was observed - - and use those words (*powerful* and *less powerful*), and no others!

You don't show the video and say "…this is *great* teacher. I will be looking for this in your classrooms." That isn't the one-way street you should travel down, because there will be too many oncoming cars heading right for you!

The videos you select will speak for themselves. Putting a label on *great* teaching would be remiss if isolating one specific style or model as paramount. The videos provide the first step toward *purposeful self-reflection* based upon observed pedagogy and the internal comparisons made by the teacher.

You will be elated when one of the teachers refers back to a video you presented, and mentions how and why they enhanced a lesson (or lessons) based upon their purposeful reflection and the video. *Gold! You have struck gold!* And again, add this to that teacher's end-of-year evaluation, because remember, teachers talk to one another!

The closest we can come to defining *great* teaching is this: *A teacher's ability to successfully use various methods of teaching while supporting a variety of learning goals and student learning styles.*

This definition is fairly simple given the complexity of the teaching process; however, it bare-bones it, and renders a complicated process down to what needs to be viewed as the end result.

I would submit that the key word in that sentence is *successfully*, and your job (and the job of the teachers) will be to *locate success for each child*. You will need to note the causative factor(s) of the lack of performance in others, and plan a teacher growth trajectory to accomplish amelioration. Please take personalities out of the equation and simply use the purity of that definition as a guide for you and the teachers and administrators.

Mantra

Some will argue that *great* teaching is difficult to define, so how could an administrator know what *great* or successful teaching is?

In my opinion, *great* teaching is extremely easy to define: you can see, hear, and measure the results over time. The blanket statement by teachers and possibly some within the cadre of the school's administrative team might be that *great* teaching is hard to define. This is an attempt to cloud an issue that is crystal clear.

There are many variables to assess when determining the effectiveness of a teacher. And the clues and/or lack of clues, the **evidence**, is all laid out in front of you. All you really need to do is *recognize what you see* and gather the pieces together to establish your points regarding their effective pedagogy within the classroom. This establishes the trajectory of the growth plan for the teacher.

The poor-quality teachers will bottom out right in front of your eyes, especially if you clearly understand and can articulate *great* teaching. The ability to differentiate between the two will obviously help you provide assistance through a professional growth plan for all your teachers, even the ones you consider highly effective, because growth is continual, and no one has ever is grown enough!

Developing a basic framework/rubric to use for the TGT, and a set of guidelines to identify *great* teaching, must be accomplished in order for you and your building-level administrators to venture out into a school and correctly identify teachers performing at the highest levels, as well as the ones who should be granted tenure, and the tenured staff requiring of significant growth.

Communism Works - - in Theory

While I try to steer clear of theoretical practices (because remember, in theory, Communism works) from time to time there are some that can serve as a foundational underpinning which are not bad to have in the back of your mind, especially for those of you who are more theory-based.

I am about to offer you three that I think will serve you well. And please do what I did: select from the smorgasbord of concepts presented in each, add them to your mind-set, shake well, and apply as needed - - and don't forget to refrigerate what's left over!

Kidder's Ethical Checkpoints

Rushworth Kidder's checkpoints are one theory I can live with comfortably. They are applicable to your process of developing a growth mind-set within the faculty regarding TGTs. The systematic approaches Kidder suggests are as follows:

1) First, recognize that there is an issue. This is very important, because it makes one acknowledge that there is actually growth potential that will benefit the students. Remember, a teacher growth trajectory is intended to support the teacher's efforts with their students, and the success of the students!

2) Next, focus on the issue and decide who is responsible for addressing the problem. This at first seems a little weird, given the focus here, but there is a strong ethical issue involved with teachers accepting compensation for job performance. Teachers are not accomplishing what they are being paid for if students are not progressing, learning, and making relevant connections to what they are being exposed to in school. I would clearly never bring this to a table when I am talking with a teacher about their growth trajectory, but it is firmly implanted within my brain, and does, at certain times, drive me, while at other times it is infuriating.

It is important to gather relevant facts - - ah, **evidence**. It is imperative that adequate, accurate, and helpful, not hurtful, information is gathered in order to make effective decisions - - decisions that are achieved by both you and the teacher, and ones based upon the **evidence**.

Kidder postulates that if two people cannot agree, then they may need to negotiate an alternate solution. Frankly, I want what I want, and what I want is for a teacher to grow.

Presenting the concept as part of her or his growth trajectory is certainly something I can live with, because I am postulating the TGT concept.

I also have patience and know that if I can get someone to take that initial first step with me, the potential for them to take another is huge, especially if the first step isn't into a bear trap!

A decision regarding the initial growth trajectory needs to be made, and I will willfully acquiesce to a teacher's desire out of the gate to help ensure further compliance down the road, because I want the road to be a yellow brick one.

Lastly, reflect on the situation and decision. One should learn from their experiences and the choices that they make. There is always a lesson to be learned, and one to teach - - and this most assuredly includes you.

SAD Formula

The SAD formula (*Situation Definition, Analysis, and Decision*) was developed by the media ethicist Louis Alvin Day. He created this formula to build important elements of critical thinking into moral reasoning. Possessing critical thinking skills allows one to take a rational approach to making decisions that emphasizes careful analysis and evaluation.

Critical thinking begins with first having an understanding of the issue to be evaluated, and then moves to identifying the issues, information, and assumptions that encompass the problem. Then one should complete the process by evaluating alternatives and coming to a conclusion. These are things that you will be discussing with the teacher in a post-observation conference.

The Situation Definition has as its main component the description of the **evidence**. As previously written, it should include a consideration of external factors. Doing this can have a significant calming effect on the teacher. The types of students in the classroom and the baggage they bring with them each and every day is something that needs to be strongly considered and ultimately factored in.

There is nothing more supportive to a teacher then when he or she knows you acknowledge and understand the extenuating circumstances that surround what ultimately is accomplished in the classroom. Strong, unified, and positive decisions many times come out of careful definition and analysis of the situation. You can determine which is the best decision after external constraints are identified and evaluated.

One significant advantage of the SAD formula is that it encourages *systematic* and *situational reasoning*.

Nash's 12 Questions

Laura Nash suggests 12 questions that can help identify the responsibilities involved in making choices. Discussion and reflection about the queries can be very helpful and useful, even though they are not all applicable for every situation; nevertheless, maintain them in your mind's Rolodex (sorry, Millennials. You will need to Google up Rolodex to see what that was).

You should answer the questions below as a self-guided litmus test. There is also some sense of a moral obligation to run through these types of exercises just so you remain ethically above the fray. Also, it is important to explore a variety of alternative solutions.

Below are the 12 questions Nash suggests pondering. I submit them to you verbatim rather than with the twist of applicability to a school venue. I will leave that up to you. I do bristle at the use of the word *problem* -- but let's go with it here.

1) Has the problem been defined accurately?
2) How would one define the problem if he/she stood on the other side of the fence (empathy)?
3) How did this issue/problem occur in the first place?
4) To whom do one's loyalties as a person or group lie as a member of the organization?
5) What is your intention in making this decision?
6) How does this intention compare with the probable results?
7) Whom could your action or decision harm?
8) Can you engage the affected parties in a discussion of the issue before a decision is made?
9) Are you confident that your position will be as valid over an extended period of time as it appears to be now?
10) Could you tell your boss, your CEO, the board of directors, your family, or society as a whole about your decision or action?
11) What is the symbolic potential of your action if understood or misunderstood?
12) Under what conditions would you allow exception to your stand, for moral consistency is very important?

Consider Kidder, Nash and SAD in the Developing a TGT

There are several similarities among the three different approaches to decision-making to consider while you are working with a teacher and co-developing their TGT. Kidder's ethical checkpoints are similar to Nash's 12 questions, in that they highlight the importance of identifying the problem and gathering information. Nash's 12 questions, however, go a little further to encourage engagement in perspective-taking. It is important see the problem from the other person's perspective, establishing empathy. SAD also states that the problem should be defined while stating the facts at hand.

When it comes to making ethical choices or decisions, there are steps that should be taken that Kidder, the SAD Formula, and Nash have in common. When it comes to making the necessary decisions, the following are steps that should be included.

First, it is important that all relevant and necessary information (aka, **evidence**) is gathered from every possible scenario you observed. This serves as the foundation. Making a decision without first collecting facts -- in our case, **evidence** -- can prove to be ineffective, and could also be unethical.

- Next, you must also identify the values as well as the principles that could change the outcome of the decision.
- Next, one should weigh the values and principles that were gathered, again, as they are likely to impact the final decision to be rendered.
- Finally, you should be able to defend your choice based on all the information and research (aka, evidence) that was gathered throughout the process. In addition, you should also ask yourself some questions that Nash pointed out.

Some of the questions that should be asked are:
- Have you accurately defined whatever the problem was?
- How did it occur?
- How would you look at the problem as an outsider, or from a different perspective?
- What are my intentions in making this decision?

What Is the Problem?

Defining or recognizing there is a need for growth is the first phase for all the approaches. If the need is not clearly established, it cannot be resolved.

One must identify the issue, along with who was affected and how they were impacted. Nash noted the problem must be defined with precision, while the SAD formula described defining the situation, and Kidder plainly stated there must be recognition of a problem. These three theories are applicable while you reflect on the situation(s) you observe, and how you subsequently use one or more of these processes in creating desirable outcomes via a TGT. Theory-based, yes, but processes that are invaluable.

A Little Chapter Closure

I think motivation is a force that infuses people with the desire to complete a task such as building toward *greatness*.

Warren Bennis (2004) attributed the success of a leader to "...his or her ability to not only relate to people, but also to engage people so that they are motivated" (p. 57). The most effective leaders do not force anyone to do anything (usually), but rather they have the ability to motivate people *to want* to do things themselves.

If a leader is to motivate people, they must allow others to clearly see what their vision and goals are, and patiently allow teachers to build toward an understanding, and hopefully appreciation and adoption of these goals and desired outcomes.

Building a common plan to reach goals is the best way to motivate a person. If everyone truly believes in the goal, they will be much more likely to want to achieve success. Motivation should involve praise, coupled with a message that more can always be done to grow pedagogically, both individually and as a collaborative group, then cutting to the bottom line of what is best for students.

Chapter 10
Pre- and Post-Observation Conferences

The first hurdle for teachers is to understand the message.
Begin with the end in mind.
~ Stephen Covey

The process of purposeful self-reflection in teachers is critically important. You need to make sure your feedback is allowing for the development of a growth trajectory process where concepts and areas of growth are built upon previous ones, and not simply a reaction to the individual observation or one piece of **evidence**.

One of your major responsibilities and efforts must be developing educators toward the concept of obtaining the very best outcomes with regard to their pedagogical practices. In order for that to occur, your feedback (feeding-back, feeding-forward, and feeding-up) must be heard, seen, understood, internalized, and subsequently applied in order for it to be effective for the teacher.

Great feedback is information that is useful, purposeful, attainable, and relevant, and can be specifically delineated and subsequently used.

As you seek *greatness* from teachers, please remember your part in this process is nothing short of your *greatness* as a support and resource for teacher growth. Leaders gain influence and credibility, and people begin to follow them, because of what they have accomplished that will propel the organization toward *greatness*.

Mindfulness, as I define it, is a combination of *self-awareness* as well as *situational awareness*. You develop self-awareness through practice of purposeful self-reflection. You strengthen it by asking for feedback from trusted colleagues. Situational awareness comes from knowing the score: what's happening and what's not happening.

Leaders need to know how the team and organization are doing, and they gain that perspective by asking questions, observing, listening, and evaluating what they have learned as a result of that intake process. The issue for you becomes how to disseminate this knowledge to others and subsequently obtain extraordinary results!

You can build upon a learner mentality by your comments when a person who's been around the block a few times teaches you something. Your comments will let people know you're a learner, and that you cherish the opinions of others. This has a tendency to put people at ease with you, and you don't come across as a know-it-all. As previously noted, if you think and act like a know-it-all because you are the principal, then you have immediately and effectively demonstrated that you really *don't* know it all.

Conspicuous Focus

I have always had a kind of bunker mentality. As the winds of change stir around the educational landscape, it is important to ground yourself and the faculty with a vision of what *great* teaching and *great* schools look and feel like. Regardless of whether there is a new mandate from the federal government, the state education department, or a new superintendent hell-bent on making a name for themselves, you need to retain your conspicuous focus on teacher growth!

There are small and time-consuming events where you work one-on-one with a teacher to provide them growth opportunities.

Smile more; talk less (Hamilton, the Musical, 2014).

Listen more than talk.

Smile more than frown.

Cover a teacher's class so they can observe other teachers, not on *their* time, but on your time.

Don't be afraid to say, "I like what you have accomplished..."...but also don't be afraid to say, "let's try this again, and here are the reasons *why*, and some possible alterations you might want to consider." This will also be considered **evidence**, should your feet be held to the fire by a union, a superintendent, or a board of education.

Engage in conversations that allow for give and take of ideas. Success is impossible sans a shared understanding of expectations.

Assist teachers in their progressive growth via a TGT and a two-way conversation about:

1) An appreciation of what constitutes greatness.

2) A knowledge of the quality of their present work in relation to the target of greatness.

3) A repertoire of practices that help them close the gap between (a) and (b). The ultimate aim in providing feedback should be to equip teachers with the ability to self-monitor the quality of their pedagogy through purposeful self-reflection.

It All Starts Here

Look at it this way: It is much easier to provide feedback about a single one-hour event that hasn't been beneficial for students than it is to provide feedback about a whole year of ineffective one-hour events. This is only possible based on your ongoing and continual classroom presence.

That message and process begins during the pre- and post-observation meetings! Regardless of what you have presented to faculty en masse, you are now sitting with the teacher, and you need to put into play what you talked about as theory to assist in teacher growth via a TGT.

By engaging on a one-to-one basis, you enhance the learning experience through a specific structure of individualization. The question is, how do you help teachers understand and visualize exemplary pedagogy?

You will need to enter the processes with this basic structural understanding and continually move forward:

- Introduction of the Teacher Growth Trajectory concept.
- Pre-observation meetings
- Post-observation meetings
- The entirety of other continual conversations about growth targets, methodology to obtain and sustain pedagogical growth, and assessment of targets presumably reached.

It will be your responsibility to understand the impact of the processes on someone who would be considered *your subordinate* (a word as previously noted that I detest, but nonetheless that is how teachers view themselves unless you change that dynamic and mind-set!).

In states where the process is tied to tenure, pay increases and, most important, the ability to retain one's job, these parameters automatically revert the process to boss-to-employee status. Therefore, it is incumbent upon you to make sure you do not get caught up in that mind-set. Yes, the teacher will think that way no matter what you say, but that doesn't mean *you* must think like that, and it will be what you do and how you do it that will influence and alter teacher mind-sets.

Enter classrooms and the process as innocent as a newborn baby. Walk in with the clear purposes of teacher growth potential and enhancement of opportunities for students in the classroom. Your comments, actions, directions, suggestions, and more are all based upon the **evidence** gathered, and are focused on pedagogical growth leading to student advancement - - period.

Wasted Authority

Having the authority based upon the nameplate on your office door and then not maximizing that authority to highest degree possible is shirking your responsibility!

Your attitude must not be that the words *authority* and *power* are interchangeable, because they are not. You are looking toward creating teacher growth through the *authority you have* to commence that process absent a teacher's self-propelled initiative.

Approaching this task via your *authority* to do so differs from having the *power* to do so. Use your *authority to assist,* and not your *power to demand.* If you look at the process from the viewpoint of the authority giving you the responsibility to encourage a TGT, as opposed to the power to demand it, adjusts your mind-set and, by extension, helps propel the teachers' mind-set into the proper place.

What you are doing is seeking to impart nuggets of information that you and the teacher can agree to work on as an area of growth.

The best dialogue is sometimes called *thinking together,* where you and the teacher are collaborators. Teachers will see ongoing and consistent dialogues as a sign of a more equal relationship that they have with you. Plus, continual dialogues may allow you to identify possible misconceptions that impede a teacher's understanding of their TGT.

Two suggestions for how to use dialogues to sustain teacher growth are:

- First, you can simply check in with a teacher to see how their TGT is going. You can ask the teacher what they think is (are) the major challenge(s) they are working on, and how they are approaching the challenge(s). The check-in is also a good time to discuss the lesson planning concept, and the kinds of things that are going on behind the lesson that are critical to a teacher's success. You may discover a problem in a teacher's lesson planning, and a simple suggestion may make a world of difference in the outcome of the teacher's performance.

The check-in process itself will also improve teacher motivation by showing them you care about their growth. The check-in also allows teachers to share concerns or ask questions in this thinking-together time that may not have come up initially, but are nevertheless relevant to the TGT. It also allows teachers to reflect on their ongoing learning experiences - - almost constantly.

- A second possibility is to use thinking-together discourse to have the teacher think through their pedagogical growth trajectory. This is an excellent opportunity for you to model thinking for the teacher. A carpenter will not just tell an apprentice how to hammer in a nail -- the carpenter will model the process.

Similarly, you can model the very thinking process you are hoping teachers will acquire and use. Teaching requires strategies that you can demonstrate. You can talk about how he or she teaches, what they plan for, and especially how they identify and deliver constructive insights that make academic work important and relevant for their students.

Feeding-Back, Feeding-Forward and Feeding-Up: Advice, How to Advance, and Understanding Why

Please let me drill down a little deeper into these concepts, since they are *critically important,* and are the underpinnings of all pre- and post-observation conference discussions.

You need to establish in your mind, and convey to the minds of members of the administrative cadre, the difference between feeding-back, feeding-forward, and feeding-up. Feeding-back, feeding-forward, and feeding-up influence a teacher's knowledge, skills, and purposeful reflective practice so they build and sustain pedagogical growth on their own. These serve to guide and sustain the teacher in their relevant TGT.

Feeding-Back: Feedback is the tool used to help the teacher learn from their attempts. It consists of information in your advisory capacity formed from *specific observable events*. Feedback must contain and be based solely on **evidence**.

Feeding-Forward: These are deliberate conversations providing specifics relating to growth based upon the harvested **evidence**, with your concrete examples leading toward a teacher's *understanding* of what you are bringing to their attention. Teacher understanding eventually must grow into self-propelled, purposeful reflection and subsequent remedial action.

Feeding-Up: Feeding-Up provides the *reason, rationale,* and/or *knowledge base* for advancement of each teacher's pedagogy. It answers the teacher's *why* question. *Why* do I need to do this, grow here, or reflect on this or that? *It helps the teacher make sense of process.* Adult learners need to see the relevance of what you are feeding them. When they understand the reason *why*, teachers are more likely to buy into the concepts that you share with them, and to develop a vision to propel them going forward. This is extremely important for adult learners!

In Which Room Do You Want this to Happen?

In the school where I was principal, my office was centrally located within the Main Office, directly across from the mailboxes and key rack. It had a large internal window, and everyone and anyone walking to and from the mailboxes or key rack easily saw what I was doing (and with whom).

The fact was, everyone could see me meeting with teachers in my office. Everyone saw him or her in there and, of course, wondered why. Was it a good reason, or bad one? Additionally, that is my home base, and not the teacher's classroom. Given the potential emotional baggage associated with the pre- and post-observation conferences, as well as meeting to build and sustain a TGT, the principal's office is not the best place to build a collaborative atmosphere. Why not go to the teacher's classroom for those meetings?

First, you can easily reference events that occurred during the observation by pointing to the area as opposed to trying to describe it from your office. It also is comfortable for the teacher, because now they are home and you are the visitor. I believe - - and I may again be Pollyanna - - that you being there is a sign of respect for the teacher, and an unspoken gesture of *let's do this together*. I allow many teachers a sense of being more at ease by going to their backyard.

However, in all candor, I did not always do this. When I knew the meeting could possibly be a contentious one, where I needed the power of the throne (my desk and/or my office), I conducted the meeting in my office. If the union people were coming, it was in my office. In some really overt cases, I had either another administrator there or, even better, I had the office secretary come in and take notes. I never wanted the he-said, she-said scenario to dull, blur, distort, or misinterpret the facts of what occurred during the meeting(s).

Logic

During observations you should be able to pick out key elements during a lesson that can impact student learning. During the post-observation conference, you can have a discussion with regard to techniques used during the lesson and possible alternatives that can more positively impact effective learning in the classroom. Open dialogues with teachers about what makes a teacher effective and what *great* teaching should look like in the classroom is also important.

Unless you set standards, individuals will not know what is expected of them. If a teacher is not provided with useful feedback, they can assume that they are being effective and meeting the needs of their students, when in fact they may not be.

How to Give Advice in your Pre- and Post-Observation Conferences

The predominant question is, what kinds of instructional strategies or approaches will enhance teacher reflection and subsequent growth?

One of the first things I try to remember is that every situation is somewhat unique. Even if I witnessed an error, I tried to come up with a better, a more comfortable term than error. However, the reality is that we all make errors, and there is no harm in it being recognized as such. It is not catastrophic.

Conversely, making the same error repeatedly is a potential catastrophe. I would certainly refrain from indicating to the teacher that there was an error. Error is the wrong word, and it would be, in and of itself, an error to use the word - - ever! What it comes down to is how the teacher is going to accept and fulfill the TGT plan that will constitute the uniqueness of your comments tailored to the individual teacher and the situation (the error).

You must take into account your relationship with the teacher, and what has transpired between the two of you in the past. It will not matter the degree to which that relationship has flourished (or may not have been so good). That will not influence, not even for a second, the fact that you will talk with the teacher and offer your advice. You will do that regardless.

The question is simply how you *plan your approach*, and a well-planned approach is critically important. Every situation is unique, so never assume you know all you need to know about an issue. If you need clarification, ask questions. Being an active, deep, and purposeful listener will not only help you give good advice; you will also exponentially increase the chances that the person will take that guidance.

A great approach is to try to imagine yourself in the teacher's situation. If you've been in a similar situation, think about what you learned, but don't rely solely on your own experiences to give advice. Imagine you are giving yourself advice for the unique circumstances the other person is facing.

Another interesting concept to grapple with while you construct your plan to provide advice is to think about the consequences of the teacher taking your advice. While you're at it, think about the consequences of him or her *not* taking your advice. If there's no significant difference between the results of those two scenarios, your advice might not be bad, but it will not be useful either. Your teacher will realize this in a heartbeat, and your credibility will be damaged.

You will be making chatter with him or her for the sake of appearing to be doing something because you are the principal. Ditto if the action you advise is impossible. If you can envision the growth path you suggest leading to a worse result than doing nothing, then your advice is probably bad.

Take your time. When possible, think long and hard about all the possible courses of action, and consider the pros and cons of each. Think about both the short-term and long-term consequences of the TGT. Very important decisions are usually very important because of their long-term impact. Think as far down the road and around the bend as possible.

Empathize

Some applications of a TGT require sensitivity and thoughtfulness. If you really try to put yourself in the other person's shoes, empathy will probably develop naturally. Even so, be very careful about how you word the TGT plan and be sensitive to the other person's feelings and emotional state. Giving advice is more than a logical exercise. It usually involves helping a person sort through conflicting efforts as much as conflicting choices. It also can be a highly emotional situation for some people.

Brainstorm with the Teacher

Sometimes there is no clear-cut "right" plan for a situation. In this case, try to help the teacher mull over all the alternatives so they can reach a conclusion, either with you or on their own (which is always best). Even for very simple questions, it can be beneficial to help the teacher develop their own advice, if only because they are more likely to consider it a positive addition to their TGT.

Make it Regular

Feedback is a process that requires regular attention. There isn't an observation season, just as there isn't a season near a school holiday or near the end of school, where teaching isn't expected. You need to be expected in a classroom at any time, on any day, walking through classrooms informally, seeing (and sensing) what is occurring there.

When something needs to be said, say it! People then know where they stand all the time, and there are few surprises. And, candidly, a pat on the back every now and then or a positive comment or two about what you saw, also keeps people on track and enhances their understanding of what track they are on.

I never had an issue letting teachers know when I thought they were doing an outstanding job, and I also never failed to let them know when they needed to spend more time concentrating on pedagogy for *my kids*, and less on the art of creating a linear display of red Xs!

Let's Meet

One way you can foster a more positive environment among the teachers would be to promote regular and active collaboration. Teachers should be given frequent opportunities to work together while they develop best practices, observe one another (and hence share positive and constructive feedback), and discuss what works for them - - and possibly why certain things did not work as well. The more teachers have an opportunity to share and work together, the more potential there is to reflect upon best teaching practices and solidify their individual TGTs.

You want to know who they met with, whom they observed and what was discussed - - with outcomes specifically delineated. This will be an important component of the pre- and post-observation conferences and your TGT notes.

For example, you are working with a teacher because of some complications with them teaching reading effectively. Your TGT discussion/comment topic *cannot be,* "You need to teach reading more effectively." That statement is weak because it is too broad. Even drilling down and saying, "Teach guided reading effectively..." is still too weak because it remains too broad. Create a strong, specific, and actionable component and comment like, "Teach students two strategies for decoding by responding to student errors at Fountas & Pinnel Levels D-F, with the appropriate prompts."

Another example might be a teacher having difficulty in one component of history/social studies. You cannot tell them they, "Need to better understand the importance of primary source documents in their teaching of history." That statement is weak and tells the teacher nothing because it's too broad. Indicating that they, "Must utilize primary source documents..." is better but still too broad. A comment that the teacher, "Needs to teach students the techniques for interpreting a primary source document..." is specific and actionable in a more defined manner.

Set a Good Example as a Collaborator and as a Boss

If you advise one thing but do the opposite, your advice will be seen as phony and hypocritical. If you do as you say, people will be more likely to respect your advice. Understand that the teacher may not follow through on your collaborative growth trajectory plan initially to the degree you would like.

How obligated is your teacher to act on the plan? That is a great question, and the word *insubordination* is a very heavy word in the teaching profession when dealing with administration. It is the trump card you want to avoid putting down on the table, because it defeats everything you have been working toward in developing trust. However, know it is available up your sleeve if you require it down the road - - but way down the road!

Understand that people will sometimes ask advice in order to bounce ideas off you, and don't be surprised if a person rejects even good advice and decides to make her or his own mistake. Live with it, and let the person live with his or her decision. At least there is an effort being shown, and the next time, if necessary, he or she will be a little more likely to follow your advice. Actually, they might even be appreciative that you let them try walking that puppy on their own initially.

According to Paul Friga (2009), effective leaders are expected to provide guidance and direction that involves thinking strategically in order to move forward. Basically, strategic thinking is a driving force which, when utilized effectively, creates a way of thinking, acting, and learning that achieves desired success (Jensen, 2014). These decisions involve a process or strategy used to address issues by establishing a growth mind-set (Google: Carol Dweck) in the teacher.

Therefore, it is essential that you establish the skill sets necessary to design and implement a *great* growth plan (TGT) that ameliorates the less-than-desirable pedagogical practices. However, the focal point for you will be your ability to effectively and efficiently identify pedagogical issues, create a growth plan to ameliorate the identified pedagogical practices (hopefully, with the spirit and enthusiasm of the teacher as your partner), and know how to use the resources or acquire the resources needed to effectively implement the growth plan.

This focal point is dependent upon utilizing key components which are a combination of interpersonal and analytical elements and skills, and which provide a framework that ensures teacher success if implemented and developed properly to establish teacher buy-in. The components provide leaders with a strategy that is a mixture of rational thinking and creativity that identifies and evaluates issues in order to implement a plan that will solve and correct the issues (Markides, 2012).

Your Ability to Influence

As you look deeper and reflect on your own abilities as a principal, according to Peter Miller (2012), improving your skills and practice means to be aware of your current skills, strengths, weaknesses, values, behavioral patterns, and your predominant ways of influencing others.

I have repeatedly used the word *influence* because it is so essential to the TGT process! It is your ability to influence via the trust and capital you have been able to develop with members of the administrative team and faculty that will sustain your efforts.

This means knowing your own leadership style and other characteristics you have, and how much of an impact you have on those you are leading. Leaders who are guiding and setting standards for others must know the importance of having the types of skills that make them effective. These skills are integral to being able to respond in an effective manner to situations pertaining to growth of pedagogy in the cohort of teachers in the school.

The foundation of transformational leadership theory is that leaders can motivate individuals to increased effectiveness through engaging their values, morale, and innate beliefs. Leaders who can influence followers in such ways create high-performing organizations (Gooty, Gavin, Johnson, Frazier & Snow, 2009). This will be put to the test during your pre- and post-observation meetings (and all other meetings involving the TGT).

As a parent, I would feel that my child was being cheated compared to students who had a teacher who didn't resist change. As an administrator, I would make it clear that the change is meant to give students a better education. It is easy to say, but also extremely true, that every single person employed in a school only has a job because of the students, which means they all have a responsibility to the students.

I would let the teachers know that if the change was truly enacted and didn't yield successful results, it would be clear that the change would not be worth making. However, either way it would certainly be worth trying.

Communication

Summarizing is key to clear and effective communication. When facilitating a pre- or post-observation conference, summarize what was discussed, and physically archive future goals, efforts, direction - - *everything*.

Always remain objective and guide the conversation toward a productive result. Refrain from interjecting too much of your own bias regarding how something can or should be done, unless you are asked.

One of the important components is getting the teacher to come to realizations on their own. You have now taught them how to fish as opposed to feeding him or her daily.

That doesn't mean you won't have an opinion about what's happening. However, to facilitate effectively, you need to keep your opinion to yourself (do not think with your mouth open) - - at least initially - - to assure a positive, long-term outcome based upon your relationship with the teacher.

You need to arrive prepared for the conferences/meetings. Have your copious notes from previous meetings either on your electronic device or in a three-ringed notebook separated by teacher (not a bad situation when you sit with a teacher and you have this tome of a binder separated by teacher. The teacher sees that *everyone* has a file, not just him or her). Trust me, the degree of seriousness, coupled with copious notes, as well as the readiness you apply to the TGT process, will be magnified tenfold by the teacher when he or she sees the folder and archived notes, ideas, direction, *successes*, and more, from previous meetings! You will not taken seriously if you go into the meeting unprepared.

The theory I have applied and have seen come to *exceptional* fruition is based upon your effort and your almost relentlessness focus, and teachers will, in fact, take greater charge of their growth because of *your* focus and determination. Your job will become easier as the teachers do more in terms of their own growth development. <u>It is as though they want to spend less time with you, so they will do more on their own</u>.

Can You Think as Fast as Usher or Bruno Mars Can Dance?

Facilitation of pre- and post-observation conferences requires fast and logical thinking, a skill that will be strengthened with practice. While you will have a game plan going in, there will be sidebars that come up on a regular basis. Be prepared!

If you're not confident in your ability to think on your feet, remember that this will develop in time as a result of your continued and ongoing collaboration with teachers on a regular basis.

And again, for the ten-zillionth time, your presence in the classroom and your ongoing dialogue with teachers will be a significant factor. You will be a given and constant entity, not merely someone who drops in a few times per school tear. *Familiarity breeds comfort.*

People-Centric

Because every aspect of what you will be doing is people-centric, it stands to reason that the most important components of the entire TGT process are the meetings that constitute the foundation and guide the development of the TGT. While there will certainly be many ongoing dialogues concerning pedagogical growth, none will be more important than the pre- and post-observation conferences. The meetings will serve to establish the formal relationship between you and the teacher, and will serve to add to or possibly detract (hopefully not) from the less formal (in the hallway and/or in and out of classrooms during your walkabouts) kinds of informal relationships that gel during a career in the same building.

Planting Seeds of Greatness During the Pre- and Post-Observation Conferences

I have previously pointed toward open dialogue with teachers about what makes a teacher *great*, and what *great* teachers should look like in the classroom, as being extremely important.

Without setting standards, individuals will not know what is expected of them. If a teacher is not provided with useful feedback, they can assume that they are being effective and meeting the needs of their students when in fact they may not be. The use of a commonly understood set of expectations, as delineated on the previous pages of this book, upon which all discussions are based, assists in creating an atmosphere that is less dominated by principal subjectivity and more about the common understanding of what will work best for student growth.

An effective post-observation conference must be constructive, specific, sensitive, and achieve a balance between the need and the road to deliver the need. To be constructive, you must offer possible routes to solutions, not merely identify areas in need of growth. Being specific means you include a specific example (or examples) of what is being recommended.

A balanced approach points out strengths as well as areas in need of growth. To appear sensitive, keep your comments and recommendations on a positive note. *Avoid the use of negative language.* The following phrases are good ones:

You may want to consider...

It would be helpful if...

It appears that...

You might indicate...

It might be useful to...

I had a clear sense of..., however, can you go into greater detail about...

How do you feel about...

How do you think your students will react if you were to...

As we move ahead, what do you think might be beneficial for your growth?

Start to think if......would be helpful.

I've seen students improve by......, maybe that's an idea you might consider.

Going forward, how might you...

What can I provide for you?

But I Wrote a Great Lesson Plan

I briefly touched upon lesson plans previously. During the pre-observation conference, you will be presented with a lesson plan for the formal observation you will be conducting.

Teaching is a dynamic entity. It is a living and breathing operation. Performed properly, it is a beautifully choreographed ballet. Done poorly, it is as awkward as twenty-eight marbles dropped on a cement floor - - and the teacher is accountable and responsible for every marble, at all times!

For this reason teaching, at times, has a definitive plan, and yet at times often goes astray and can meander. Therefore, pedagogy cannot fit any pre-written script - - ergo, the uselessness, in my opinion, of well-written lesson plans once the lesson has started.

I have been privy to many, many lesson plans, and most looked sensational. University professors spend a tremendous amount of time working with undergraduate education students on creating outstanding lesson plans. No one can minimize the importance of a well-thought-out plan, and the lesson plan creates the blueprint and the mind-set of what an effective lesson looks like from the planning perspective. The thought process, in and of itself, is invaluable.

However, once the lesson-planning portion is complete, it is time to teach the lesson. *There can be a large gap between what was planned and what was effectively delivered!*

As you observe a well-taught lesson, you would look for teaching that was done by someone who is somewhat flexible throughout her or his lesson (as necessary). Sticking to the lesson plan because the principal is sitting in the room and has a copy of the plan - - regardless of where the lesson is heading - - is folly.

You aren't going to care if the letter of the lesson plan is not adhered to. There are appropriate teachable moments that crop up and more than justify heading in an alternate direction.

You are not observing the lesson plan the teacher had in mind, but rather determining did the lesson *that actually took place* achieve positive outcomes for the students? Regardless of the lesson plan, you are observing students engaged and involved in their learning. At the culmination of the lesson, students should be asked to apply their knowledge to complete a rigorous task, one they should be adequately prepared for based upon the attributes of the lesson.

The degree of student success in implementing the task should be used as a measurement to determine whether they acquired skills and can apply them. The important component is not the lesson plan itself - - but rather, *did it work!* Too many times teachers are satisfied with "...oh, I taught that according to the lesson plan..." but the important question is, what did the students learn?

It is the only valid determining factor of success.

Pre-Observation

A pre-observation clarifies expectations for the observed and the observer. Pre-observation conferences allow the conversation to begin around the work that is going to be viewed in the classroom.

It will be impossible and not fair to both you and the person you are observing to delineate here the specifics of what you should discuss. There are a myriad of topics and directions where you might be headed, which are determined by what has transpired previously in terms of the effort both you and the teacher applied to the teacher's TGT.

However, having postulated this, there certainly are some fundamental, broad-based structures that you will be looking for in any lesson, regardless of the pedagogical status of the teacher.

Post-Observation

Post-observation discussions are where the rubber meets the road. It is the most delicate of conferences that you will encounter, because inevitably the teacher is seeking approval for what he or she did and nothing - - n-o-t-h-i-n-g - - will be heard or processed by the teacher unless or until you either blatantly commit your approval or disapproval and/or the teacher formulates in his or her mind your response to the lesson.

It is best if you clear the air initially, just to get that issue out of the way, so appropriate focus can be maintained from that point on.

This is where your collaborative structure and the ethos you have attempted to formulate with the teacher for their TGT will be clearly evident. We have learned through the work of Paul Bambrick-Santoyo (2010) that **evidence** can be leveraged to make impactful changes in the pedagogical profile of the teacher. Conversations should be specifically focused by you being well-prepared and using specific **evidence** during your post-observation meeting.

A post-observation conference responds to the important *so what* questions (although those are not the actual words I would use. However, they are my thoughts, and I need a response).

The foundational question is always, _what was your reason behind a specific decision or decisions that you made for the lesson, and did it/they work_? How do you know the students mastered the skill and/or objective of the lesson? I saw you do this in your classroom; now what? Where do you go from here, and how can your practice be built and fostered?

A Little Chapter Closure: A Ratio of 2 to 1

The pre- and post-observation conferences must always conclude with a review of what was discussed, specifically what the teacher will be doing, and your contribution in terms of what you can provide the teacher to assist in meeting *the collaboratively developed* TGT goals.

It is critically important that you use G-d's standard provision of two (2) ears and one (1) mouth. You must use that as your ratio of listening to talking. The more the teacher sees you deeply and intentionally listening with the purpose of understanding what the teacher is trying to accomplish, the more they will not only feel in charge of their professional growth, but the more they will subsume as their part of this relationship.

You are not feeding them, you are teaching them to fish. The specificity of a teacher's growth trajectory should never be based upon theory, but rather on an actionable response to make the trajectory of utmost use.

Can the result of the growth plan be measured, and how, and what are reasonable expectation of the result? This will be an important component of the pre- and post observation conferences.

Chapter 11
Teacher Comments

Faculty Readiness

The following is what a sampling of what teachers have said they expect from the observation process. Please take an active role and notice how many times the words *improvement* and *weaknesses* are used, and think about what it indicates or implies about the mind-set of those who are being observed. What does it tell you?

I would expect the observational process to be an accurate measure of my classroom performance. The observation should be a part of my overall assessment, but is the one piece of assessment where my administrator will be able to watch and draw conclusions from what they see me doing. *~ Lauren C.*

As a teacher, you hope the evaluation process is includes no bias. With the Danielson model, it makes sure that the observations are **evidence** based, which is extremely important. As a teacher, you also hope that the evaluation process is fair and equitable. Each subject area and each teacher should be observed through the same eyes. *~ Maureen C.*

As a teacher, I expect the observation/evaluation process to serve as a reflective practice of my performance in the classroom. Teachers should use feedback garnered from observed lessons (when constructive) to guide future lesson planning and instruction. The observation process can be interpreted as a form of professional development, because it encourages teacher growth. Both veteran teachers and novice teachers alike can benefit from outside guidance and support that can be gained throughout the observation process. ~ *Lori P.*

As a teacher, I expect the observation process to be reflective of my overall teaching and to give constructive feedback that will improve instruction in my class. ~ *David J.*

As a teacher, I think the expectation is that the observation should be helpful and reflective. That I should become familiar with my strengths and areas for growth and that the administrator will be providing be feedback to help me, Not as a "gotcha, you suck at..." ~ *Mary M.*

As a teacher I hope to think that the expectations would be of growth and collaboration. I strongly believe that most teachers have a strong desire to improve their practice and, if done with integrity, would accept criticism if it is grounded in data and pedagogical research. ~ *Rochelle S.*

As both a teacher and a principal, my expectations of the observation process are the same. I expect the observation to be a part of the assessment of a teacher's efficacy, but certainly not the only means. I want the observations to be demonstrations of what is already known and expected from a given classroom teacher. If teachers and administrators have consistent communication, the observation becomes a smaller piece of a bigger puzzle. What does the student data indicate? What do the students in the class say when discussing their educational experience in the classroom? What are the ongoing class projects and goals? These are essential measures that can't be ascertained from forty-minute observations. Again. The formal and informal observations should be used to solidify what we already know, not as an illuminative or exploratory process. ~ *Beshamie M.*

As a teacher, I would expect to be observed and evaluated by an unbiased professional. This professional should be able to present corrections to my teaching, and do so in a manner that does not demean. This constructive building, will allow me to see my flaws and revise them accordingly. I would expect that post observations meetings should feel free of condescension. Ultimately the goal of this professional is to build on my strengths and show me how to build up my weaknesses. ~ *Morgan W.*

My expectation of the observation/evaluation process as a teacher is a way for a building administrator to get a better idea of what goes on in your classroom and to see the interactions with the students. I also feel the administrator is there to give an opinionated view of the lesson as if they were the student. This can allow the teacher to make improvements to the lesson. ~ *Nate C.*

My expectation of the observation/evaluation process is to highlight my areas of expertise and constructively point out areas needed for improvement. Human beings are not perfect and we could all use room for improvement. ~ *Bobbie S.*

The evaluation/observation process is stressful on both the teacher and the principal. However, the experience can be a comfortable one for both if the parameters of the evaluation are clear to both. The teacher seeks a clear and fair system where the expectations are attainable. If something is newly implemented, then appropriate support should be provided in order for the teacher to be successful. ~ *Andy D.*

From a teacher's viewpoint, the observation/evaluation process should help me to identify areas for improvement and/or suggest or introduce alternate teaching methods that help to enhance my ability to reach students. ~ *Robert B.*

What frustrates me the most about the teacher observation processes is how contrived it seems. It is very planned and coordinated and in my opinion, even the most ineffective teachers can "look effective" for a formal observation. I wish it could be more consistently done with more collaborative supervision where a supervisor (principal etc.) could have ongoing informal observations and ongoing conversations and reflection throughout the entire school year. APPR in our district has made the observation process even more ineffective, again in my opinion, because the paperwork required for the process is so time consuming, administrators have to spend hours upon hours for each teacher for 1-2 observations. This time could be better spent in conversation with the teachers and on more frequent observations. ~ *Erika S.*

The paperwork, specifically the time spent filling out the pre-observation components. It is so much time on my part and the part of the administrator to review it and comment on it. The fact that we have a 10-minute observation component that is performed by a third party frustrates me. Ten minutes does not allow anyone to get insight into a classroom, and a third party observer does not know me at all. How can that be an adequate measure of my performance? ~ *William F.*

I think the time spent by administrators, pre-conferencing and post-conferencing, is not the best use of their time, especially if they are observing a master teacher. Perhaps the pre- or post-conference could be at the teacher's or administrator's discretion, if they are deemed to be a master teacher. I would think that administrators have at least 3-4 hours of time invested in the pre-conference, conference, post-conference, and write ups, multiplied by a staff of 50? 60? That's a lot of time spent per staff member on just the announced observations. ~ *Stan V.*

I think the announced observations are too planned, and unannounced observations give a much more accurate view of the classroom and what takes place on a daily basis. I would love to see the announced observations taken out completely and only unannounced observations occur. Then the pre-observation conference becomes moot, and you only need a post-conference. ~ *Jessica T.*

I have a very self-reflective nature and I am always looking at my lessons and how I can make them better. I am always trying new instructional methodologies and researching techniques that I can use in my classroom. Typically I mention my reflection in my pre-observation conference, as I speak about the lesson as I have completed it in the past and how I have changed it to meet the needs of my current class. In the post conference, I will bring up my honest thoughts about how the lesson went, and how I will potentially change the lesson the next time I give it, or how I did modify it at a later lesson that day (since I teach 4 math lessons each day). ~ *Talia Q.*

I am a firm believer that everyone can learn and everyone can develop no matter how long they have taught. A teacher should never keep doing things the same way every year, because they will never grow, and they will stop meeting the needs of their students. ~ *Roberta P.*

I feel that I am supported in being an important member of the school and attending various professional development opportunities. However, I do not feel supported in receiving feedback on my craft or my instructional delivery. Granted my supervisors are supportive when approached with questions, but otherwise there is little offered for growth. ~ *Sandra P.*

I try to be as self-reflective as possible and adjust my instruction to meet the varying needs of my students. Thankfully my supervisors have a deep knowledge of the program and do back decisions that are made to benefit our students. Therefore, when being observed the supervisors recognized that it is often to adjust and change on the fly to properly address students learning and negative behaviors that occur in the classroom. I meet with or at a minimum have a discussion with one or both of my supervisors at least 2 times per week, I also know that I can go to them at any time.

Overall, I would say that we work very well together to address changes that can be made to the program for individual students and to changing strategies based on student needs. But there is very little discussion of curriculum or teaching strategies during these conversations. ~ *Linda K.*

My supervisors generally have a strong knowledge of what is occurring in our classrooms, so it often feels like observations are just going through the motions. As I said earlier, they are usually a nice pat on the back and ego boost, but I would never rely on that information to full assess my teaching practices. There is so much that goes on in our program on a daily basis that a 45-minute snapshot does not address the true knowledge and abilities of our teachers. ~ *Jodie M.*

My expectation when I am observed and evaluated is twofold. 1). I have expectations of myself to do the best job I can and demonstrate that I am effective in the areas of the rubric and/or how I help students learn. 2). I expect and truly like the evaluator to critically evaluate me...meaning seriously assessing and examining both strengths and weaknesses. Additionally, I would expect thoughtful feedback and suggestions that will help me to be the best I can be. ~ *Russell O.*

I had an observation last year that was frustrating because my principal was very brief with me during the post-observation. I got very little feedback (positive or negative) and it was very unrewarding. It also did not drive me to make any changes. I think the lesson was overall good, but I'm sure it could have been better. I would have liked to hear what he enjoyed and what he thought I could improve on. ~ *Cynthia D.*

As a teacher, I expect the observation/evaluation to constructively and objectively assess my abilities in the classroom. Specifically focusing on pedagogy, content and classroom management. Additionally, there should be some dialogue to address what was observed and to address anything was may have been missed, overlooked, or to provide details as to why a particular occurrence happened. ~ *Stephanie C.*

As a teacher my expectation are for the observer to be objective. Ideally, I would expect someone who can provide honest feedback and mentoring throughout the school year prior to the evaluation. Then during the time of observation, the teacher can be confident knowing that there hard work will be recognized. ~ *Jannine A.*

As a teacher I would crave observations that highlight my strong points and make me reflect on my own practice. I would expect that feedback would be immediate and manageable in the sense that what is told to me by my administrators can be implemented right away and I can then be observed again to make sure I am using the observation as a tool to improve my practice. ~ *Julie C.*

As a teacher my expectations of the observation/evaluation process are that they will be a resource to provide feedback, praise, and possible criticism to the way my classroom runs and my lessons. I definitely don't think I am perfect and I do appreciate feedback. I think with my students, who I could have for 4 years, I get stuck in my past experiences with them. I might not see a new behavior or skill that someone else might pick-up on as an outsider. I think however this type of "instrument" would be time consuming and especially this year leaders are also facing a lot of responsibilities and expectations. I still however hold out hope that this is how they will be utilized. ~ *Jared D.*

Simply explaining the process and the way we teach and learn math is not enough. It has to go deeper. So how does this happen? Below are some things that I have seen effective leaders to have not people only accept change, but embrace it as an opportunity to do something better for kids. ~ *Nancy P.*

Model the change that they want to see. Although this might seem extremely "cliché", it is the most imperative step for any leader in leading the "change effort". Many organizations talk about the idea that people need to be "risk-takers", yet they are not willing to model it themselves. Until that happens, people will not feel comfortable doing something different. It is also the difference between talking from a "theoretical" to "practical" viewpoint. People will feel more comfortable taking a journey to an unknown place if they know that someone else has taken the first steps. Although I believe in the idea of distributed leadership, the idea of "leaders" is that they are also ahead; they have done things that have not been done before. ~ *Mayra M.*

Leaders need to be "elbow deep in learning" *(Author's note: Wow! What a great way to put it)* with others, not only to show they are willing to embrace the change that they speak about, but to also be able to talk from a place of experience. ~ *Karlisha B.*

The word "change" is terrifying to some because it makes them feel that everything that they are doing is totally irrelevant. Rarely is that the case. I have seen speakers talk to an audience for an hour and people walk out feeling like they were just scolded for 90 minutes (O.K., I did the math but I left it as Nathanial sent it to me – scary) on how everything that they are doing is wrong. It is great to share new ideas, but you have to tap into what exists already that is powerful. When you show people that you value them and their ideas and not in a fake way which is pretty easy to read through, they are more likely to move mountains for you and for themselves. Strengths-based leadership is something that should be standard with administrators to teachers. ~ *Andrea C.*

Bring it back to the kids. What does an 80% to a 90% tell us about a kid? That they are now 10% better? Most educators got into the profession because of a strong passion for helping kids, so when we reduce who a child is to simply a number, or teaching simply to a process, we lose out on why many of us became educators. To help kids. A 10% difference does not create the same emotion as watching a student talk about something they learned or have done. Don't let a grade tell a story; let the kids do it themselves. ~ *Maryanne S.*

The way the process is currently set up in my program leads to the observation being a "dog and pony show," with little or no constructive feedback being offered. Last year my post-conference occurred on the last day of school (a half day), less than an hour before the school year wrapped up. My observation was very positive but there was absolutely no discussion of growth or things to work on in my teaching. ~ *Regina M.*

I personally would like to work my supervisors to develop goals for the school year for me as a teacher rather than just the SLOs that address student growth and achievement. While I know that this is part of the TIP process, and not necessary for effective or highly effective teachers, I believe that it could improve the way we all teach. Additionally, I would like to have the post-conference address more instructional issues and offer suggestions for improving my craft. It is an ego boost to hear how great things are and be highly effective, but that does not make me better or show me how to improve. ~ *Renata D.*

I have been in a school and watched an administrator encourage his teachers to embrace something different in their practice, and he made that change impossible to do. Giving the answer that "we need to change the policy before you can move forward" not only encouraged the detractors, but it killed the enthusiasm. When "...yeah but..." was the most commonly used phrase in his leadership repertoire, he might as well just learn to say "no"; it's essentially the same thing. The most successful people in the world rarely follow a script, but write a different one altogether. Are teachers doing something better "...because of you..." or "...in spite of you?" If you want to inspire change, be prepared to "...clear the path..." and get out of the way so difficult that change can happen. ~ *Rebecca W.*

I am very close to my administrator who performs my observations, and I get along with her and my AP extremely well. I think she takes the observation process very seriously. I was one of the model observations that my Principal and AP performed to make sure they were similar in their ratings of teachers. I think my principal has given me fair and appropriate observation that I earned, not one based on our relationship. My interactions with my principal and AP have always been positive. I have never gotten the impression that my principal sees the observation process as routine, but it is definitely a process that is overwhelming to her based upon our conversations.

Pluses for our interaction: My principal knows how I load myself up with responsibilities and committees until I don't have time to breathe. My principal will tell me no for a committee I want to sign up for despite my fight to be on it. I truly feel that she cares about her staff and looks out for them.

Minuses for our interaction: It's hard to wear the different hats when my principal is also someone that I consider a friend. It's hard to have a "friend" conversation and also hard to have a "colleague" conversation because I feel the lines are blurry. ~ *Bryan B.*

I enjoy observing other teachers in order to develop my own classroom. For a short period of time, three years, we were encouraged to develop a "Professional Growth Option." This gave release to time to do research and peer observations based on a goal selected by a team of teachers. This was more work than the traditional observation but also more rewarding professionally. This did not mesh with the micro-management of a new principal and the program was terminated. I and other teachers expressed our disappointment and attempted to provide data and narratives to show the clear benefits. We were told to get over it and get with the program or else. Then it actually became worse; Common Core and APPR – enough said. ~ *Elise B.*

If we are working towards a continual growth mindset, then these observational conversations are narrow-minded in their scope when limited to only how we view the growth of the teacher. Perceiving this opportunity as necessary for the teacher, but not necessary for the administration is a design flaw. Having administration in the classroom, witnessing new ideas, and/or reflecting on their own views of what works in the classroom is a relevant part of growth. This is an unfortunate consequence of using these observations to rate teachers, rather than to evolve the thinking of the observational process.

I personally feel that I am encouraged to grow by administration; however, the observational process does not necessarily support it. This growth is usually supported by the less formal reflective conversations that occur throughout the year that do not focus solely on my own actions. Rather this is fostered by talking about the multiple views of my practice, including the views from the administration, paraprofessionals, and students. These conversations encourage my views and knowledge to go beyond my own walls of experience by observing others. ~ *Sheri M.*

An effective teacher can be recognized no matter what the area. I am a music teacher that does intimidate supervisors unfamiliar with the terms and execution. This can also be the case in a foreign language class. While the supervisor may not be able to help either teacher with content specifics, he should be able to observe whether or not students are engaged. Are they active? Can you see improvement? Are the students willing to participate? Does the teacher respond to the class?

It is frustrating at times when a supervisor tries to turn my class into something it isn't so that it fits in their data box. For example, a conclusion of a music class may be a run-through of the music performed to measure understanding, improvement, or to review and reflect on class objectives. One of my supervisors insists that we stop and write an exit ticket. While I can appreciate the suggestions and can see the value of the closing strategy, it is frustrating that she fails to see any value in a different type of closing that is just as beneficial to the students and perhaps more beneficial considering the subject. ~ *Sam F.*

Usually I do feel very supported in my professional growth. I have had some meaningful pre-observations about teaching philosophy. I like it when the pre-observation is 25% about the upcoming lesson and 50% teaching philosophy and 25% building issues (working with team members).

I've had some excellent feedback received from post-observations that made me feel good about the work I do, and some tips that were easily implementable to immediately improve my craft. The nicest thing an administrator has said to me is "If my child was in this school, I would want them to be in your class!" ~ *William C.*

I happen to like the primary observer I have had for the past few years, he is kind and interested in the students. He is interested in educational dialogue, but his hands are tied philosophically by his superiors and, sorry, APPR. The only way we work together is at post-observations when he rattles off the same obligatory recommendations his former supervisor demanded he include in all observations. I have high hopes for him now that he has tenure and a new supervisor. ~ *Michele G.*

Conclusion
Greatness is a Journey of Continued Growth

To lead people, walk beside them...when the best leader's work
is done, the people say, we did it ourselves!
~ Lao Tsu

Unthinkable

And now let's address the unthinkable.

The TGT concept *appears* to not be working!

Despite your meticulous planning and outstanding implementation practices, the TGT concept has gone over like a lead balloon with some of the faculty members - - the red-X'ers and a few more.

I cannot suggest strongly enough that you don't take your canoe out of the water and move onto the next concept and/or initiative. First, because teacher growth is way too important, and the TGT will be working well with some faculty members, and second, the benefits of the perspective of supporting student achievement demands and warrants your continued commitment.

When a person doesn't do something suggested to them, often our immediate assumption is malicious intent. As a result, a *moral reactive attitude* toward the person can develop. This attitude, which often expresses itself as taking offense or anger, arises in people as a result of a moral judgment that is made about someone else.

It is possible that the teacher decided not to incorporate your input into their pedagogy, but I would prefer to think that isn't likely (until I am proven wrong). A more likely answer is that the teacher didn't understand the feedback, and/or they didn't understand how to apply it.

The important point is to take emotion out of the conversation and focus instead on supporting the teacher's need to grow pedagogically. You may initially feel a moral reactive attitude, like being offended, but you need to take that out of the equation when you're speaking to the teacher.

A moral reactive attitude would only put the teacher on the defensive and create a negative impression of you in the teacher's mind, which would then make future feedback even less effective.

It is better to work on discovering *why* the teacher is not applying the feedback. You could point out that he or she still seems mired and has not effectively applied the concepts outlined in the TGT. Invite a continued discussion on the topic to see why the teacher is not applying the growth strategy.

Where to Start?

Applying the technique of *listening* is a good way to start the conversation with a teacher who does not seem to be paying attention to you or getting the message that you've been trying to send during the past few months!

Start by asking them questions about how they feel about their performance. Where do they think their most important area of growth needs to be focused? You have presented this information and advice, and you don't see them heading in that direction. What do they think of the advice and/or what do they think of their performance? Do they think they are actually incorporating it and you have simply missed it? The most direct question after months of getting nowhere might be, *"Why are you unwilling to use my input?"* "Unwilling" is clearly the operative word, and will definitely spark a reply!

Ask them to just start talking, and it is important in these moments to do your best not to have a second conversation going on in the recesses of your mind, formulating a response to their comments. In other words, do not have preconceived answers or rebuttals in your mind, because that, as previously mentioned, interferes with your ability to listen to the teacher.

One fundamental technique of marriage therapists is to require one person to speak to the other side while the second side remains silent. Then, when the first side's finished speaking, the second side repeats back to the first side what they heard. This forces the couple to listen without having that second conversation going in their minds about how they are going to respond no matter what comes out of the other person's mouth.

Starting with a question, having the teacher open up -- you can certainly prime the pump by starting with what you've been seeing and what they have been doing via the **evidence**. Then ask them what they think. They'll probably appreciate the question, and you might hear some surprising answers. They may think they've been doing what you have been asking them to do, and don't understand how what they're doing doesn't match what you have been asking. Maybe there is some other problem, and they will acknowledge it or become introspective about what the problem might be, which might help them get past it, or help you see a way to help them get past it. Or maybe they will just retire!!!!!!

Starting by asking questions and then just listening. This is a great way to start the process of getting through to teachers who seem to be putting up a barrier between you and their TGT.

Hit the Pause Button

Another major model for managing your moral reactive attitude reactions is pausing between act and intent, especially when you are upset.

There's an interesting story involving Abraham Lincoln and the battle of Gettysburg. Meade, the Northern general, defeated Lee, the Southern general, and actually had Lee on the run. Lee reached the waters of the Potomac, which had swelled, making it impossible for him to cross back into the South. In essence, Meade had him where he wanted him. Lincoln ordered Meade by telegraph to attack Lee and effectively end the war. But Meade did the exact opposite. He waited, and while he waited, the waters receded and Lee was able to cross the Potomac, thus extending the war.

Not surprisingly, Lincoln was furious. Meade had disobeyed a direct order. He wrote a letter expressing his anger to Meade, telling Meade he had extended the war, and that he had disobeyed him. What is interesting is the letter was never sent. It was discovered in Lincoln's belongings long after he died. He had decided sending the letter would be of no benefit. The act was done, he was not going to change what happened in the past, and it could only anger Meade. Bottom line, it would not have moved things forward, and so Lincoln simply did not send it.

This is a really good illustration of the idea of pausing between act and intention. So you might even try that in your general feedback to teachers. Prepare what you want to discuss with the teacher, taking notes at the very least, but perhaps writing it out. And if you know you're upset about it, just let it sit for a day - - let it grow some hair! Think about it the next day. You might re-analyze your approach. It is really important to take a second look at it. Even one angry bit of feedback can ruin the relationship.

It's important to ask yourself if what you are saying/writing is really going to get the teacher to change their pedagogical practices. Very often getting upset/disappointed at someone just causes them to dig in their heels, to harden their position.

So ask yourself if you *are simply expressing your anger - - venting - - or are you providing information or advice that will improve the person's pedagogical practice?* It is important to distinguish between these two, and pausing to gain some perspective may help you do that.

Blind Spot

Next, there's something called the Expert Blind Spot that you need to be mindful of and avoid. The idea is that experts come into a situation with a background context that allows them to filter the information they see and put it into a context that makes it easier for them to understand what is relevant and what is not relevant.

Teachers lack that! This can be why they leave out certain parts of a lesson and/or overlook, or even discount segments that are needed in their TGT. As an expert you may attribute missing information to laziness, assuming they are not trying hard enough, they are not thinking through the lesson, goals, and desired outcomes of the TGT. But in reality they may not be able to pick out those points as well as you can.

So you might want to engage teachers in the form of a question about how to think through the formation of an effect of their TGT. You can provide advice on how to do so.

There's nothing wrong with sending a message to a teacher about what is important in their TGT. That will give the teacher a huge advantage in developing pedagogical skills. You are providing the background expertise that allows them to develop correctly, and keeps them from going off in the wrong direction. This will help them, and make your job easier in the long run.

Try to put yourself into the shoes of the teacher, someone who is just coming to you for a consultation about the TGT, and when you do that, you may realize that they could be missing a lot of information, which can cause them to be confused or go in the wrong direction.

People Don't Do Things *to* You, but Rather *for* Themselves

It is important not to take things personally when teachers are putting up barriers. A good mantra to keep in mind is that *people don't do things **to you**, but rather **for themselves***.

There is some reason why they're doing what they're doing, some reason why they believe it is *in their best interest*, and presumably they have the same goals you have. They're there to grow, they're there to keep their job (sorry to sound so mercenary), and so they don't want to fail. There is something driving them, or moving them, to do whatever they are doing or not doing.

Let's go back to the Lincoln example. There is some reason why Meade disobeyed Lincoln and did not pursue Lee. He had a lot of injured, and maybe he didn't want to move the injured. Maybe he believed his men were exhausted. Maybe he decided he didn't want to outrun his supply lines. Maybe Lincoln thought he needed to develop a strategy first.

Presumably Meade was on Lincoln's side, in that he wanted to win the war, but being on the battlefield, and from his position, he saw things that Lincoln did not see, which led him to make a different decision. Lincoln's wife would very often complain about Southerners, and Lincoln would say to her, "Don't be too harsh on them, because they're doing what we would do if we were in their situation." Talk about empathy!

So keep in mind while you are working with teachers on their TGTs that they are not acting out of malice, but rather what *they think is in their best interest*. So presumably, if they are not doing the right thing, in my mind then they do not know what their best interest is, because what's in their best interest is the success of their students - - especially when they are working with me.

It is a failure of knowledge!

Think about this, and it will help you in your communication with them.

Oh, and by the way? Please understand that in my mind - - and I will assume in your mind as well - - their best interest translates to me as what is best for *my kids*. It is the only interest I really care about!

Too Much of a *Great* Thing

Finally - - yes, there is a *final* finally. If a teacher just does not understand or isn't applying certain feedback from you, it is possible they're simply overwhelmed by too much of it.

Consider how many different topics you are covering in your feedback. Our mind can only absorb a certain number, and very few topics at any one time. If teachers are overwhelmed, they are simply dropping balls. In that case, you might want to simplify. Focus on only one or two things at the most. It will take time for the information to sink in, because most people don't master things overnight. Again, we are not databases that can passively absorb the material and then be ready to go. It may/will take time.

You do not need to cover all the topics at once. You're not going to turn them into a Socrates. You just need to move the needle forward. If the needle is not moving forward with what you are doing, then try a different approach.

You are growing teachers and growing enhanced opportunities for kids - - and please allow me to remind you, they are _your_ kids. That, in and of itself, supports choosing to continue - - the re-examining of the specifics of your program to see where tweaks might make a difference, and then renewing your efforts.

What to do?

Well, maybe you have planted your TGT seeds too deep or too close together!

Reflect! Speak with some people for whom the TGT is working well and don't be afraid to ask how and why it's working for them. Then retrace your footsteps with anyone for whom it does not appear to be working well.

I am not referring to the recalcitrant red-Xer's, but the good people who have made significant effort, and compare their success with those of limited success. You then need to go to your special place, your Palace of Solitude (and just so you know, the Fortress of Solitude is already occupied) and reflect on your efforts, conversations, processes, and your involvement in the process.

How can you improve A, so that B is engaged for the benefit of C, and what is it that is missing? Sounds too nebulous? Well it is, and if you gave others the same advice I just gave you, you really stink at what you are trying to do! It is just that, lacking specifics, it is hard for me to formulate an all-encompassing blanket response of remediation. However...

Let's Try These on for Size

- Maybe they didn't understand the individual components of the process.

- Maybe they didn't understand the need.
- Maybe they were suspicious of it and would not commit.
- Maybe they didn't understand what was in it for them or the students.
- Maybe they couldn't connect their responsibility to the TGT strategies and so they quit trying.
- Maybe they felt it was not collaborative enough.
- Maybe they decided to take a wait-and-see attitude to observe what happens to the others first.
- Maybe they absolutely disagreed with the TGT concept.
- Maybe they felt it was too much work on their part, and decided "just return me to the old system."
- Maybe they felt this was a project the administration created to make themselves look good for the superintendent or BOE.
- Maybe they felt they had no way to provide feedback on the TGT process and/or initial results.
- Maybe they felt they did not possess the skills to truly be reflective and make the TGT process work.
- Maybe they felt they didn't know how to measure their growth.
- Maybe they felt they didn't have enough time.
- Maybe they felt overwhelmed.
- Maybe they believed there were members of your administrative cadre who just gave the TGT process lip service and didn't take it seriously.
- Maybe they felt the process was insulting their previously established ability.
- Maybe they felt resentment, believing you used the observation process as a tactic to drive involuntary compliance.
- Maybe they just wanted their hand held a little more.
- (or maybe they felt if they dragged their heels long enough you would give up and go away.)

Anything in life worth achieving takes time and patience!

Very rarely do we achieve a goal immediately after starting out. It is rare to achieve it without a series of events occurring between starting and culmination, events that could be beneficial, or could be catastrophic!

A process comes with certain obstacles that either encourage or discourage us from continuing toward our goals. Overall, those experiencing the journey through the difficult components of the process and through to the end result can experience great satisfaction.

When you are working with a cohort of teachers, the means to the end will be individually addressed, with an occasional speed bump or two on the road, but eventually it will come to positive fruition.

Everyone participates. Everyone will be listened to and heard. Everyone will share the joy and sense of accomplishment! The difficult component is that while it is a faculty-wide endeavor, *it is individually developed.* The team is playing, but as individuals. It is not a football, baseball, soccer, or lacrosse team; it is a tennis team, with everyone playing individually.

You have a responsibility to develop workforce capabilities and a continuous growth mind-set in order to cultivate sustainable teacher growth, which manifests itself in increasing student success. You need to develop an understanding of the factors that shape individual reactions in order to cultivate collaborative agreements between you and the teachers, but one teacher at a time. This is not a group endeavor.

Think of an end result where teachers seek you out, ask your opinion, share enthusiasm with you, and are comfortable having you walk into their classroom. These actions speak volumes about the relationship you have built.

You Have the Keys

You need to understand that achieving professional growth goals through the process of TGTs based upon observations will not be unproblematic. Consequently, it will require *perseverance* on your part, and test your ability to motivate that perseverance in your teachers in order to establish and maintain a dynamic ethos of professional growth.

To accomplish this task, you must motivate the staff to fill vital connective roles within the school. Understanding the strengths of each staff member and their ability to add to the growth trajectories of others allows you to involve the staff to the maximum.

For all the good that can come from collaboration and unity, it is ultimately how you mold and critique each teacher's vision of their pedagogical practices that will allow faculty members to find success. In essence, *you hold the keys that may either open or lock doors.*

To accomplish this momentous task, you must remain true to your educational core values while holding staff accountable for upholding these values as well. A leader of such importance must require staff to display *professional maturity* at all times, while actively being a facilitator and mentor to those who are teaching ineffectively.

Such a principal is the glue that holds together a community of learners to seek "...a cause beyond oneself" (Glickman & Gordon, 2014, p. 35). If successful, you will be a voice of reason, confidence and perspective that is so vital in any school wishing to achieve *greatness!*

In *The Four Agreements*, Don Miguel Ruiz (1997) wrote about how to live your life and have personal freedom. He asserts that there are four agreements everyone should live by:

1) Be impeccable with your word.
2) Don't take anything personally.
3) Don't make assumptions.
4) Always do your best.

Within *great* schools, teachers are constantly striving to find growth that allows them to improve on their less successful endeavors. For them to partake in this methodology, the feeding-back, feeding-forward, and feeding-up provided by you will be indispensable.

Great schools, therefore, harbor "effective educational leaders to help their school develop visions that embody the best thinking about teaching and learning" (Leithwood & Riehl, 2003, p. 3). This unity of vision is what will drive the faculty forward while you and your colleagues, who are all paddling in the same direction, strive for professional success.

It is through this cohesiveness of values that school-based cohorts develop a vision and compilation of best practices that encourage and motivate others to aspire toward professionalism, while at the same time creating an ambitious, determined mentality.

Take to heart that *great* principals can have different personality traits. Some are quiet and shy (introverts, like me) while others are energetic and unreserved. However, all successful principals have one thing in common. They are principals who are able to understand and visualize that the success of the school is *not their success*; it belongs to the teachers and *my kids*.

Banking Knowledge

You are charged with the <u>responsibility to identify what constitutes *great* teaching</u> based upon your student population. There isn't anything that can't be learned from books, journals, or articles.

However, *great* teaching cannot be learned from or achieved by reading a book. You will have the daunting task of overseeing dozens and dozens - - hundreds - - of students each year, and dozens and dozens of teachers teaching.

You will spend time watching, listening, reviewing assessment data, and discussing with teachers the most effective method to teach specific types of learners. These observations and discussions are what initiate the process of placing teachers on appropriate growth trajectories (and enters them into a purposeful, reflective practice - - and never underestimate what has occurred within your own growth trajectory as you look, listen, and learn).

You will be growing as a principal, as an expert in sound and effective pedagogical principles, and each lesson you observe (good, bad, and/or downright ugly) and every conversation you will have with a teacher (about their cooperation, lack of cooperation, or even antagonism), and every growth trajectory you plan together will increase your knowledge base and abilities.

Never discount or underestimate your own growth during the entire process. *It will be massive!* You must *bank* this knowledge and call upon it when you make decisions about pedagogical effectiveness. You must call upon the knowledge when you sit and discuss developing growth trajectories with colleagues.

Teaching is an art, not a science, and the more time I spend around teachers (and I am into my 43rd year of being an educator), I admire *great* teaching more and more every day, and I am thrilled that I have helped to create a school where *great* teaching was present just about *every single day*. I felt privileged to walk into many of the classrooms of *great* teachers, and I felt a reverence about being there. Trust me, you will know *great* teaching when you see it and feel it!

One Simple Fact That Needs to Resonate with You

Now you have completed the book, I want to thank you for buying it, and I hope it will make *at least* a little difference in the success of *your* (future) *students*.

There is a bottom line that I want you to be aware of, and to practice religiously. Otherwise everything on the preceding pages will just be cannon fodder.

Nowhere in this book - - and please go back and check - - did I ever use the terms *"__my__ school"* or *"__my__ teachers!"*

I never even thought to use the *"my"* word in that context at any time during my administrative career -- *and it has made all the difference!*

Appendices

The following are record maintenance forms that are self-explanatory and will afford you an opportunity to keep track of the pre- and post-observation conference topics and the teacher's Growth Trajectory, as well as referencing ancillary meetings surrounding the teacher's TGT. These are not part of any formal component of the observation process, but serve as notes to yourself.

Record keeping is extremely important, not only to keep everyone and everything straight in your mind, but also because it has a larger and more significant purpose. These forms and your strict adherence to them in front of and while conversing with your teachers sends a definitive message that what you are collaborating on with them is extremely important.

Your best defense is a great offense, and should things go south between you and the teacher, having copious notes of not only what transpired at meetings but, in fact, when those meetings took place, will be indispensable.

A: Pre-Observation Conference

School Year:		Date of Conference:	
Teacher:		Grade Level/ Department:	
Teacher Status (P1, P2, P3, Tenured):		Type of Class:	
Scheduled Date of Observation:		Number of Students in Class:	
Administrator:		School:	

Topics Discussed:
Carryover Focus from Previous Post-Observation Conference:
Carryover Focus as Outlined in the Teacher Growth Trajectory (TGT):
New Area(s) of Focus for the Forthcoming Coming Observation:
Topic/Intent/Goal of Lesson:
Set of Activities Proposed:
Student Assessment Proposed:

Administrator's Initials:	Teacher's Initials:

B: Post-Observation Conference*

School Year:		Date of Conference:	
Teacher:		Grade Level/ Department:	
Teacher Status (P1, P2, P3, Tenured):		Type of Class:	
Date of Observation:		Number of Students in Class:	
End Time of Observation:		Start Time of Observation:	
Administrator:		School:	

Topics Discussed:
Carryover Focus from Pre-Observation Conference:
Growth Trajectory (TGT) Outcome(s):
Adjustments to the TGT:
General Notes/Comments:

Administrator's Initials:	Teacher's Initials:

* Attach a copy of the written observation report when available

C: Record of Formal and Informal TGT Discussions[*]

(other than formal Pre- and Post-Observation Conferences)
Teacher: _____

Date	Time	Topic(s) Discussed	Resources Provided/ Actions Suggested	Admin. Initials	*Teacher Initials

Page ___ of ___

(Make reference of date of meeting in your desk calendar.)

* Teacher Initials only indicates that he or she was present during the meeting.

D: Teacher Growth Trajectory (TGT) Plan

School Year :	_____-_____ in _____ Year of the TGT	Date:	
Teacher:		Grade Level/ Department:	
Teacher Status (P1, P2, P3, Tenured):		Type of Class:	
Date of Observation:		Number of Students in Class:	
End Time of Observation:		Start Time of Observation:	
Administrator:		School:	
Focus and Outcome(s) from Previous Year (if this is not the first year of the TGT):			
Carryover Focus as Outlined in the ongoing Teacher Growth Trajectory (if different from above):			
Growth Trajectory (TGT) Adjustment(s):			
Next Year's TGT Focus:			
General Notes/Comments:			
Administrator's Initials:		Teacher's Initials:*	

* Teacher's Initials only indicates that he or she was present during the meeting.

E: Teacher Support Log

Teacher:	
Grade Level/Discipline:	
Administrator:	
School Year:	20__ - 20__

Date	Focus Area	Teacher To Do: Teacher's Initials	Administrator To Do: Administrator's Initials	Next Mtg

Page ___ of ___

References

Abdullaha, N.A.W., DeWitt, D., & Alias, N. (2013). School improvement efforts and challenges: A case study of a principal utilization information communication technology. Procedia - Social and Behavioral Sciences. 103, 791 – 800.

Arias, E. G. (1996). Bottom-up neighborhood revitalization: participatory decision support approaches and tools. Urban Studies Journal—Special Issue on Housing Markets, Neighborhood Dynamics and Societal Goals, 33(10), pp. 1831-1848.

Ball, D. L., & Forzani, F. M. (2011). Teaching skillful teaching. Educational Leadership, January 2011, 40-45.

Bambrick-Santoyo, P. (2010). Driven by data: A practical guide to improve instruction. Jossey-Bass.

Barth, R. S. (2001). Teacher leader. Phi Delta Kappan, 9, 443-449.

Bennis, W. (2004). New Zealand Management, 51 (5) 3-5.

Boekhorst, J. A. (2015). The Role of Authentic Leadership in Fostering Workplace Inclusion: A Social Information Processing Perspective. Human Resource Management, 54(2), 241-264. doi:10.1002/hrm.21669

Boyum, V. S. (2012). A model of servant leadership in higher education (Order No. 3503142). Available from ProQuest Dissertations & Theses Global. (1009052822).

Bradley, B. H., Anderson, H. J., Baur, J. E., & Klotz, A. C. (2015). When conflict helps: Integrating evidence for beneficial conflict in groups and teams under three perspectives. Group Dynamics: Theory, Research, And Practice, 19(4), 243-272. doi:10.1037/gdn0000033

Brooks, D. The Road to Character, 2015

Bryk, A. and Schneider, B. (2003). "Trust in Schools: A Core Resource for School Reform". Educational Leadership, Volume 60 (6). Retrieved from: http://www.ascd.org/publications/educational-leadership/mar03/vol60/num06/Trust-in-Schools@-A-Core-Resource-for-School-Reform.aspx

Collins, J. (2001). Good to great - Why some companies make the leap... and others don't. New York: Harper Business.

Cordeiro & Cunningham, W. (2013). Educational leadership: A bridge to improved practice. New York: Pearson

Costello, K. (2014). Don't Forget, Administrators: Listen, Care, Try. Women in Higher Education, 23(10), 18-19. doi:10.1002/whe.20123

Cottrill, K., Lopez, P. D., & Hoffman, C. C. (2014). How authentic leadership and inclusion benefit organizations. Equality, Diversity and Inclusion: An International Journal, 33(3), 275-292. doi: http://dx.doi.org/10.1108/EDI-05-2012-0041

Cottrell, D. (2002). Monday Morning Leadership: 8 Mentoring Sessions You Can't Afford to Miss. Dallas, Texas: CornerStone Leadership Institute. ISBN: 9780971942431

Covey, S. R. Principal-Centered Leadership. Fireside Publishers, 1992.

Covey, S. R. (2013). The 7 Habits of Highly Effective People. Powerful Lessons in Personal Change. New York, NY. Simon & Schuster. ISBN-13: 978-1451639612

Crippen, C. L. (2006). Servant-Leadership. International Journal Of Learning, 13(1), 13-18.

Darling-Hammond, L. (2009, December). Recognizing and Enhancing Teacher Effectiveness. The International Journal of Educational and Psychological Assessment, 3.

Datta, B. (2015). Assessing the effectiveness of authentic leadership. International Journal Of Leadership Studies, 9(1), 62-75.

deWitt, F. C., Greer, L. L., & Jehn, K. A. (2012). The paradox of intragroup conflict: A meta-analysis. Journal of Applied Psychology, 97(2), 360-390. doi:10.1037/a0024844

Drucker, P. (2014). Peter Drucker quotes. Retrieved from http://thinkexist.com/quotation/leadership_is_not_magnetic_personality-that_can/294628.html

Duckworth, A. (2016, p.185), Grit the Power of Passion and Perseverance

Dufresne, P. & McKenzie, A.S. (2009). A Culture of Ethical Leadership. Principal Leadership, 10(2), 36-39.

Ericsson, A. & Pool, R. (2016). Peak, secrets from the new science of expertise, Bodley Head, 78.

Friga, P. (2009). The McKinsey engagement: A powerful toolkit for more efficient & effective team problem solving. McGraw-Hill

Glasser, W. (1998). The quality school. New York: HarperCollins.

Glickman, C. D., Gordon, S.P., & Ross-Gordon, J.M. (2014). Supervision and Instructional Leadership: a Developmental Approach. Upper Saddle River, NJ: Pearson Education, Inc.

Glover, E. (2007, September). Real Principals Listen. Teachers as Leaders, 65(1).

Gooty, J., Gavin, M., Johnson, P., Frazier, M., & Snow, D. (2009). In the eyes of the beholder: transformational leadership, positive psychological capital, and performance. Journal of Leadership & Organizational Studies. 15(4). 353-367. doi: 10.1177/1548051809332021

Gray, S. and Streshly, W. A. (2008). From Good Schools to Great Schools: What Their Principals Do Well. Publisher: Corwin Press

Gray, J., Kruse, S., & Tarter, C. J. (2015). Enabling school structures, collegial trust and academic emphasis: Antecedents of professional learning communities. Educational Management Administration & Leadership, 44(6), 875-891.

Green, R.L. (2017). Practicing the Art of Leadership: A Problem-Based Approach to Implementing the Professional Standards for Educational Leaders (5th ed.). New York: Pearson.

Greenleaf, R. (1989). The servant as leader. Indianapolis, IN: The Robert K. Greenleaf Center.

Haar, J., & Foord, K. (2012). Gauging effectiveness: how to know whether your district's PLCs are contributing to better student outcomes. School Administrator, January, 33. Retrieved from the Gale database.

Hackett, A., Renschler, L., & Kramer, A. (2014). Health education in practice: employee conflict resolution knowledge and conflict handling strategies. Health Educator, 46(2), 22-27

Harris, I. (2016). Capacity building activities for educational stakeholders for improving the quality of education. Üniversitepark Bülten, 5(1), 26-37. doi:10.22521/unibulletin.2016.512.3.

Hocker, J. & Wilmot, W. Interpersonal Conflict, 2nd. Ed. Wm. C. Brown Pub. 2013, p.236

Hocker, J. L., Wilmot, W.W. (2014). Interpersonal conflict (9th ed.). New York, NY: McGraw-Hill.

Hoyle, J.R., English, F.W., & Steffy, B.E. (2005). Skills for Successful 21st Century School Leaders: Standards for Peak Performers. Lanham, MD: Rowman & Littlefield Publishing Group.

Hoyle, J.R., English, F.W., & Steffy, B.E. (2005). Skills for Successful 21st Century School Leaders: Standards for Peak Performers. Lanham, MD: Rowman & Littlefield Publishing Group.

Hughes, R.L. & Ginnett, R.C. & Curphy, G.J. (2009). Leadership: Enhancing the lessons of experience (6th ed.). New York, NY: McGraw-Hill Irwin. ISBN: 9780073405049.

Johnson, C. E. (2013). Meething the Ethical Challenges of Leadership: Casting Light or Shadow. Thousand Oaks: Sage.

Kouzes, J. M. & Posner, B. Z. The leadership challenge – 4th Edition. 2012. Jossey-Bass, San Francisco.

Lunenburg, F. C., & Ornstein, A. C. (2012). Educational Administration: Concepts and Practices. Belmont, CA: Wadsworth Cengage Learning.

Marion, R. (2005). Leadership in education: Organizational theory for the practitioner. Long Grove, IL: Merrill/Prentice-Hall.

Markides, C. (2012). Think again: Fine-tuning your strategic thinking. Business Strategy Review, 23(4), 80-85.

Marsh, C.J., & Willis, G. (2003). Curriculum alternative approaches, ongoing issues (3rd ed.). Upper Saddle River N.J.: Merrill Prentice-Hall.

Marshall, E. W. (1995). The collaborative workplace. Management Review, 84 (6) 13-18.

Maulding, W. S., Peters, G. B., Roberts, J., Leonard, E., & Sparkman, L. (2012). Emotional Intelligence and Resilience as Predictors of Leadership in School Administrators. Journal of Leadership Studies, 20-29.

Miller, B., (2014). Looking inward: How self-reflection strengthens leaders. https://www.linkedin.com/pulse/20140910151050-240215-looking-inwards-how-self-reflection-strengthens-leaders

Miller, P. (2012). Self-reflection: The key to effective leadership. http://works.be-press.com/cgi/viewcontent.cgi?article=1132&context=peter_miller

Moxley, R. (2002). Focus on leadership. Servant leadership for the twenty-first century. John Wiley Sons, Inc. New York. Retrieved from http://www.wiley.com/

Northhouse, P. (2013). Leadership: Theory and practice (6th ed.). Thousand Oaks, CA: Sage Publications.

Novak, D. (2012). Taking people with you: The only way to make big things happen. New York: Portfolio/Penguin.

Nwogbaga, D. E., Nwankwo, O. U., & Onwa, D. O. (2015). Avoiding school Management Conflicts and Crisis through Formal Communication. Journal Of Education And Practice, 6(4), 33-36.

Peppers, G. J. (2015). National Teacher Education Journal, 8 (1), 25-31. Retrieved from: http://www.ntejournal.com/

Prieto-Remón, T. C., Cobo-Benita, J. R., Ortiz-Marcos, I., & Uruburu, A. (2015). Conflict resolution to project performance. Procedia - Social And Behavioral Sciences, 194, 155-164. doi:10.1016/j.sbspro.2015.06.129

Pysh, P. (2011). *The Diary of a West Point Cadet*. Saxonburg, Pennsylvania: Pylon Publishing.

Riveros, A., Newton, P., & Burgess, D. (2012). A situated account of teacher agency and learning: Critical reflections on professional learning communities. Canadian Journal of Education, 35 (1), 202-216. Retrieved June 9, 2012 from EBSCOhost database

Ruiz, D-M. (1997). The Four Agreements. San Rafael, Ca.: Amber-Allen Publishing, Inc.

Sandholtz, J. H. (2011). Preservice teachers' conceptions of effective and ineffective teaching practices. Teacher Education Quarterly, 28-42.

Sinek, S. (2009). Start With Why: How Great Leaders Inspire Everyone To Take Action. New York, NY: Penguin Publishers.

Sullivan, L. G., & Wiessner, C. A. (2010). Learning to be reflective leaders: A case study from the NCCHC Hispanic leadership fellows program. New Directions for Community Colleges, 2010(149), 41-50. doi:10.1002/cc.394

Thacker, K. (2016). The art of authenticity: Tools to become an authentic leader and your best self. Hoboken, NJ: John Wiley & Sons. ISBN 9781119153429.

Thomsen, M., Karsten, S., & Oort, F. J. (2016). Distance in schools: The influence of psychological and structural distance from management on teacher's trust in management, organizational commitment, and organizational citizenship behavior. School Effectiveness and School Improvement, 27(4), 594-612.

Treasurer, W. (2009). Courageous Leadership. Wiley, San Francisco, CA.

Tschannen-Moran, M., & Hoy, W. K. (2000). A multidisciplinary analysis of the natures, meaning, and measurement of trust. Review of Educational Research, 70, 547-593.

Tucker, C. (2008). Implementing and sustaining professional learning communities in support of student learning. Alexandria: Educational Research Service.

Sternberg, D. (2012). The Principal: Traversing the High Wire with no Net Below. 79 Places Where the High Wire Can Be Greasy. Pittsburgh, PA: Dorrance Publishing. September 2012.

Sternberg, R. (2014). Robert Sternberg quotes. Retrieved from http://www.brainyquote.com/quotes/authors/r/robert_sternberg.html

Stibitz, S. "How to Really Listen to Your Employees." Harvard Business Review, January 30, 2015. https://hbr.org/2015/01/how-to-really-listen-to-your-employees

Vodicka, D. (2006). "The Four Elements of Trust". Retrieved from: https://www.nassp.org/portals/0/content/54439.pdf

Wiggins, G. (2012) Seven steps to effective feedback. Educational Leadership 70(1), pp10-17.

Zisa, J. (2013). Listen to serve: Servant leadership and the practice of effective listening. The Greenleaf Center for Servant Leadership. Retrieved from www.greenleaf.org

Made in the USA
Middletown, DE
07 August 2021